"*The Leadership Integrity Challenge* provides a unique a␣␣␣␣ch for understanding the qualities and character␣␣␣␣␣␣␣ emotionally wise leader. In the current ␣␣␣␣␣␣␣␣ corporations are struggling to regain t␣␣␣␣␣␣␣␣ for leadership that embodies integr␣␣␣␣␣␣␣␣ ability to build a strong team. This i␣␣␣␣␣␣␣␣ CEO who is building a team or assessing a␣␣␣␣␣␣␣ Dr. Morler clearly identifies the levels of emotiona␣␣␣␣␣␣ty as a basis for determining a team candidate or, in the case of an existing team, who stays and who goes."
　　　　—Lou Thompson, Jr., former CEO,
　　　　　　National Investor Relations Institute

"In *The Leadership Integrity Challenge*, Ed Morler provides practical distinctions, clear insights, and an inspiring vision of integrity and leadership. His book challenges all leaders to work on themselves. This is not only a must-read, but a book that those committed to ongoing growth will refer to over and over again."
　　　　—Eleanor Bloxham, President, The Value Alliance and
　　　　　　Corporate Governance Alliance; author of
　　　　　　Economic Value Management and
　　　　　　Value-Led Organizations

"Dr. Morler's impressive work struck me on a gut level, for here was the blueprint, clearly, of what I needed to do to more fully live my potential. Its poignant truth was both scary and exciting. I felt compelled to read on. I was not disappointed. This is a must-read for those courageous souls who take the warrior's journey of fundamental change—be they heads of state, CEOs, or those on a path of personal growth."
　　　　—Orlando Villanueva-Cortes,
　　　　　　former Professor, Purdue University

"*The Leadership Integrity Challenge* teaches us how to respond versus react and live a life of emotional maturity. This is required reading!"
　　　　—Bill Keener, Regional Credit Director, Regions Bank

"This book is a gem! It is focused, relevant, insightful, actionable, and filled with useful anecdotes and quotes. It flows and develops beautifully, has depth, and makes sense from A to Z. It is indeed a how-to book of substance."
—Larry West, EVP (retired), Banc One

"Ed Morler's book guides us on our personal paths to higher maturity levels as well as making it possible for us to guide others. Taking on the integrity challenge is not an option—it's a must!"
—Richard Love, philosopher

"*The Leadership Integrity Challenge* is a very practical, intelligent, and resourceful guide on creating authentic leadership within yourself and others. It makes you think and provides the means to put concepts into action. This is a book I highly recommend."
—Marjorie Weingrow, Director, SAGE Scholars Program
UC Berkeley; Chair., Business and Leadership Forum,
Commonwealth Club of California

"Invaluable! An insightful presentation of the key elements that shape how we deal with life and relationships. It eloquently points out why integrity is about growing up—personally, professionally, and organizationally—and how we can go about it. It should be, at a minimum, a foundational text for any program dealing with personal growth or interpersonal skill development."
—Rod Pieper, Executive Coach

"Presence, impact, power, the list goes on and on. Dr. Morler presents a guide for not only monitoring and managing our own emotional maturity levels, but those of our associates, families, and friends as well. He encourages us to embrace our emotions and responsibly express them, allowing them to work for, rather than against us. Dr. Morler has sounded a call for leaders—real leaders: Do you have what it takes?"
—Latoya Love, student, University of Wisconsin

The Leadership Integrity Challenge is offered to you as a gift from the Santi Company.

We believe that acting with integrity is the foundation of global operational excellence, outstanding performance and a fulfilled and happy life.

May this book contribute to your success and well-being.

Very best regards,

John D. Santi Sr.

THE
LEADERSHIP
INTEGRITY
CHALLENGE

ASSESSING AND FACILITATING
EMOTIONAL MATURITY

EDWARD E. MORLER, M.B.A., PH.D.

SANAI PUBLISHING
SONOMA, CALIFORNIA

Available through:
Amazon, Barnes and Noble, Baker and Taylor, and Ingram

Discounts for bulk orders are available
through Sanai Publishing.

Sanai Publishing
1140 Brockman Dr.
Sonoma, CA 95476, USA
Phone: (707) 935-7798; Fax: (707) 935-3642
www.SanaiPublishing.com

Copyright © 2006 by Edward E. Morler, Ph.D.
All rights reserved. No part of this book may be used or
reproduced in any manner whatsoever without the written
permission of the author, except in the case of brief, credited
quotations embodied in critical articles and reviews.

First Edition, December 2005
Second Edition, October 2006
Printed in the United States of America
Typeset by LAFingGraphics.com
Index by Doug May

LCCN: 2005929121
ISBN: 0-9768643-2-0

Categories: business, education, psychology, leadership,
integrity, ethics, self help.

Soon to be published in Chinese and Spanish.

With love and affection, I dedicate this book
to my wife, De Morler. Her love, patience, and
support have helped me look into my own
self-imposed limitations and inspired me
to greater sensitivity and compassion.

ACKNOWLEDGEMENTS

The contents of *The Leadership Integrity Challenge* are a synthesis of concepts and practical applications from many disciplines: psychology, organizational theory, quantum mechanics, chaos theory, philosophy, metaphysics, religion, education, and business. The basic concepts and dynamics are not new. Many have been expounded as ideals since the dawn of civilization. The only thing original here is how they are organized and presented.

Many individuals have contributed to this current integration. Their critiques and suggestions have been invaluable and are very much appreciated. Any mistakes, omissions, awkwardness, or lack of clarity are solely my responsibility.

I want first to thank my wife, De, for her loving patience and support for a project that became much more time-consuming than anticipated. Second, I am indebted to General Jack Chain, who patiently read a number of drafts, made many valuable suggestions, and became a good friend in the process. Similarly, Lou Thompson, former CEO of the National Investor Relations Institute, and Jack Krol, former CEO of DuPont, also devoted significant time reviewing and providing insightful comments on focus and direction. Many thanks to developmental editor, Mary Lobig Giles, and copy editors Katrina Mather, Ricky Weisbroth, and Beth Blevins. In addition, I would like to express my appreciation to Lorien Fenton, Desta Garrett, and Debra van Stigt for their professional administrative and technical support. I wish to express special thanks to Amelia Behm, my exceptionally competent associate of seventeen years who tolerated, with aplomb, the numerous attempts of earlier versions.

Many others have reviewed various sections or drafts and provided feedback and support. These include: James Andracchi, acquisitions integration manager, Metavante; Huguette Anhalt, screenwriter; David Arrigo, senior chief petty officer, USN; Eleanor Bloxham, president, The Value Alliance, and author of *Value-Led Organizations*; Melissa Booth, executive director, Executive Leadership International; Robert Booth, EVP and senior credit officer, Cadence Bank; Jack Carlsen, senior chief petty officer, USN; Betty and Richard Connor, lifelong friends; Judy and Bill Elbring, co-founders, LifePartners; Rich Everett, COO, West Marine; Bruce Fabric, M.D., psychiatrist; Dawson Faulk, entrepreneur; Ben Gerson, senior editor, *Harvard Business Review*; Andrew Hahn, Psy.D., founder, Guided Self-Healing; Lois Hart, Ed.D., executive director, The Women's Leadership Institute; Ellen Heffes, managing editor, *Financial Executives International*; John Horen-Kates, president, Vail Leadership Institute; Karla Jacobs, CEO, Jacobs Creative; Bill Keener, regional credit director, Regions Bank; Jack Labanauskas, editor, *Enneagram Monthly*; Fleur Lee, artist; Latoya Love, student, University of Wisconsin; Richard Love, philosopher; Ellen Masterson, partner, PricewaterhouseCoopers; Doug May, CTO, The Intuitive Edge; Ron Morgan, director of human resources, Nektar Therapeutics; Mike Morler, real estate investor; Ron Ostertag, former CEO, General Semiconductor, Inc.; Rod Pieper, executive coach; Gail Regan, vice chair, Cara Operations Limited; Jared Rosen, co-author of *The Flip*; Jan Sue Rossini, friend; James Sprayregen, head, Worldwide Restructuring Group, Kirkland and Ellis; John Santi, Jr., principal, Santi Company, LLC; Robert Vanourek, chairman, Vail Leadership Institute; Orlando Villanueva-Cortes, former professor, Purdue University; Lesley Ward, Ph.D., psychologist; Marjorie Weingrow, director, SAGE Scholars Program, UC Berkeley; Larry West, EVP (retired), Banc One.

Thank you all

CONTENTS

5 Emotional Maturity

8 Facilitating Emotional Maturity

FOREWORD

by General John T. "Jack" Chain, USAF, Retired, Former Commander in Chief of the Strategic Air Command

The Leadership Integrity Challenge is a seminal work on a critically important subject. It deserves the attention of everyone who desires a world where integrity is not a cliché but a living presence. I have been very fortunate in my life and career to have known and worked with people and organizations of integrity. Regardless of the pressures, which can be many, and the consequences of decisions, which can be significant, living in an environment of integrity creates clarity and an inner sense of what is right action. When that is missing, chaos abounds and bad things happen, including losing a sense of the meaning and value of integrity itself. For sanity and good judgment to prevail, an environment of integrity is not simply desirable—it is necessary. Integrity truly is the vital factor.

Recent corporate scandals have demonstrated a level of greed and fraud the likes of which we have not seen before. Nevertheless, they have also been a gift, for they have created an awareness of the vital importance of integrity and the huge cost of its lack. These scandals have been a powerful stimulus to look more deeply at this problem. Issues of governance, compliance, potential conflicts of interest, and reporting and accounting procedures are being looked at with more scrutiny than ever before. Some of what comes out of this will be helpful. Some may only divert us from the underlying issue of how we are to create an environment of integrity, not simply ensure compliance to some arbitrary set of rules and laws. Clear standards and better procedures are necessary, but while they may be contributing factors, they are not in themselves causative or transformative.

The Leadership Integrity Challenge addresses causative and transformative factors in depth. Dr. Morler has not only taken this much-talked-about, but little understood, subject of integrity and made it understandable, but also provided a model and means to expand its presence. He looks at integrity with its many facets: how it relates to our maturity and sense of purpose; how it affects our ability to deal with change; how it influences our perceptions, attitudes, authenticity, contributions, and leadership potential; and how it affects our ability to enjoy life.

Dr. Morler clarifies how we can let go of our self-imposed limitations, expand our power of choice, and facilitate others to do the same. He emphasizes that we can choose to live an empowered life with integrity at its core and do so along with others of like intention. He expands upon and goes beyond emotional intelligence to emotional maturity and shows how its development is the key to creating more integrity in our life.

The Leadership Integrity Challenge should be a priority read for any executive, supervisor, manager, or aspiring leader. It has a breadth and depth that deserves careful study. Anyone who takes the time to read this will find many useful applications, across all cultures, from personal growth to leadership development. It is particularly useful for leaders who are serious about developing an organization of integrity. I hope it gets the attention it deserves.

Jack Chain,
Summer 2005

INTRODUCTION

Live your best and act your best and think your best today, for today is the sure preparation for tomorrow and all other tomorrows that follow.

—Harriet Martineau

When Bruce was mistakenly given a one–hundred–dollar bill instead of the ten dollars due him, he hesitated for a moment, then mumbled "thank you" and quickly walked away.

Carol didn't say anything when she noticed her boss padding expenses. After all, her review was coming up, and besides, it wasn't her money.

Peter knew there was a potential conflict of interest, but the "smart people" were doing it and had been for years. Not going along seemed not only naive but foolish.

We do not have to look far to find numerous examples of self-serving or dishonest behavior. We live in a world that largely views integrity as inconvenient, impractical, or naive. The blatant arrogance of many of those involved in recent corporate scandals and the broad-scale devastating impact of this selfish and unethical behavior has awakened public awareness to the magnitude and cost of these irresponsible behavior.

Such extreme examples of greed and fraud may seem shocking. Yet how often, in our own environment, have we ignored, minimized, or accommodated questionable behavior to avoid

1

confrontation or protect our own interests? How often have we turned a blind eye toward breaches of integrity? How often have we been less than authentic in our own communication? Abuse of any nature—from simple lies to massive corporate fraud, from highway litter to rainforest destruction, from individual acts of bigotry to large-scale acts of terrorism—negatively impacts both the individual and the greater world. The accumulative costs, emotional and financial, are enormous.

As Bill George eloquently states in his highly acclaimed book, *Authentic Leadership: Rediscovering the Secrets to Creating Lasting Value*, "Somewhere along the way we lost sight of the imperative of selecting leaders that create healthy corporations for the long term. We need authentic leaders, people of the highest integrity, committed to building enduring organizations. We need leaders who have a deep sense of purpose and are true to their core values. We need leaders who have the courage to build their companies to meet the needs of all their shareholders, and who recognize the importance of their service to society." *The Leadership Integrity Challenge* addresses these very issues.

When integrity is missing, decline and decay are inevitable. The absence of integrity always precedes crises of character, vision, vitality, and human dignity. We can foretell the future of an individual, an organization, a society, or a culture by the values it prioritizes and upon which it acts. An entity with values and priorities based on the bedrock of integrity will thrive.

Integrity is much more than legal, moral, or social compliance. Clarifying what is acceptable behavior and obtaining agreement and compliance with those behaviors is often a needed first step. However, compliance actions, by themselves, do little to shift fundamental attitudes. We can spend a disproportionate amount of resources on the presenting problem (symptom) rather than its cause, virtually ensuring that the problem will resurface and, like some viruses, morph into a more virulent form.

What we need, beyond clear communication and rules of acceptable behavior, are programs that actually facilitate an environment in which integrity is, in fact, the reality, not simply defined by compliance with some contemporary social or legally mandated standards. We need to understand the dynamics at a fundamental level. From that understanding we must develop and use *core competencies* that address integrity itself, not just the symptoms of its lack.

To do so, it is helpful to observe a basic characteristic of integrity. Integrity is binary in nature: it is on or off. We may generally be people of integrity, but at any particular moment, we either have it or we do not. Since development tends to be a cumulative process, how then do we facilitate the development of integrity and do so without imposing self-righteous judgments?

Even people who truly understand the vital importance of integrity often have little idea how to assess it, much less facilitate its development. Our culture is often a major inhibiting factor, tolerating and often promoting appearance over substance, frequently at the expense of honesty and authenticity. Consequently, recognizing the difference between individuals of integrity and pretenders can be a real challenge. It's no wonder that leaders are honestly confused about how to evaluate much less facilitate the development of integrity. One may be emotionally intelligent yet have little real ability to apply that intelligence to the varying circumstances of life. That ability is the heart of emotional maturity.

The key is to recognize the relationship between integrity and emotional maturity. Like the two strands in the double helix of our DNA, emotional maturity and integrity are inextricably interconnected. Developing and expanding our emotional maturity enables us to act with integrity more of the time.

The fact is that most of us still have some growing up to do, some much more than others. As with integrity—either we are emotionally mature or we are not. However, with emotional maturity, we can distinguish relative degrees or levels of immaturity. By understanding these levels, we are able to assess our own and others' level of emotional maturity. From that understanding *we have the means to develop skills in facilitating movement toward greater emotional maturity.*

By facilitating the development of emotional intelligence *and* maturity (individually and organizationally) we set the all-important framework for manifesting an emotionally mature environment of integrity with all its strengths and benefits. The more emotionally mature an organization's employees, the more likely that organization's ability to attract more like-minded people of integrity.

The real leaders and change agents are those who set the tone and do what is necessary to ensure the development of a truly integrity-rich environment. *The most critical responsibility and long-term priority of enlightened leadership is to facilitate the development of emotional maturity.*

Executive Summary

PURPOSE

To help develop *core competencies* fundamental to moving toward a saner world where integrity is the norm.

OVERVIEW

Our integrity is our bottom-line. It defines our humanity and our future. The worldwide presence of ignorance, greed, hurt, and destruction evidence a lack of integrity and responsible leadership. History, up to and including the present day, provides more examples of destructive leadership than it does of constructive leadership.

Responsibly making needed change, doing the right thing, acting with integrity—all come down to a fundamental attribute—emotional maturity. When emotional maturity is lacking so is integrity. Raise emotional maturity and individuals become more secure, discerning, responsible, productive, and happy. From that empowered foundation, knowing what is right and acting on it increasingly becomes an effortless, natural occurrence. *We will have sanity and justice only when we have more emotionally mature people leading others to increasing levels of responsible behavior.*

The Leadership Integrity Challenge directly addresses this need. It acknowledges, but moves beyond, the symptoms and compliance issues surrounding the lack of integrity. It focuses on causal factors. For the leader, the educator, the executive, and the individual user, it *provides an effective, teachable means to develop core competencies in assessing and facilitating emotional maturity.*

These core competencies are:

- **Fundamental to understanding ourselves and others**
- **Vital to personal growth**
- **Key to effective communication**
- **Essential to leadership development**
- **Invaluable to creating a culture of integrity**

The underlying principles are universal and apply to all people—across culture, religion, nationality, gender, personality, and socioeconomic status. They are potent tools. Competently applied to client relations, sales, negotiation, management, or supervision, they can have significant bottom-line impact. Implemented with integrity, they generate an environment of integrity.

WHO BENEFITS

- **Leaders desiring to create an emotionally mature environment of integrity**
- **Executives and managers responsible for execution**
- **Educators who lay the foundation; parents, teachers, coaches, trainers, mentors and therapists**
- **Those in sales, negotiation, and customer service**
- **Anyone interested in personal growth**
- **The organization, society, the planet**

THE DNA OF A FULFILLED LIFE

Chapter Summaries

Chapter One: Leadership—Making Change an Opportunity addresses the issue of change and the role of leadership and emotional maturity in dealing with change. It defines and looks at the interrelationships among presence, responsibility, power and empowerment. It reviews the dynamics and conditions that create or allow limiting and dysfunctional behavior.

Chapter Two: The Emotionally Wise Leader details the qualities and characteristics of emotionally wise leadership. It outlines and recommends a seven-step process to facilitate the development of emotional maturity and integrity. The chapter also provides suggestions to optimize training effectiveness.

Chapter Three: Integrity—The Vital Factor provides greater clarity to the meaning and importance of integrity; indicates how it lays the foundation for vision, principles, and character; stresses the costs when integrity is lacking; and suggests how to put integrity into practice.

Chapter Four: Emotional Intelligence and Beyond looks at emotions—their meaning and their purpose—and how we use and abuse them. It expands on the concept of emotional intelligence and acts as an emotional-intelligence primer for understanding emotional maturity.

Chapter Five: Emotional Maturity takes a deeper look at emotional maturity: what it is, why we so often act like self-centered children or self-important adolescents, and what we can do to start growing up.

Chapter Six: The Levels and Impact of Emotional Maturity introduces the six levels of emotional maturity/immaturity, details the attitudes and behaviors of each level, and shows how the levels can be used as a measure to objectively assess states of emotional maturity.

Chapter Seven: The Power of Communication reviews some of the communication basics often forgotten but needed to translate convincingly the concept of emotional maturity into practical, achievable reality.

Chapter Eight: Facilitating Emotional Maturity develops, based on the emotional-assessment tools presented in previous chapters, the how-to of facilitating individuals to higher levels of emotional maturity and integrity.

Epilogue: A Call to Leadership emphasizes the need and the opportunity for individuals to stand tall and guide us toward a saner world where integrity actually is the foundation of our choices and actions.

Appendix: Understanding Personality defines personality, introduces the Enneagram of Personality, and integrates the six levels of emotional maturity with the nine personality drives adding dynamism to the Enneagram and increased specificity to the levels.

1

LEADERSHIP—MAKING CHANGE AN OPPORTUNITY

You are not here merely to make a living. You are here in order to enable the world to live more amply, with greater vision, with a freer spirit of hope and achievement. You are here to enrich the world, and you impoverish yourself if you forget the errand.
—Woodrow Wilson

"Outstanding!" Tom was ecstatic. He had just learned of his acceptance by the company that topped his wish list of potential employers. This company was recognized as a leader in its field. It had a reputation for being highly profitable, and it paid excellent salaries. Its benefits program was exemplary. In addition, perhaps best of all, it was an easy commute. Tom was on cloud nine.

Alas, Tom discovered the internal climate at the company was not as portrayed. Almost immediately, he noticed a slew of seemingly arbitrary—and contradictory—directives sent via email from his division head. When he queried a colleague about it, the colleague told him it was not considered prudent to question the division head's judgment—on anything. "If you like working here," the colleague said, "you don't want to get on her bad side." It was also obvious that little meaningful communication existed among divisions or even between departments in the same division, making Tom's job particularly difficult. He was continually frustrated by having to work with so many individuals who were unwilling to share information.

After several months, Tom thought things might be improving when management assigned him to the company's Leadership Development Program. The assignment was considered an excellent career-enhancement opportunity. However, he was soon disappointed to learn that the program's content and emphasis had little, if anything, to do with leadership. Rather, it was about how to ensure strict adherence to the company's historically very successful sales strategy.

People were not happy when Tom started questioning the truthfulness of claims being made by the sales and marketing departments. Things went from bad to worse when he asked about some dubious financial arrangements. Tom's colleagues hinted rather strongly that his questions indicated a naïveté about how the "real world" operates. Increasingly he heard, "It's not an ideal world Tom, you have to be practical;" "Just do your job and let others worry about theirs;" and "You have a great job. Don't look a gift horse in the mouth." Unable to deny the obvious, Tom realized that management's touted open-door policy was a sham. Its values-based policy was a figment of the public relations department's imagination. Being a "good team member" seemed defined as not bringing up problems.

These were not isolated incidents. By cutting off feedback, management was alienating many employees, including key players. As a result, management was not adapting to the changing competitive environment. Quarterly sales and financial pressure precluded the needed changes from being considered, much less implemented. To Tom it was clear that current management policies were undermining the company's future. Unless major changes were made, current profitability would not remain sustainable.

Tom loved the money he was making, but he did not like what he was seeing or how it made him feel. He could not just ignore the problems, as some seemed to do, and he was frustrated that he was not more personally effective. Those few people with whom he could share his concerns acknowledged the problem but felt as powerless as he.

Tom realized that the major problem the company was facing was not a lack of salable products or technical skills. The people weren't bad, but their unwillingness to confront issues on all management and employee levels did indicate lack of principle and weakness of character. This translated into a lack of responsible action. Neither leadership nor integrity were among the company's strong suits.

With growing alarm Tom noticed that a number of the people he'd met when he started had moved on. He was not happy himself and knew he needed to start looking elsewhere, though he had some concerns about leaving. "How will leaving so soon look on my resume? Will I be able to land a job that pays as well? Will I be able to handle the new mortgage payment? Why is it," Tom wondered, "that even when the need is obvious, change is so difficult?"

FACING THE CONFUSION, DOUBT, AND FEAR OF CHANGE

When problems grow requiring change, will doing anything less than making those changes resolve the issue? The simple and obvious answer is no! Yet we continually avoid needed changes. Why? Because it means moving into the unknown, doing something different—not doing what is familiar or comfortable. It means not being able to rely on the old skills, connections, images, and pretences that previously seemed to work. Change, therefore is threatening because always associated with it is some degree of confusion, doubt, and fear.

Leadership is about motivating others to move beyond their comfort zone into the unknown, to let go of some old ways of being, doing and having, and to try on new, often initially awkward, attitudes and behaviors. Consequently, from those asked to change, there will always be some level of resistance; some responsively appropriate and helpful, some reactively inappropriate and not helpful.

Substantive change therefore requires commitment—the willingness to face and deal with all the predictable resistances that confusion, doubt and fear generate—from both leader and follower. Key to effective leadership is the underlying commitment to learn to differentiate and evaluate responsive versus reactive resistance and decide and act accordingly. Without responsible (versus reactive) commitment, our desires and dreams remain little more than fantasy. Without integrity, there is no real responsive commitment.

Too often, fearful, emotionally immature individuals are not willing to confront the predictable resistance to even desperately needed change. They claim that they will—then don't follow through. They are stymied by fear. They rationalize a decision to stay with what is familiar because it feels much safer than facing their fears and dealing with the inevitable resistance to change.

The familiar may have been perfectly adequate and appropriate in the past, but today, that familiar environment may not support the desired result. Change will occur, but unless the discernment and flexibility of emotionally mature leaders are truly present, that change is unlikely to be the change needed.

Emotionally immature people are paralyzed by their fear and reactively resist and fight change. Mature people face their confusion, doubt, and fear, and appropriately respond. They demonstrate resilient, proactive behavior in the face of change.

We must never lose time in vainly regretting the past nor in complaining about the changes which cause us discomfort, for change is the very essence of life.

—Anatole France

Meaningful change requires a positive self-image, courage, and commitment. These qualities are inherent to integrity. Without integrity, meaningful change is impossible. When real change is needed and is ignored, or only "fixes" are applied, both leadership and integrity are missing.

We must always change, renew, rejuvenate ourselves; otherwise, we harden.

—Johann Wolfgang von Goethe

It is only when we believe things to be permanent, that we shut off the possibilities of learning from change.

—Sogyal Rinpoche

SUBSTITUTING FIXES FOR LEADERSHIP

When integrity and real leadership with their inherent emotional maturity are lacking, needed change does not occur. Instead, a culture of resistance and rationalization develops.

Tremendous amounts of time and energy are spent on posturing, looking busy, protecting turf, and covering one's back. Personal values are compromised. Problems are magnified. Some form of crisis is inevitable and will not be resolved by tweaking the system and returning to what is familiar and comfortable.

Improvement is an important aspect of being efficient, effective, and appropriate. Improvement makes a good thing work better. Fixes add improvements to what is already irrelevant. Fixing is a way to resist and therefore avoid dealing with the difficult issues of real change.

If you modify or fix what is no longer relevant and expect it to work under the new conditions, you may as well try to protect the country by painting World War II fighter planes; giving them new engines, wheels, and controls; training pilots to fly them; and expecting them to survive dogfights with modern jet fighters. It is not only fuzzy thinking, but costly; deadly for the pilots, and a sure strategy for defeat.

Fixes are neither efficient nor effective. They squander time, money, material, and most of all, human capital. They are wasteful and potentially fatal, especially during times of rapid change. Fixes deflect focus away from what is actually needed. The fix may buy some time and thereby appease some political constituency, but it never lasts. If real change is needed, fixes only exacerbate the problem.

Fixes frustrate competent personnel and stifle innovation and creativity. They build up expectations that do not materialize, which in turn dashes hopes, creating even greater frustrations and eventually apathy. This makes it even more difficult for the next person in charge to gain support for needed changes when the crisis eventually looms even larger. Implementing fixes is one of the surest ways to create mediocrity. If continued, fixes ensure the departure of the best and brightest.

Sometimes the existing paradigm needs reinforcement or development. Sometimes it needs breaking and replacing. The latter is the most difficult and is usually resisted. Regardless, it takes wise leadership to know what to do and when and how to do it. *It takes the perspective and discernment of emotional maturity to distinguish among (1) fixing, (2) appropriate improvement, and (3) the need for transformational change.* To create transformational change, to stand tall and do what's right, takes guts.

Your behavior is actually creating structures that future humanity will inhabit. Therefore, choose your acts very, very well.
—Ken Wilber

REAL LEADERSHIP TAKES GUTS

Real leadership takes others and us into new territory. It creates an environment where people stretch old boundaries, try the untried, take risks, fail often, learn more about themselves, contribute, and grow. It takes courage to face the confusion, doubt, and fear that accompany any real change; to risk losing one's carefully crafted public image; and to persist through the inevitable resistance to any change. All of this boils down to willingness to face personal fears, which is what real courage is all about. Leadership takes guts, i.e., willingness to face and deal with whatever is present.

The desire for safety stands against every great and noble enterprise.
—Publius Cornepius Tacitus

You have to have courage. I don't care how good a man is, if he is timid, his value is limited.
—Theodore Roosevelt

Points to consider:
- **What do you not want to confront? What decision or action are you avoiding?**

- **Whom are you avoiding?**
- **If you had the courage, what would you do to make your environment a better place?**

- **What part or aspect of that vision can you do now?**

PRESENCE—BEING IN THE MOMENT

Presence is the quality of being in the now, fully engaging the present environment, regardless of what that environment is. Buddhists refer to this as mindfulness. Our ability to be present lays the foundation for discernment, which in turn makes it possible for us to respond effectively to whatever situations we face.

We can fully discern what is happening in the moment only when we are in the now. When we are not present, we miss information, lose discernment, and limit our ability to make sound decisions; we cannot respond optimally. Being stuck in old patterns is a way of not being present. Unfortunately, some people use this pattern to avoid dealing with any unpleasant situation responsibly. Procrastination is an avoidance of being responsible *now*.

The experience of being present with what is, is the experience of facing the truth. Any avoidance of experiencing what is, positive or negative, is an avoidance of the truth. Children and adolescents lie because they are afraid and insecure. Truly emotionally mature individuals have the awareness to know that real responsibility includes the willingness to face all truths.

Being emotionally mature means having the self-confidence and sense of security to deal with whatever a truth may be and to respond (versus react) by taking positive action to the best of one's ability. As Eckhart Tolle points out in *The Power of Now*, it is our ability to be present with what is, that is the foundation for our ability to respond and be truly powerful.

In Presence, we simply experience what is and respond in love versus react in fear.... In Presence, we are available to all the resources within and through us, and we are fully at choice about how we use them.
—Kathy Eckles

RESPONSIBILITY—THE ABILITY TO RESPOND

Responsibility is the ability to respond to and constructively deal with whatever is—the bad as well as the good. It should not be confused with social mores of expected behavior, which often have little relevance to what is occurring in the present and tend to be imposed as responsible behavior.

Responsibility involves becoming increasingly more self-referential, with each person honestly assessing and owning his or her unique part in creating or contributing to a situation, and then acting to make things better. *Responsibility is our willingness to be the source of our life and it incorporates the realization that everything we do, including what we choose to avoid, has impact.* Responsibility is about owning and being accountable for that impact, and having the ability to respond (versus react) to the impact of forces outside of ourselves. It is being "response-able."

Leadership is not rank, privilege, titles or money. Leadership is, ultimately, responsibility, and it is the ultimate responsibility.
—Colin Powell

Responsive versus Reactive Behavior

Being responsive is being in the moment, being aware, and being able and willing to discern and differentiate relative priorities and take appropriate, constructive action. *Responding is taking responsible action in the moment.* Responsive individuals are those who listen and are willing and able to face and deal with whatever situation is at hand to the best of their ability, given the resources available. Only when one is responsive can one be responsibly proactive.

A reactive person is one who, in the past, was unable or unwilling to confront certain situations. Because the individual avoided these situations, the situations never resolved. Consequently, they act like magnets, keeping the individual's attention stuck in the past. To that extent, the individual is literally unable to observe, much less respond to, what is actually occurring in the present. As a result, the ability to develop discernment and differentiation skills is significantly limited.

With any additional avoidance, the stuffed energy accumulates, resulting in an increased feeling of overwhelm. For this reason, when people are reactive rather than responsive, their emotions and behaviors appear to be, and are, exaggerated relative to the present circumstances. They are reacting to the accumulated energy of the past, which the current situation often only restimulates. The greater the repression, the smaller the stimulus needed to create a reaction, the greater the reactivity, and the more hostile or despairing that reactivity will be. When a person is reactive, he or she cannot and will not be responsibly proactive.

The outward attack that often accompanies reactivity is often a projection of an individual's repressed anger at himself for his unwillingness to take responsibility for his own behavior. The intensity of the attack (not necessarily the volume, for the attack can be covert and passive-aggressive) is an indication of the degree of repression, fear, and denial present within that individual.

The opposite of responsibility is reactive judgmental blame (see "Blame," page 171). It is also doing something only because one feels obligated. Responsibility viewed as a burden is not responsibility at all, but a victim's or martyr's way of controlling and avoiding responsibility.

As people feel overwhelmed, their willingness to take responsibility for their impact declines exponentially. Truth becomes increasingly skewed and, depending on the extent to which a person feels overwhelmed, that truth can become totally inverted. For example, when overwhelmed, what one person accuses another of is sometimes literally what he or she has done to the other person.

A man never describes his own character so clearly as when he describes another.
—Jean Paul Richter

Any time we avoid being responsible, we automatically limit ourselves. The more we avoid responsibility, the more we allow ourselves to be controlled by things and circumstances "out there" and the greater is our sense of being powerless. We wind up acting like victims and become ineffective complainers.

The more personal responsibility we assume for our actions, the more potential we have to direct toward achieving what we truly want. We are only flexible and able to create anew when we are responsive. When reactive, we are neither flexible nor creative.

When responsible people find themselves feeling upset, they recognize that their feeling is a message that something's wrong. They quickly respond and transmute that upset energy into doing something constructive about the situation. *Expanding awareness is about being more present to whether we are responding or reactive.*

FALSE RESPONSIBILITY

I don't know the key to success, but the key to failure is trying to please everybody.
—Bill Cosby

A distortion of true responsibility is taking inappropriate responsibility for another person's actions or emotions. Helping other people help themselves is one thing. Taking responsibility for others, as in rescuing them, reinforces the message that they cannot handle the situation but the rescuer can. That generates a "better than/less than" relationship. This acts as an invalidation of the rescued person and is arrogant behavior by the rescuer.

Chronic rescuers feel they do not or will not have value unless they are rescuing someone. Therefore, they need someone to rescue and are very successful at creating needy relationships. This behavior inevitably leads to increased dependency, self-pity, victimhood, resentments, and mutual recriminations. It is what creates codependency, which is always destructive to all parties.

Another form of false responsibility is using the mask and lie of being the "nice-guy." A nice-guy does not honestly confront others with their irresponsible actions, justifying that being honest might hurt their feelings or would not be gracious. However, those seemingly pleasant avoidances, more often than not, are little more than glib attempts to hide and excuse an unwillingness to face and deal with anything uncomfortable.

The chronic nice-guys tend to have a limited inventory of what they think they can be. They also usually have a large inventory of what they cannot or should not be. The nice-guys may avoid overt conflict and be socially acceptable, but if successful, that behavior keeps them from dealing with their own fears. It also blinds them to their inherent strengths and talents. To top it off, this nice-guy's behavior deprives others of potentially valuable feedback. Consequently, their communication is inauthentic and untrustworthy.

Avoiding dealing with irresponsible behavior in the name of graciousness does nothing to end such behavior, and can actually reinforce it. This is especially true when people play the victim game of purposely trying to gain sympathy to deflect the negative consequence of their irresponsible behavior. It is a destructive game of manipulating and controlling through weakness. Allowing it to continue is disempowering to all parties.

As we recognize the vast difference between true gracious respect and superficial pleasantries to avoid dealing with certain issues, we open the door to experiencing and modeling greater presence and authenticity, thereby gaining effectiveness and respect. *If we do not recognize and own the impact of all our behavior, we continually make ourselves the victim of forces outside of ourselves and feel more and more out of control and powerless.* (See "What is Rage?", page 140.)

POWER—THE ABILITY AND THE WILLINGNESS TO ACT

Power is both the ability and the willingness to act. Ability without willingness to use it generates nothing. Likewise, willingness without ability has no power. Both ability and willingness must be present.

Power is a potential; it is not an action itself. That is why powerful people seldom have to actually demonstrate their power. Their recognized willingness and ability to act often is all that's needed to get the desired response.

Power stems from an ability to hold a position. Try pushing a heavy object while standing on a patch of ice—you have no solid position from which to establish traction. Similarly, when a person is insecure, frightened, overwhelmed, or has low self-esteem, there is no solid foundation from which to generate anything.

Real power is based on an individual's fundamental sense of security and positive self-esteem. It is not conditional on anyone else's actions or approval (see "Self-Esteem versus Other Esteem," chapter 6, page 214). People who are secure do not need to resort to threats or manipulation; insecure people often do.

True power has nothing to do with intimidation or manipulation. Would-be leaders use various forms of intimidation, manipulation, and invalidation to hide their insecurity and force others into fear or apathy. The only power they have is the power we allow them.

Repressive behaviors are manifestations and symptoms of false power, of a perceived need to have power and control over someone or something as compensation for a lack of real power and a feeling of being out of control. Because false power is based in insecurity, it has no substantive foundation and thus usually collapses *if responsibly confronted*. In the meantime, it can do a lot of damage. All tyrants are fundamentally insecure.

Irresponsible behavior indicates a lack of real power. Correspondingly, lack of power indicates lack of responsibility. *Increased responsibility always generates increased power.* If you feel powerless, ask yourself, "what responsible decision or action am I avoiding?" See if you can find a pattern of similar avoidances.

Being willing to honestly observe our own behavior is, in itself, empowering.

Most powerful is he who has himself in his own power.
—Lucius Annaeus Seneca

Points to consider:
- What are you doing that you don't want to do?
- What are you unable to do that you say you want to do?
- How willing are you to do what's necessary to develop that ability? What do you refuse to do?
- Is your refusal based on ethical principles or fear?

EMPOWERMENT—GIVING OURSELVES PERMISSION TO ACT

Power is about potential, and empowerment is about manifesting that potential. The key is giving ourselves the permission to act and assuming the authority (owning our authorship) of our action or inaction. As with power, both aspects—permission and authority—must be present. *If we do not give ourselves permission to act, we cannot do anything, regardless of the potential available. When we deny our authorship—that is, our part in either creating or allowing the situation—we forgo any authority to change the script.* Empowerment is the direct result of our willingness to take responsibility and be accountable for our impact.

People speak of empowering others. However, true empowerment is not and cannot be given by some other person or entity. It can only be given to us, by ourselves. Others only can provide a supportive environment (or not). Developing that environment is a vital element to organizational success and longevity. Its achievement is a measure of truly effective leadership. *Becoming empowered is always the result of personal acts of responsibility.*

A good leader inspires one to have confidence in him; a great leader inspires them to have confidence in themselves.

—Sun Tzu

The key to self-empowerment is to first own the truth of the following statements:
- Whatever we do (or do not do) has impact.
- We create or allow our reality.
- We reinforce that to which we give our attention.

The degree to which we allow, own, and actualize these points is the degree to which we build a foundation for empowerment. Realize that whenever we find ourselves reacting (feeling put upon, upset, or blaming) rather than responding (dealing with a situation constructively), we are denying that we have impact and, instead, we are focusing our attention on how the external world has victimized us. *Whenever we disown any of our impact, good or bad, we give our power away.* This reinforces a disempowered perception. However, because we do have impact, we have contributed at least something to the existing reality. Therefore, that perception cannot be valid. In this sense, there are no victims, only volunteers.

Points to consider:

- Name something specific that you are not doing that you would feel good about doing.
- Is there any reason you cannot possibly do it?
- What is stopping you? Are you stopping yourself?
- Consider taking your "stop" off and give yourself permission to start—if you really want to. What would be your first step?
- It is your creation. Are you willing to acknowledge your authorship?
- How will you begin your next chapter?

GOALS—AN ANCHOR TO THE FUTURE

What the mind can conceive, it can achieve.

—W. Clement Stone

Clear goals set an anchor into the future, provide a focus and help to keep us from wandering aimlessly, wasting time and resources. To the degree we are unclear about personal goals, we will have difficulty relating to and being motivated by organizational goals, even if the latter are clearly stated. There is little basis for alignment. With no perceived alignment, we will be frustrated, upset, and complain. To optimize the result for all parties, goal setting needs to address personal goals first, professional goals second, and organizational goals last and ensure that all are in alignment with and supportive of one another. If organizational goals are unclear, people with focused personal goals are more likely to be creative and responsible in helping to clarify organizational goals and aligning them with their own.

More often than not, management violates this sequence with organizational goals receiving dominant attention at the expense of individual aspirations. When that occurs, the individual tends to become frustrated and distracted. The cost to both the individual and the organization can be huge.

When it becomes clear that personal goals are not in alignment with organizational goals, those individuals need to move on *for everyone's benefit.* The clearer individuals are about where personal and organizational goals do align, the more passionate and mutually beneficial is the relationship.

The tragedy of life doesn't lie in not reaching your goal. The tragedy lies in having no goal to reach.

—Benjamin Mays

Follow your bliss.

—Joseph Campbell

Points to consider:

- **Are your needs and aspirations being adequately addressed?**
- **Have you clarified, for yourself, what they are?**
- **How can you more responsibly address them?**
- **How can you align your needs in a way that contributes to your organization's well-being?**
- **What, specifically, can you do?**
- **Are you willing to do it? If not, why not?**

BUTCHER, BAKER, CANDLESTICK MAKER
—WHEN ARE YOU WHICH?

Every position in an organization requires and makes use of multiple and different skill sets. There are times when we need to use our technical skills. There are times when we need to manage and there are times we need to lead. This is true for anyone and everyone in the organization, regardless of title or position.

However, it is important to differentiate the skill sets and know when each is required in the moment. It is important not to confuse leadership with management. *Managers deal with what already exists. Leadership is about breaking ground—it is about motivating others to unexplored heights and new territories.*

Honestly look at yourself and what you do in your current job, keeping in mind that different functions and responsibilities are needed at different times.

Points to consider:

- To what degree are you a leader, a manager, or a technician? When are you which?
- Are you being a technician when you should be a manager, or otherwise enacting one role when you should be fulfilling another?
- You may find yourself doing what is familiar or what you are good at, but is that what you need to be doing now?
- It may be useful, but is it a top priority at the moment?
- Which functions or subjects do you tend to avoid? What are you doing instead? How do you rationalize

doing so? Is it a chronic pattern? What is it costing
you? What is it costing the organization?

- What could you be doing that might be of even bigger
benefit to you and the organization? Why aren't you
doing it?

GOOD POLICY APPROPRIATELY APPLIED

Policy is a set of standards and procedures intended to provide
guidelines to help an entity function optimally. Good policy
develops from experience that has shown the organization is
better served when certain actions are taken and less well served
when those actions are not taken. As circumstances change,
organizational policy needs to adapt accordingly. Problems arise
when leaders are reluctant to initiate changes when policies
that were appropriate and successful in the past are not so
today. Sometimes a policy is generally appropriate, but can
be inappropriate or even destructive with regard to a specific
issue. Bureaucratic executives, out of fear, apathy, or ignorance,
blindly adhere to policy no matter how currently inappropriate or
destructive it is. "It's policy!" On the other end of the inappropriate
continuum is the hotshot who ignores or violates appropriate
policy. Functioning on either end of that continuum indicates a
problem of discernment, judgment, and/or willingness or ability
to take appropriate action. Good executives—emotionally mature
executives—realize that good policy is not a static set of standards
and procedures but an evolving one that needs to be adhered to,
except where it is obvious that it would be detrimental to do so.
Effective executives have the discernment and judgment to know

when to enforce rules or policies and when to make exceptions to them.

Points to consider:

- Does your organization have an organized, understandable set of policies and procedures?
- Do you know what they are or how to access them when needed?
- Are they based on what experience has shown works, or are they little more than a set of arbitrary rules?
- Are they applied with appropriate, responsible flexibility; applied blindly; or cavalierly or apathetically ignored?
- What do you believe needs to be done to improve your organization's policies and procedures? List your top three recommendations.
- What would your first proactive step be?
- What's stopping you, if anything, from taking it? (Be brutally honest with yourself. Your personal clarity here is what's most important.)

OBSTACLES TO CHANGE

The following are examples of attitudes and behaviors that tend to limit constructive change.

Over-Managed and Under-Led

Former head of the Strategic Air Command, General Jack Chain, continually emphasized, "You lead people and manage things." Yet how often do leaders confuse or abuse this principle, with the all-too-common result being that such leaders wind up treating people like things that need to be managed rather than individuals who need to be motivated by competent leadership?

We live in a world that, with rare exception, rewards managers but avoids developing leaders. Why? For the most part, managing ensures that what needs to be done is done within an existing system—a familiar system. Good management requires an understanding of the existing system and keeping it efficient and effective. Leadership is about getting others to move beyond the familiar. When people actually lead, they upset the old familiar system and its vested interests. *Managing the familiar tends to be much less threatening than leading people into an unknown and much less predictable future.*

Both managing and leading require many of the same underlying skills and qualities—for example: good communication, emotional intelligence, and emotional maturity. However, *competent leadership demands, in particular, an ability to motivate others to stretch boundaries.*

Managers generally focus on planning, organizing and controlling how work gets done, while leaders must foster change.
　　　　—Robert L. Joss, Dean, Stanford Graduate School of Business

Points to consider:
- **How often do you stretch boundaries?**
- **Are you encouraged and supported in doing so?**
- **Do you over-manage and under-lead?**

- What problems concern you?
- To whom can you communicate your concerns?

The We're Successful Syndrome

If an organization's leadership becomes enamored with the success of what has worked—particularly with their own success within that structure—they can become emotionally dependent on retaining the status quo. In doing so, they blind themselves to the needs of an evolving environment and rationalize their resistance to any substantive change. "Look at how successful we are. We want people who can make the existing system even better. We don't want people upsetting a proven success formula."

This viewpoint effectively disallows true leadership development. Though programs may retain the title of Leadership Development, what is effectively allowed and offered instead are programs limited to management, as opposed to leadership development. The impact of this restricted and often misleading focus is that the adaptability and innovation needed for sustainability decline.

Sustainability, especially in a competitive environment, *depends on keeping an effective balance between managing a working system and leading it into new arenas.* In a dynamic environment, that balance is critical. Lack of balance is always evident in failed or declining organizations. Unless that dynamic balance is re-established, organizational success predictably becomes history. An organization caught in the "We're Successful" syndrome requires the courage of true leadership, not solely the skills of well-paid managers doing what worked before.

In times of change, those who are ready to learn will inherit the world, while those who believe they know will be marvelously prepared to deal with a world that has ceased to exist.

—Eric Hoffer.

Points to consider:

- **What non-contributing or destructive behavior is your organization doing simply because it worked in the past?**

- **In what ways has your organization been exploring new frontiers, innovating, and taking risks?**

Their Numbers Are Up

How often do we see obviously dysfunctional, emotionally immature people maintain their position and even be rewarded or promoted because their financial numbers are up? Mature leadership expects that positive, appropriate results be achieved. The viability of an enterprise depends on it. Numbers are a way to measure those results. They can be very helpful, if the appropriate measures are used.

Organizations are complex, and it can be helpful to simplify the measures that can expedite decisions and actions. However, when short-term financial or political factors play a significant role, these numbers are sometimes reduced to one or two bottom-line figures. Important factors that constitute real productivity and have long-term implications are often ignored or rationalized away. When that occurs chronically, the actual results are an inefficient use of resources, repressed communication, frustration, decreased morale, and the eventual loss of the best and the brightest.

When a dysfunctional executive's bottom line figures are up, more often than not, those figures are not valid indicators of real productivity. Valid, positive results that do occur are more likely to be despite the person's actions, not because of them. *When an obviously dysfunctional executive is kept in place because his numbers are up, something is being denied or ignored.* It is a sure sign of weak leadership—ignorant of or unwilling or unable to deal with what needs to be confronted.

To sin by silence when they should protest makes cowards of men.
—Abraham Lincoln

Points to consider:

- **How careful do you need to be in discussing topics like this in your workplace?**
- **Have you ever mistaken an upswing in your financial numbers for success?**
- **Besides the numbers, what other indicators help you to determine if what you are doing is effective?**

Mind Reading Required

How often do we see authenticity replaced with partial truths or outright lies? To what degree is a person expected to read between the lines of most communication? How often have we been kept on hold waiting for a decision that had already been made but was intentionally not communicated?

Communication of this type occurs continually in organizations. It always results in frustrations, inefficiencies, and loss of trust. The degree to which an organization's leadership condones, encourages, allows, and does not confront lack of honesty and authenticity, directly indicates that leadership's lack of maturity and integrity (which is always rationalized).

Points to consider:

- How would you describe the quality of your immediate group's communication?
- How authentically does your supervisor communicate?
- How authentic is your communication with your supervisor, peers, subordinates, and family members?
- To what degree is misleading or meaningless communication part of your daily interactions?
- How have you dealt with this type of situation in the past?

But I Intended to Do It

Intention is a necessary precursor to results, especially when you are trying to initiate change. Try to do something—get out of your chair—without intending to do so. You can't do it. Conscious or unconscious, our intention is fundamental to what we allow in our perception of reality.

If we are willing to look, we can have a reliable means to understand anyone's actual intentions, including our own, by observing what we actually wind up doing. What intention would someone need to create that result? For example, Judy was supposed to accomplish X. Instead, Y resulted. She said, "But I really intended to do X." That statement simply is not true. She got Y. Therefore, at some level, conscious or unconscious, her intent was Y, not X—or a stronger Y intention overrode the X intention. She may have consciously wanted to do X but unconsciously had a stronger intention to do Y.

If someone is having difficulty executing what he needs to do, particularly when he supposedly has the skills to do so, look to his intention. The motive will be different than the person has claimed. Behind the actual intention, conscious or unconscious, will be some emotion upon which the person is fixated. It is usually hostility (overt or covert), fear (real or imagined), grief (stuck in some loss), or apathy (why bother?). All are various symptoms and degrees of feeling overwhelmed.

If an individual is exhibiting any dysfunctional symptoms, often simple observation shows a person feeling insecure and over-whelmed—often denied. Continuing dysfunctional behavior is the manifestation of a self-sabotaging intention or belief (again, conscious or unconscious). Addressing the symptoms—that is, the overt behavior—will not provide more than temporary relief. The underlying intention or belief needs to be brought to light and its motivation recognized, acknowledged (owned), and addressed. *The Power of Intention*, by Wayne Dyer, addresses the potential of this dynamic. (Also see section IIIc, page 55, and "The Genesis of Limitiation," page 164.)

Points to consider:

- Think of an instance when your stated intention was different from your results. Are you aware of what your actual intention was?

- What were you reluctant to communicate, acknowledge, address, or confront?

The Genesis of Crazy-Making

In studying schizophrenic behavior, Dr. Gregory Bateson observed that a person's mental state appeared to be much more dependent on the interaction between the individual and his or her environment than on what was going on with his or her internal mental processes. With that observation, Bateson wanted to determine the kind of environment that could or would trigger schizophrenic behavior.

Based on additional studies, Bateson developed the theory of the Double Bind, a process and set of conditions which tend to create schizophrenic behavior. Drs. Chris Argyris and Donald Schön did a parallel study of organizations. They observed an almost identical process and set of conditions that result in schizophrenic behavior. That process and those conditions are the following:

1. The situation involves someone with authority over another.

2. The person with authority gives a direction or an order to a subordinate, along with some threat (implicit or explicit) of negative consequences for noncompliance.

   Example: "If you want a promotion, make sure I know everything that's going on!"

3. The authority then gives a contradictory instruction containing a threat. Example: "You're always telling me the problems. I want solutions, not problems. You had better start getting it right!"

This creates the Double Bind of "Damned if I do, damned if I don't." The following are what make the Double Bind crazy-making:

1. The authority makes two contradictory intentions or requirements that cannot be discussed and includes some form of threat. For example: "What contradictions? You're creating problems where there are none!"

2. The authority makes what cannot be discussed undiscussible but pretends this is not so. For example: "What do you mean we can't talk about it? You know I have an open-door policy on everything!"

3. The authority ensures that the other person feels he or she cannot leave the situation. Example: For senior executives, this deterrent may be in the form of "golden handcuffs." For others, it simply may be a tight labor market or concerns about a negative reference.

The most troubling aspect is not that an organization has contradictions, but that the contradictions are undiscussed or, worse, undiscussable. Opening the door to resolution demands an honest assessment of one's own role in a situation and a willingness and ability to discuss contradictions.

"Schizophrenergetic" (crazy-making) behavior is more prevalent in organizations than most people realize or are willing to acknowledge. It significantly reduces the likelihood of implementing needed change. This is particularly true in times of increased stress. How do we stay sane and responsibly proactive in complex environments, which can, naively or not, create schizophrenergetic behavior? Crazy-making environments can be righted if competent communication skills and willingness to dialogue are present. One of the most important things we can do is recognize how we may be contributing to schizophrenergetic behavior. If you observe crazy-making behavior, ask yourself, "How am I either creating, allowing, or contributing to this situation?" *If we don't recognize and take responsibility for our part, how can we ask others to take responsibility for their part?*

The Silo Effect

How often do we observe a lack of communication and interaction among groups in the same organization? This isolating behavior, known as the Silo Effect, severely limits potential synergies of strategic and functional alignment. The loss of cross-selling opportunities among departments and divisions is but one example.

Reasons for this lack of communication can range from simple introversion into assigned tasks to significant turf issues. Regardless of apparent causes, the Silo Effect stems from insecurity based in real or imagined fear. That persisting fear is a result of issues not being confronted and addressed. This avoidance of responsibility must be recognized and brought to light if the organization is to capitalize on its potential. *The degree to which the Silo Effect persists is directly indicative of insecure, apathetic, arrogant, or incompetent management and leadership.* When present, it requires priority attention.

Well-designed and well-delivered communication programs, along with competent coaching, can be very helpful in relieving the Silo Effect, as can the Communication Clearing Process outlined in chapter 7, page 257. However, all will be for naught if people are afraid to speak their truth. *The presence or absence of a safe environment in which honest communication and true dialogue can flourish reflects directly what senior management actually wants and is willing to allow.*

The presence of spontaneous, authentic communication is an indication that senior management is relatively secure and has a healthy sense of self-confidence and self-esteem. This indicates emotional maturity at the top management level and suggests a positive prognosis for the organization as a whole.

The willingness and ability to honestly confront repressed communication has a greater impact on organizational effectiveness than personal charisma, management style, incentive programs, technical expertise, or product uniqueness. Those can be valuable, and sometimes vital, but they will not be utilized to the extent possible if repressed communication—of any nature—is present.

When the Silo Effect is lessened or eliminated, synergies occur; productivity and morale rise, often dramatically *Effectively dealing with the Silo Effect, or any communication deficiency, should be a priority of senior management.* (See section "Dealing with Repressed Communication," chapter 7, page 241)

Points to consider:
- How prevalent is the silo effect in your organization?
- Between which groups is it most noticeable?

- How would you evaluate the effectiveness of those groups' management?
- If you were CEO, what would you do?

LOOKING FOR A FEW HEROES

A leader's job is to ensure an organization's growth and development. To be sustainable, an organization needs to show a return on its resources. How that return is achieved must be accurately communicated to the organization's stakeholders.

Moreover, most people will agree that the current corporate financial reporting process is dysfunctional. Its short-term emphasis misallocates resources that often have costly long-term consequences. Even more significant, the process breeds dishonesty, manipulation, and fraud.

So, how can corporate leaders move beyond the numbers game? They can start by communicating to the investment community what factors drive long-term value in their companies. Professor Baruch Lev of the Stern School of Business at New York University states that more than half of the market value of S&P 500 companies is due to non-financial factors. Some of these are: quality of management, execution of corporate strategy, corporate reputation and brand, innovation in developing new products or services, research and development efforts, patents, use of human and intellectual capital, and alliances and business relationships. These non-financial factors are more difficult to quantify.

For many leaders, it is easier to hang their hats on quarterly financials than do the work needed to provide a more comprehensive (and honest) perspective. The resulting reports are misleading and incomplete, and therefore lack integrity. By focusing more attention beyond just the short term, leaders can move the discussion toward the actual factors that provide real value.

We need leaders who are willing to stand tall; stop creating purposefully misleading smoke screens; and insist on a forthright process where we all can learn and together cocreate a new standard of honest reporting that better serves all stakeholders. Where are these courageous paradigm-shifting heroes?

There's a politically incorrect definition of a pioneer: the guy with the arrows in his back. That's fundamentally what any of us who are trying to push the envelope are up against.
—Ken Wilber

Unless an organization sees that its task is to lead change, that organization will not survive. It is therefore a central 21st Century challenge for management that its organization become a change leader.
—Peter Drucker

THE DNA OF EMPOWERMENT

2

THE EMOTIONALLY WISE LEADER

If your actions inspire others to dream more, learn more, do more and become more, you are a leader.

—John Quincy Adams

The maturity of an organization's leadership lays the foundation and sets the tone for everything that follows. It determines the organization's priorities and ultimately its contribution to its stakeholders and the world.

The previous chapter looked at the difficulty people and organizations have in dealing with even vitally needed change. It briefly described some of the more common issues that arise and suggested that we are better served, individually and organizationally, by the presence of greater emotional maturity.

This chapter looks at the characteristics of emotionally wise leadership and outlines a process to facilitate the development of an emotionally mature organization built on integrity. It also identifies training concerns that, when addressed, help to optimize the developmental process and impact. Subsequent chapters clarify and develop specific aspects of that process.

THE EMOTIONALLY WISE LEADER— QUALITIES AND CHARACTERISTICS

Emotionally wise leaders share certain definable qualities and characteristics that set them apart. They behave in the following ways:

- Live by, consciously relate to, and act from fundamental values (developed in chapter 3)
- Do not repress feelings; express and use them in ways that contribute positively
- Have a sense of purpose; contribute in a way that extends beyond themselves
- Have presence; listen to and acknowledge others
- Have a healthy sense of perspective and balance
- Authentically walk their talk; are willing to share their ideas and feelings with honesty, sincerity, sensitivity, and compassion
- Can see the big picture without losing sight of the current situation
- Respond to their environment rather than react to it
- Are aware that everything they do and say has impact; are responsible and accountable for that impact
- Have the flexibility and resiliency to change their behavior when their impact does not create the result they want

- Are willing to honestly look at themselves and acknowledge their shortcomings and their strengths
- Have the discipline, determination, and persistence to correct their shortcomings, expand current strengths, and develop other strengths
- Are secure within themselves; are willing to ask for and receive help
- Are willing to let someone else take charge if that person can do a better job
- Have the capability and willingness to develop intimate and lasting relationships
- Do not, and will not, tolerate irresponsible or unethical behavior
- Help others help themselves
- Encourage, develop, and facilitate dialogue
- Have sensitivity to and respect for the dignity of all with whom they come into contact, and thus create an environment in which individuals are respected for who they are and feel safe to expand and grow
- Have well-defined and clearly communicated boundaries of behavior (principles)
- Have character, vision, and vitality
- Are able to assess and evaluate relative priorities, which allows them to make sane decisions and act simultaneously with humility and a sense of confidence, even under difficult or rapidly changing circumstances
- Are adaptable and know which role to play when

- Are trustworthy and trust people who have earned their trust
- Have the courage to try new things, make mistakes, and learn from their mistakes
- Have the determination to deal with and persevere through the inevitable resistance to real change, their own as well as that of others
- Have integrity (See chapter 3)

To live in the company of men-at-their-best is the finest thing possible. How can a man be considered wise, if when he has the choice, he does not live in such surroundings?

—Confucius

A foundation of emotional maturity enables a leader to see the big picture; make strategic decisions, changes, and commitments; and innovate, follow through, and get the desired results, executing it all with sensitivity and compassion. These characteristics are extolled but seldom consistently observed. While leadership style and methods vary considerably, the demonstration of these qualities enables the emotionally wise leader to inspire commitment and action from others in ways that contribute to everyone's expanded well-being and awareness.

These qualities, rare in most, remain consistent and persistent in emotionally mature individuals of integrity. They provide a *competitive advantage* and lay a solid foundation for generating additional competitive advantages in the future. However, these people are human, by no means perfect, and make many mistakes because they are willing to try things their more timid associates are too afraid to attempt. While they make mistakes, they seldom repeat the same ones because they consciously make a point to learn from each one.

Emotionally wise leaders realize they are living in a dynamic universe and that survival itself depends on their ability and willingness to work with that dynamic rather than fight or resist it. Emotionally wise leaders act on this awareness. From their secure foundation they easily step where others fear to tread. They are therefore naturally innovative and creative.

Emotionally wise leaders know that the key to organizational emotional maturity and to an organization's vitalization rests on selecting people with the greatest potential for making a positive contribution. *Wise leaders realize that hiring, developing, and supporting emotionally mature people of integrity must be among their primary goals.* They make sure that they implement supportive strategies and policies. They look for and proactively facilitate the development of emotional maturity in others. Whatever form it takes, their priority is to create an emotionally mature organization of integrity. They are willing to do what it takes to achieve that. *Integrity is the core of truly great leadership.* It is developed in depth in chapter 3. (See "Integrity and Greatness," page 99.)

Example is not the main thing in influencing others. It's the only thing.
—Albert Schweitzer

Points to consider:
- **What is your top priority for the next year (Hint: To what do you give most of your attention)?**

- On your list of priorities, how far from the top is the development of emotional maturity? Honestly, is it a real priority at all?
- Are you so busy with other things that you just don't have the time to work on emotional maturity?
- If so, how long has this been going on?
- Given your organization, if you were CEO and wanted to create a profitable, sustainable organization of integrity with high morale and an outstanding reputation, what would be your priorities and their order of importance?
- What would be your first action?

SELECTING, DEVELOPING, AND RETAINING THE EMOTIONALLY MATURE

The more emotionally mature people of integrity present within an organization or group, the greater its potential positive impact. These people are mentally and emotionally present; have a strong sense of self-worth; and are secure, willing to learn, and open to new ideas. Their perspective is broad, balanced, and relatively free of prejudices and rigid ideas. Emotionally mature people are therefore the most capable of meeting their own needs and optimally using their inherent talents, and developing appropriate functional skills. Consequently, they can best meet client needs and thereby offer the greatest potential for making a positive contribution. Their selection, development, and retention are critical to optimizing success.

When leadership is weak, certain out-of-proportion tendencies occur. Personnel selections are almost entirely based on factors other than integrity and emotional maturity. Hiring practices can range from hiring yes-men to a sole emphasis on hiring people with a particular functional expertise. Functional competence *and* experience are vital to organizational success. However, they are secondary to emotional maturity and integrity. Emotionally mature individuals have little need to defend ideas or positions. These individuals tend to be responsible and adaptive, easily learning what needs to be done. *Placing little real attention on integrity and emotional maturity is one of the costliest, yet most common, rationalized mistakes of many executives.*

It is critical to make the correct choices about which individuals to select for training and development programs, in terms of optimizing results and return on investment. Well-designed, competently delivered, and appropriately reinforced training programs can have a very positive impact—when delivered to emotionally mature people.

Unfortunately, management often selects personnel for development programs based on job title or function rather than emotional maturity. Often, that includes emotionally immature people. Because such individuals are frequently feeling overwhelmed, they are reactive rather than responsive. Their defensive reaction precludes being open to new ideas, change or growth. Therefore, training the emotionally immature is, more often than not, a waste of resources.

Retaining these individuals is always costly and hurtful to the organization. Emotional immaturity always diverts resources—mental, emotional, and physical. It also does harm to the individuals because supporting dysfunctional behaviors prevents them from facing their immaturity.

Only by attracting the best people will you accomplish great deeds.
—Colin Powell

VITALIZING THE ORGANIZATION AND OPTIMIZING PERFORMANCE

Despite the profound impact of integrity, many leaders focus their attention and energy elsewhere, not fully comprehending that even seemingly minor lapses of integrity can take a huge toll on individual dignity and morale. These lapses also have enormous financial and environmental costs.

Because integrity and emotional maturity are so vital to an organization's long-term success, the first priority of leadership is to evaluate the emotional maturity of senior staff, as those individuals set the tone and resonance for all employees under them. Since like attracts like, these senior staff will attract and select those who are of a comparable emotional level.

We too often fail to recognize that our integrity profoundly affects our actions, feelings, relationships, results, and happiness. Accurate evaluation of our own integrity has a direct impact on our self-image, self-respect, self-esteem, and self-confidence. *Lack of integrity inevitably creates problems. Authenticity and honest communication are the first to suffer.*

Without addressing causal factors, actual and potential problems do not go away. They magnify. Every decade or two, the corporate business world explodes into a rash of scandals, which creates a flurry of finger pointing and blame, as well as demands for tougher rules and laws. These explosions recur largely because, as problems become apparent, society does nothing to address them or attempts to do something by focusing primarily on dealing with symptoms. Often society does not recognize, much less address, the underlying cause or causes.

In response to recent scandals, passing new laws or clarifying and requiring adherence to expected behaviors may be helpful, even necessary, initial steps. However, those expected behaviors must align with the individual's fundamental values. A sense of personal ownership must also be present. If these conditions are not met, the result will be, predictably, little more than superficial social compliance. Lacking real ownership, compliance begins to wane and more outside enforcement mechanisms are required. Clarifying what is expected is a positive step and may address some legal and public relations concerns. However, to comply with someone else's standard does not constitute or create integrity.

The following section outlines a process to expand emotional maturity and integrity, thereby vitalizing organizational growth and performance.

THE RECOMMENDED PROCESS

This process is comprised of seven steps, starting with securing a commitment from senior management, and leading to a continual reassessment of each step or aspect of the entire process.

Step I. Secure Management Commitment

Ensure that senior management is committed to the primacy of integrity and emotional maturity in all organizational processes. This includes relationships outside the organization as well the process of selecting, hiring, developing, promoting, and retaining people within the organization. When such a commitment to organizational integrity and emotional maturity is truly present, the positive resonance and energy of the entire organization often rises dramatically.

Management's committed intention itself must be authentic and complete. Anything less will be misleading and foster cynicism, misallocation of resources, and undermine leadership credibility. This intention must be communicated passionately and persistently throughout the entire organization. (See "A Word of Caution: The Impact of Self-Image," this chapter, page 62.)

A cup of water to put out a cart load of burning firewood is an inadequate response.
> —Chinese saying

Note: To optimize effectiveness, Steps II and III should be implemented concurrently. *Subsequent chapters are devoted primarily to developing the clarity, models, and means to facilitate these two steps.*

Step II. Educate the Organization

If an organization truly intends to revitalize itself with integrity and emotional maturity as its foundation, then everyone in the organization needs to understand the following points:

- What emotional maturity and integrity actually are and their interrelationship
- Their vital importance
- Management's commitment to developing an emotionally mature organization of integrity
- How to evaluate integrity and emotional maturity
- How to facilitate the development of emotional maturity—personally, professionally, and organizationally

It's not enough to do your best. You must know what to do and then do your best.

—W. Edwards Deming

Step III. Facilitate Individuals to Empower Themselves

No business is successful, even if it flourishes, in a society that does not care for or about its people.

—Eugene C. Dorsey

Treat people as if they were what they ought to be and you will help them to become what they are capable of being.

—Johann Wolfgang von Goethe

III-a. Develop presence. Presence, discussed in chapter 1, is the quality of being in the now with one's full attention fully engaging the present environment regardless of what that environment is. It is mindfulness. Presence is the foundation of discernment upon which integrity stands and is the platform for personal power.

When individuals are mentally or emotionally distracted, they miss information, lose discernment, and limit their facility for decision making. The result is a less-than-optimal response.

If they are stuck in old patterns, they are not present, and cannot and will not act responsibly. Responsibility is a component of and integral to true power. Without presence, people cannot operate with integrity or be truly powerful.

III-b. Eliminate repressed communication. Repressed communication is the bane of most organizations and the major cause of the Silo Effect (described in chapter 1) The willingness and ability to confront repressed communication honestly has a tremendously positive impact on leadership and organizational effectiveness. Other virtues may exist in an organization, but they will not be fully realized as long as communication is repressed. (See "Dealing with Repressed Communication," chapter 7, page 241.)

There is a direct correlation between the degree of repressed communication and the degree of a person's or an organization's emotional maturity. It follows that when repressed communication is released, cocreation, real collaboration, and true teamwork can manifest. Then creativity can expand, along with innovation, efficiency, effectiveness, productivity, customer relations, and cross-selling. This constructively impacts morale, turnover, profitability, and susceptibility. The Communication Clearing Process, outlined in chapter 7, page 257, can be very helpful in facilitating more open communication. However, personal example by the organization's leadership remains the most important influencing factor.

III-c. Find and transform limiting beliefs and self-sabotaging patterns. Fortunately, recent advances in energy psychology make finding and transforming limiting beliefs a relatively easy process. Of particular note is the work of Andrew Hahn, Psy.D. His innovative process called Guided Self Healing elegantly locates the original cause of the problem, including limiting beliefs, and transmutes its energy toward constructive growth. His forthcoming book, tentatively titled *Accessing Our Hidden Wisdom: Accelerating Personal Growth*, will be available in 2007.

In *Power Versus Force*, David Hawkins, M.D., Ph.D., evaluates from a macro perspective relative states of awareness. His research points out that even a few people of integrity with fewer limiting beliefs can have an enormous influence in shaping our world.

III-d. Develop a positive self-image. An individual's self-image sets his or her boundaries. If people expand their self-image, they expand their ability and willingness to cocreate and contribute. They can enhance their self-image only if they are willing to look honestly at themselves. Most people are too insecure to undertake this process on their own. Providing an organizational environment and support system in which honest, competent self-assessment and authentic communication are the norm not only attracts individuals with a positive self-image but also facilitates everyone's self-image development.

All that we are is the result of what we have thought.

—Buddha

The Self-Image Process (outlined in chapter 7, page 258) can be a useful and profound process for significantly expanding a person's real self-image. Done glibly, it is a waste of time.

III-e. Help the able be more able. Recognize and develop individual underlying strengths, inherent talents, and hidden or repressed passions. Along with selecting emotionally mature individuals and providing programs to eliminate repressed communication, an organization must provide an environment that nurtures individual development. Leadership that truly wants an organization to grow and capitalize on its full potential cannot afford to ignore individual development. An organization comprised of the emotionally mature individuals will create such an environment. They proactively take the following actions:

- Help individuals recognize, determine, and uncover their own values, strengths, and talents; when those are found, passion follows. (See "The Value of Competent Coaching," chapter 8, page 291.)

- Place individuals in jobs and on assignments in which their talents and proclivities can best be used, encouraged, and developed; focus on building upon individual unique strengths (*People Pattern Power: The Nine Keys to Business Success,* by Wyatt and Marilyne Woodsmall, provides methods to easily assess individual strengths and optimally align them with functional skill needs.)

- Assist individuals who are not performing up to their full potential; do not delay in removing and replacing individuals who are unwilling to do so. (See "Willingness—The Determining Factor," chapter 5, page 175.)
- Provide competent facilitation, coaching, and training where needed for personal, professional, and organizational growth

Everyone has talent. What is rare is to recognize it and then have the courage to follow the talent to the unknown place where it might lead.
—Sandra Day O'Connor

Step IV. Cocreate the Organization's Vision, Core Values, Strategic Intent, Strategic Objectives, and Operating Principles.

Unless an organization incorporates cocreation, the best its leadership can ever expect is willing compliance—a far less motivating energy. Cocreation provides individuals with a feeling of involvement, participation, and contribution, which greatly increases their sense of determination, commitment, and ownership. Some call this energy passion; some call it heart. The degree of cocreation and heart energy present corresponds directly to the level of emotional maturity present. The higher that level, the greater is an individual's fundamental sense of security, ability to let go of what is no longer working, openness to consider different opinions and options, ability to authentically dialogue, and willingness to stretch into the unknown.

A group of individuals collaborating from this foundation generates a world of exciting possibilities not previously considered. However, the cocreative process will be a sham to the degree that emotional maturity and Steps I through III are taken superficially.

An organization's *vision* provides a picture of the ideal. The extent to which emotional maturity and integrity are present within the organization determines not only how big and how compelling the organization's vision can be, but also the probability of manifesting that vision to its full potential.

Imagination is everything. It is the preview to life's coming attractions.
—Albert Einstein

In addition, the degree of emotional maturity and integrity in an organization will become evident in the organization's *core values*; the de facto values the organization actually operates from and which determine its behavior. When core values align with and support *essence values* (developed in chapter 3) positive synergies happen quite elegantly. When a company's core values ignore or violate essence qualities (for example, "profit at any cost"), difficulties inevitably manifest.

Understanding our organization's actual core values is key to choosing priorities that optimize production viability. To the degree that Steps I through III are in place, an organization can achieve greater depth of meaningful purpose, which includes and goes beyond increased profitability.

An in-depth look at an organization's core values provides its members an opportunity to make choices that are more informed.

This is the base that provides a sense of potential real contribution that generates passion, creativity, and commitment, opening to possibilities not previously imagined.

Strategic intent is that impeccable focus and intention so compelling that the vision will necessarily manifest (e.g., surpass XYZ corporation in profitability; destroy the enemy's ability to resupply). The strategic intent generates the broad, key objectives known as *strategic objectives*, which provide the framework for executing the organization's vision and values, e.g., cash flow to cover at least XXX% of fixed and variable costs. It is important to ensure that all strategic objectives are mutually reinforcing. If one does not obviously reinforce the others, it is probably not a strategic objective.

All subsequent plans, programs, projects, goals and resource allocations must contribute to one or more of the strategic objectives or be eliminated. If they do not contribute, they divert resources needed to attain those objectives. Without strategic objectives to provide a benchmark, there is little or no coordinated focus, and resources are either dispersed, diluted, or otherwise wasted.

Operating principles are boundaries of individual and organizational behavior that support the attainment of the strategic objectives and help manifest the vision. Violating those boundaries of behavior expends resources on things that distract rather than support that movement. Operating principles should be clearly defined, stated, understood, committed to, and honored. When an organization imposes rather than cocreates these boundaries, their workability and value is limited. The vision, values, strategic intent, strategic objectives, and operating principles must all be in alignment and mutually supportive. Cocreating these key elements provides the foundation for an organization's overall vitalization.

Competing for the Future, by Gary Hamel and C. K. Pradhalad, offers excellent suggestions and insights to help facilitate this process. The Institute of Cultural Affairs' *Winning Through Participation*, by Laura J. Spenser, also offers methods to facilitate the cocreative process.

Cocreation brings focused intention into being and adds passion to the sense of teamwork and commitment. However, in the absence of emotional maturity, cocreation and teamwork will not occur and the vision will remain little more than a flight of fancy, misdirecting potential and wasting resources.

Step V. Codevelop Strategic and Operational Plans

Out of a focused vision, core values, strategic intent and strategic objectives, people within an organization develop appropriate and focused intention, meaningful actions, and a positive self-image. Without bonds of integrity, these can easily shift toward becoming inappropriate and dispersed intention, inadequate action and a negative self-image. The cocreative process, once established, can be duplicated throughout the organization.

Another book by The Institute of Cultural Affairs, *The Art of Focused Conversation*, contains many participatory exercises for codeveloping plans and addressing business issues.

Step VI. Implement Plans, Programs, and Projects

This is where the effects of the previous steps will be demonstrated. As emotional maturity develops, sane, creative, responsive behavior expands exponentially, elegantly addressing changing needs. Increased productivity and morale should be obvious.

Ample resources—publications and organizations—are available to support management in implementing processes. *Managing by the Numbers*, by Kremerr, Russuto, and Case, is a common-sense guide to financials and their meaning, and is a resource for making performance measures accessible.

Step VII. Reassess

Reassessment and adjustment of Steps I through III make Steps IV through VII clearer and flow more smoothly. If synergistic results are not forthcoming, then there is a high probability that one or more of the previous steps has likely been skipped, glossed over, or misapplied.

COMMON MISTAKES

What is the use of running when we are on the wrong road?
—Bavarian proverb

The process is most effective when the seven steps are undertaken in the suggested sequence. In many instances, an organization attempts Step V, planning, with few of the prior steps adequately in place. Without the compelling vision and strategic objectives of

Step IV in place, developing plans, goals and budgets does little more than tweak the existing system. Without a vision and aligned strategic objectives, management will devote resources primarily to planning and implementing improvements to the status quo. They may avoid ineffective fixes, but without a compelling vision, the emphasis will be much more myopic, and will do little to truly invigorate the organization, deal with a changing competitive environment, foster innovation, or lead the organization in needed new directions.

Attempting to do Step IV, cocreating a compelling vision, without Step III, facilitating individuals to empower themselves, significantly reduces the chance of a truly compelling vision being created and manifested. Without Step III, the best one can hope for is willing compliance to someone else's vision rather than the much more expansive energy and motivation that is generated from a truly cocreated vision.

Similarly, implementing any parts of Step III will have greater impact to the degree that Step II, educating the organization, is in process. Step II simply will not happen to any meaningful degree without the intention and commitment of senior management, Step I.

A WORD OF CAUTION—THE IMPACT OF SELF-IMAGE

Self-image is a crucial part of change. What individuals are capable of achieving is limited by the actual image they have of themselves. In fact, they will not obtain results that exceed that self-image. If, by fortuitous circumstances, results exceed that image, they cannot endure. Either they simply collapse, or the individual will sabotage those successes. What we manifest reflects our actual self-image. The "size" of our self-image and the substantive contribution and wellbeing we allow to manifest directly correlates to our actual, not social, level of emotional maturity.

The initiation of the seven-step process creates a synergy and a tremendous amount of energy, attention, intention, expectation and excitement with amazing speed and magnitude.

However, if the leader's actual self-image is smaller than the vision the group cocreates, it is a formula for disaster. A leader with a low self-image is a leader with a corresponding lack of emotional maturity, despite any public relations image or posturing to the contrary. That person will not allow the creation of an organization with a high level of emotional maturity. Consciously, or unconsciously, as irrational as it is, that person will regard an emotionally mature organization as a threat to his or her survival. As leader, he or she will sabotage the accomplishment of the vision until it contracts enough to be in alignment with his or her actual self-image. He or she will rationalize and justify every sabotaging act.

When leaders allow this to occur, needed changes are not made. Opportunities are lost, and expectations, initiative and morale are severely deflated. As a result, the leader's successor will have an even more difficult time initiating any revitalization program because of disillusionment or apathy resulting from previously unfulfilled management initiatives. People begin to think, "This too shall pass," and passive resistance to any management initiative becomes the norm. This illustrates why accurate assessment of management's real intention is crucial (Step I, page 52).

Our actual self-image, not some differing public persona, is the foundation for what we will manifest. It directly correlates with our actual integrity and emotional maturity. It therefore follows that *a person's integrity and emotional maturity should be among the Board of Directors' top criteria in CEO selection and retention.*

POTENTIAL IMPACT

Adequately implementing and reinforcing Steps I, II, and III offers the greatest possibility for optimizing the selection, development and retention of an outstanding, emotionally mature leadership. It also encourages the growth of an organization in which all members feel they are learning and growing, and therefore are excited about the organization's future and their part in it. They then view change as a welcome challenge and opportunity.

When responsibly and persistently implemented, these steps result in the creation of an organization with a reputation for integrity, honesty, adaptability, collaboration, innovation, excellence, reliability, outstanding customer service and exceptional personnel development. This greatly contributes to long-term viability and profitability in an environment of high morale and low turnover.

What a new face courage puts on everything!

—Ralph Waldo Emerson

Points to consider:

- Can you find evidence of each step, I through VII, in your organization? If not, which steps are lacking and what can you do to begin working on them?

LEADERSHIP FACTORS

Life has many nuances, subtleties and complexities. Leadership, as a part of that complexity, has many interacting and interdependent factors (Table 2.1). The arrows indicate the interactiveness of the various factors and the general direction(s) in which the energies flow to manifest perceptions of reality. A positive/negative manifestation of any of these factors correspondingly reflects in them all.

You cannot have a proud and chivalrous spirit if your conduct is mean and paltry; for whatever a man's actions are, such must be his spirit.
—Demosthenes

Table 2.1 shows integrity as one of a number of interrelated factors. Importantly, integrity is also the wholeness of all the interrelated factors (developed further in chapter 3). Those factors synergistically integrate to create responsible presence, the essence of emotionally wise leadership. When integrity is lacking, those factors lack real substance, are not fully utilized or effective and do not contribute to a synergistic whole. Opportunity and potential are lost. When such is the case, leadership is glib, superficial and ineffective: in effect nonexistent.

This country cannot afford to be materially rich and spiritually poor.
—John F. Kennedy

TABLE 2.1 - Leadership Factors

						→	
Presence being in the moment; facing the difficult issues *now*	↕	**Courage** willingness to confront one's fears, state an unpopular opinion	↕	**Responsibility** ability to respond—versus react—to whatever is present	↑	**Integrity** spontaneous responsibility; essence of emotional maturity	
Self-respect honoring one's own emotions	↕	**Self-confidence** knowing you can cope with whatever is	↕	**Self-esteem** one's self-evaluation	↑	**Self-image** perception of one's impact potential	
Communication attention, intention, and duplication	↕	**Rapport** affinity, respect for others	↕	**Reality** mutual agreement	↑	**Understanding** awareness and ability to apply it	
Dialogue authentic two-way communication	↕	**Collaboration** with mutual concern	↕	**Compassion** and caring	↑	**Trust** faith that one will deliver what is promised	
Values consideration of importances	↕	**Principles** behavioral boundaries that maintain values	↕	**Vision** ideal scene of a better, bigger future	↑	**Vitality** excitement and passion for expanded possibilities	
Power ability and willingness to act	↕	**Character** adherence to principle	↕	**Empowerment** giving oneself permission and authority to act	↑	**Cocreative Action** responsible alignment of imagination, desires and expectations	
Intention impeccable focus, force and direction	↕	**Determination** strength of intention	↕	**Perseverance** persistence in overcoming resistance	↑	Impact Results Growth	↑ Satisfaction Happiness Joy

OPTIMIZING TRAINING

I am defeated, and know it, if I meet any human being from whom I find myself unable to learn anything.
—George Herbert Palmer

Over the last several decades, thoughtful leaders have made significant progress in understanding organizational, managerial, and leadership dynamics. Increasingly, senior management has been viewing practical implementation of these concepts and approaches as an investment rather than a cost.

Yet for all the good ideas, the excitement, and the shift of awareness, few of the hot new concepts have manifested their hoped-for potential. Some were more difficult to apply than anticipated. Some turned out to have more fluff than substance. Some good ideas were simply oversold beyond their functional use. Some otherwise excellent concepts failed simply because of poor execution or insufficient reinforcement.

Barbara, an executive vice president of a large national bank, said she would be sending over what she thought was a good management article. Barbara is a very competent manager of both people and tasks. She definitely is goal-oriented and does get results. She also does everything she can to encourage, develop and "grow" her people, not just functionally but as human beings. She has been very proactive in this area and, in fact, has initiated numerous human-development programs for her staff. She brought in experts and hired consultants. She did all the "right things." Nevertheless, few of these programs have met with any real success. Her group attained outstanding results, but more because of her leadership skills and sensitivities than because of the human-development programs. She spends a great deal of time personally coaching her people, accomplishing what the programs could not. Overall, she is an enlightened and exceptional executive.

Barbara said she strongly agreed with the article's emphasis that management development should be focused not on generalized human-development issues but solely on the functional requirements of the business objectives. Of course, business objectives and the functional capabilities to achieve them are important and critical to an organization's survival and success. But why would a competent, enlightened, caring individual who is honestly concerned about the well-being and growth of her staff be in such strong agreement with this exclusively functional focus? Her consistently disappointing experience with developmental training programs eventually convinced her that such programs did little to increase job performance. Unfortunately, that impression is often valid for a number of reasons.

Common reasons for mediocre, poor, or no results include the following:

1. No program at all, or, a pretense of one
2. Wrong focus—not addressing actual needs
3. Poor design and/or poor execution
4. Inappropriate teaching methodology
5. Poor selection of participants

6. Wrong sequence
7. Limited scope
8. Missed synergies
9. Inadequate follow-up support and reinforcement

Underlying the above reasons is a superficial or nonexistent understanding of the dynamics involved in creating successful outcomes of developmental programs. In contrast, many programs are well thought out by knowledgeable people who address real needs. Many are both competently designed and delivered. However, it is also true that relatively few programs have adequate follow-up and reinforcement, and that inadequacies in any one of the above elements could destroy the program's effectiveness. In reason number five, poor selection of participants, lies one of the biggest but least acknowledged problems.

Selecting Participants by Emotional Maturity

Emotionally mature people tend to be the most open, quickest, and most responsible students, and the most likely to creatively integrate and use their experience in a responsible, productive manner (developed in chapters 5, 6 and 8). *Unfortunately, there is often little correlation between who is selected for training and the selectee's level of emotional maturity.*

Furthermore, the emotionally mature people who could really benefit from well-designed programs tend to be lumped with all the others. Most trainers teach to the lowest common denominator, results, with rare exception, are predictably mediocre. No one wins. The biggest losers are the organization and those mature individuals who could have really benefited but for the lowered standard of delivery which accommodated people, many of whom should not have been there in the first place.

Without competent evaluation of employees' emotional maturity, leadership and interpersonal training programs are bound to fall short of expectations. Technical and procedural skills training focused to attain particular business objectives become the default emphasis. Certainly, programs should target business objectives and develop functional skills to attain them, but not as the only or even primary consideration. *When maturity level is the primary but not exclusive consideration, management succeeds in developing well-rounded, responsible people providing a sound, long-term organizational foundation.* Following are some other factors also key to training effectiveness, which are frequently ignored or under-emphasized.

Doing the Right Thing in the Most Effective Sequence

One significant reason why excellent concepts often do not fulfill their potential is that management has not ensured that the prerequisite foundational skills are in place or actively being developed. Unless skills and attitudes such as presence, listening, acknowledging, respecting the dignity of others, and the like are present, management will fail to optimize those resources.

When leaders incorrectly assume such foundational abilities are present, or regard them as "too basic for our sophisticated people," or simply ignore them, they do not address the actuality that a large percentage of employees (and the general population) unfortunately lack these basic skills. That shortfall has a significant impact on overall training effectiveness and organizational performance.

Similarly, cocreating a vision and a set of values is a critically important part of optimizing organizational and human capital. However, if leaders attempt such cocreation without first dealing with the repressed communication present, they significantly reduce the possibility of the cocreation occurring. The same is true for any team-building program. Recognizing and appropriately addressing foundational prerequisites can contribute greatly to optimizing training effectiveness.

Developing Critical Mass

Critical mass is that state reached when a process becomes self-sustaining. In training, *critical mass occurs when management provides sufficient reinforcement and sufficient volume,* or percent of target population trained, *to reach a new norm.*

Excellent, well-designed, well-received programs, delivered in the optimal sequence, often never reach their full potential simply because they were not sufficiently reinforced or delivered to enough people to accrue critical mass. When leadership does not reinforce new desired behavior, individuals naturally tend to revert to the older, more familiar, comfortable behaviors. Lack of sufficient volume and reinforcement of good programs is one of the most wasteful and costly mistakes management teams continually make.

Furthermore, management selection of participants based on their emotional maturity significantly reduces the numbers required to gain critical mass because these people go on to encourage and lead others to responsibly demand, create and support needed programs.

Also, many training courses are stand-alone programs. Frequently, with only minimal extra effort or cost, a program can be redesigned to reinforce aspects of other programs creating synergy as well as movement toward critical mass.

Including Overlooked People

Why do some people learn and others just don't get it? There is a significant minority of bright people who assimilate information and learn differently than the way expected or taught in most educational institutions or programs. In the typical training course, these people are not exposed to needed information in a way that they can assimilate and use. Such training is not helpful, either to them or to the organization, with the result that both are deprived.

Recent research on how and why individuals think and assimilate information has provided valuable new insights into the learning process. Only recently have educators begun to understand and acknowledge some learning disabilities that were previously regarded as a source of embarrassment, denied, and/or ignored. As Ronald Davis and Eldon Braun point out in their book, *The Gift of Dyslexia*, some characteristics previously judged as dysfunctional can become a source of strength and unique ability when understood and supported.

The same is true as well of Attention Deficit Disorder (ADD and ADHD). Understanding the various ways different personalities track and learn can be critical in optimizing the learning experience. An additional excellent resource is *The Enneagram Intelligences: Understanding Personality for Effective Teaching and Learning* by Janet Levine.

Incorporating various learning needs in training and program design and implementation makes a significant difference in increasing training effectiveness. It can expand significantly the number of people actually reached in the training process.

FUNDAMENTALS IN PLACE

An organization will optimize its potential and use of resources to the degree the following are actually in place:

- Competent, committed, emotionally mature leadership
- Appropriate foundational concepts and programs
- Participant selection based on emotional maturity as a primary consideration
- Competence in program design and delivery, including synergistic reinforcement
- Programs and actions delivered in an optimal developmental and reinforcing sequence, including appropriate supportive activities such as competent coaching and mentoring
- Programs delivered in sufficient volume and concentration to attain critical mass

THE DNA OF LEADERSHIP

3

INTEGRITY—THE VITAL FACTOR

Attention, alertness, awareness, clarity, liveliness, vitality are all manifestations of integrity, oneness with your true nature.
—Sri Nisargadatta Maharaj

Susan quietly slipped the stapler into her purse. "It really isn't stealing," she told herself. "The waste around here is unbelievable. They'll never miss it. Besides, Betty and Peter have practically equipped their entire home offices from here. And management, what do they do to deserve those big bonuses and expense accounts? I deserve something, too!"

Meanwhile, twelve floors above, Eric was preparing for the board meeting. Recently, a few members had been asking for more detail on the offshore projects. He reasoned, "Sure, the way the projects are set up a few of us will do well—and why shouldn't we? The projects are all technically legal. However, the Board is not operationally involved enough to fully comprehend the de-tails. Too much information could be misunderstood. Better provide the minimum. No use creating unnecessary problems.

75

Besides, the Board has never really understood, much less appreciated, what I've done for this company. Last year's bonus was a joke."

When we do something that we know isn't right, our automatic defensive reaction is to justify that action. We often project blame to distract ourselves, as well as others, from looking at our own irresponsible acts. Not all of us are willing to look at how or why we exhibit those behaviors. However, for those of us who truly desire more integrity in our lives and are willing to look, what can we do?

To use an analogy, author and Nobel Peace Prize nominee Thich Nhat Hanh, when speaking of peace said, "There is no way to peace; peace, itself, is the way." In the same way, there is no way to integrity, integrity itself is the way. In other words, if we want more integrity in our life, we must act with more integrity.

Become the change you want to see in the world.
—Mahatma Gandhi

However, that seems to be more easily said than done. How do we live and model integrity when most of us can't even state with precision what integrity is or differentiate it from morals, principles, or character, and few of us seem to understand or appreciate the real cost of its absence? Integrity remains a somewhat nebulous ideal rather than a present and continual part of our lives and behaviors. Dictionaries provide little clarity; they tend to define related concepts in terms of each other. We need to take a deeper look at this elusive factor—

what it actually is and its qualities, aspects and impact. Then we may be in a better position to have integrity itself be the way.

As we consider the qualities and characteristics of integrity described in this chapter, we'll see that they are those of emotionally wise leaders (described in the previous chapter) and also those of emotional maturity (described in subsequent chapters). From that integrated perspective, we are better able to use those qualities and characteristics to become more emotionally mature and live wisely with integrity more of the time. Our competence in doing so depends largely on our clarity about and willingness to adhere to those things that are of fundamental importance to us as human beings—our values.

ESSENCE VALUES AND SOCIAL VALUES

Try not to be a man of success but rather try to become a man of value.
—Albert Einstein

Values are qualities, symbols, or things that we consider to be important. Some values are more fundamental than others, not better but more fundamental. We refer to the most fundamental values as *essence values*. All others, including those derived from external sources, we refer to as *social values*. Both have their place and both need to be clearly differentiated and understood.

Man's activities are occupied in two ways—in grappling with external circumstances and in striving to set things at one in their own topsy-turvy mind.
—William James

Essence values are those energetic qualities foundational to our very being, characterized by: 1) a presence that contributes to a more positive, supportive environment; 2) inclusiveness versus exclusiveness; and 3) independence of—but responsibly considers—context, circumstance, social mores, or external sources of acceptance. Examples are: authenticity, honesty, empathy, compassion, allowance, generosity, love, and forgiveness.

Essence values keep us in touch with our true purpose, power, and ability to make real contributions. They do not vary with time or context. When they are not our priority and senior standard, perspective is lost, priorities confused, decisions suboptimal, and authority abused. Since essence qualities are inherent to our very being, we cannot lose them but we can lose touch with them. That's when we get in trouble—make excuses rather than be responsible—and get further into the dung!

Social values, though sometimes desirable, helpful, and appropriate, are not fundamental or inherent to our being. They are created by and learned from our environment of what will (and will not) be acknowledged, admired, rewarded, and supported by the contemporary world. Social values can include such things as wealth, possessions, recognition, acceptance, admiration, praise, influence, titles, position, social status, and so forth. They also include group considerations (morals) of right and wrong, good and bad. Social values can and do change with time and context. *Indicators of the level of emotional maturity present are how much contemporary social values, their emphasis, and relative importance, align with and support essence values—*

and what an individual or group is willing to do to ensure alignment.

A characteristic of social values that differentiates them from essence values is that they do not have, consistently, the three characteristics of essence values mentioned above. Loyalty is an example, for as highly regarded as it may be, it can be context-dependent, exclusive, and involve outside approval.

This is not to depreciate social values for they absolutely have their place and can inspire and contribute significantly. There is nothing inherently right or wrong with social values, or doing or having what they represent, unless they conflict with essence values and behaviors. When they do not conflict, they can complement essence values and add a wonderful richness to life.

However, *we must keep social values in perspective, with our intention anchored in essence qualities.* For example, how often do we observe people pretending essence qualities for social purposes? How often have we seen the rewards for obtaining results take priority over obtaining those results with integrity? How often have we observed information being misrepresented so that someone less deserving gets the promotion?

When we pretend essence qualities, e.g., *act* compassionate, loving, and so on for social reasons (be accepted by the group, look good, be admired, etc.), we are not living essence values but performing them. Essence values such as love, honesty, and compassion may be stated as a group's values, but, *unless they are owned and lived by individual group members, they act as little more than social fluff.* This lack of authenticity creates additional problems internally (feeling dishonest) and externally (lack of trust). Authenticity is the foundation of trust; of ourself and others.

Essence values must have priority if we want to move beyond lower order needs and behaviors (survival, security, and belonging) to experience and meet higher order needs (esteem, actualization, and aesthetics; developed further in chapters 5 and 6) and thus manifest a greater sense of contribution and fulfillment. When social values override essence values, intolerance of differences among groups expands and becomes a major source of continuing strife and misery. When social values complement and support essence values, we observe secure, happy people creatively and collaboratively making positive contributions. *The degree to which social values actually support essence values is a measure of the level of emotional maturity of that individual, group, organization, or culture.*

We need to clarify for ourselves what roles we want essence values to play in our life. We need to evaluate thoroughly whether our current social values and behaviors support essence values or ignore them. Do the organization's actual core values (those they actually operate from—may be essence or social) align with and support essence values? If we truly view living essence values as a priority, that clarity can provide a foundation for elegantly differentiating actually living essence values or pretending to do so. Only when an organizations's core values actually are in alignment with, support, or are identical to essence values, does the foundation exist for the creation of a truly noble emotionally mature enterprise of integrity. Only when we make the choice to grow up will we not allow conflicting social considerations to co-opt essence values.

It's not hard to make decisions when you know what your values are.
—Roy Disney

Don't call it education unless it has taught you life's true values.
—Author unknown

Points to consider:
- **What is your highest priority value?**
- **When did you last violate it?**
- **What was your rationalization?**
- **List the values that you would like to be a key part of your life. How many are essence values?**
- **Pick an essence value and do something you have not done before to make it more a part of your life. Try another one.**

WHAT IS INTEGRITY?

Integrity is the spontaneous assumption of responsibility or, simply, spontaneous responsibility. Once the need is clear, people of integrity spontaneously do the responsible thing. It is about responding—not reacting—now! It is about being responsible and accountable for our choices and actions—now! If the action is not spontaneous it is not one of integrity but is influenced by something else, by what is deemed socially or politically acceptable. There are no shades of gray with integrity.

We may generally be people of integrity, but on a particular subject at a particular time, we have it or we do not.

The anatomy of integrity is being present (presence/spontaneity) and responsive (response-able/responsibility) to whatever is (wholeness/inclusion). Having integrity is being responsibly able and willing (power) to face whatever needs confronting in the moment.

Dictionary definitions of integrity include uprightness of character, honesty, the state or condition of being unimpaired, the state of being complete or undivided, nothing left out, whole, uncorrupted.

Understanding the concept of wholeness is key to understanding integrity. If we desire to heal, grow, transform, become empowered, we first must recognize we are not separate from but part of a whole. We are not islands but rather part of a dynamic interconnected and interdependent world. Integrity is cross-contextual, i.e., its presence or absence correspondingly impacts *all* arenas of life. Therefore, everything we do, every act—loving or hostile, caring or indifferent—correspondingly affects the whole of which we are a part.

Do unto others as you would have them do unto you.
—Jesus of Nazareth

Recognizing our part in a greater whole makes us appreciate essence values; it produces the wisdom, and allows the courage, to make essence values our standard and our stand, and to make their corresponding behaviors our priority. From this holistic perspective, we can confidently recognize and do the right thing.

Recognizing our own impact helps us to be sensitive to others' needs as well as to our own. It helps to establish a presence that keeps us from feeling fragmented and allows us to have impeccable focus when we so choose. It helps us realize we do have choice. It enables us to deal elegantly with whatever needs a response. With that recognition and presence, we become increasingly aware that we can contribute—that we as individuals can make a difference.

Think of integrity as a defining vibration with a very positive energy. When we add that vibration to any system, it creates a new, more positive synergistic resonance. When integrity is lacking, we lose the expansiveness and power of that synergy.

When we break integrity, we abandon our power., i.e., the ability and willingness to act. Lack of integrity indicates, "I am unable or unwilling to fully respond (I am not response-able)." To compensate, we play the insatiable pretense game.

We feel stress when we sense we may not be able to deal with the entirety of what is occurring. It is a message that something needs to change. If we ignore the message and do not make the necessary change, the stress builds, and we eventually feel overwhelmed.

Overwhelm, i.e., the inability to integrate and deal responsibly with the entirety of what is, results in trauma. Despite social pretenses to the contrary, operating with a lack of integrity is always traumatic. It negatively affects all levels of human activity—physical, mental, emotional, and spiritual. The ability to integrate means being willing to face all aspects of our current reality, which includes embracing fear. As in quantum mechanics, observation itself literally transforms the object being observed. *Looking at our fear face on allows us to integrate and synergistically use its energy.*

If we want to be people of integrity, we need to honestly own how actually willing we are to commit to the following:

- Face our present reality and circumstances
- Assess priorities based on essence values
- Act on those assessments, recognizing that everything we say and do has impact
- Start living essence values

Integrity is living essence values.

THE IMPACT OF INTEGRITY

Everything we do or don't do has impact. Whether we decide to work late, take a vacation, hire or fire an employee, merge a company, do nothing, or confront any difficult situation, each decision has impact. Because we do not live in a vacuum, everything we do has some impact on the larger world. The more positive our actions, the more positive our impact. Conversely, the more negative our actions, the more negative our impact.

When we are willing and able to respond to whatever needs to be dealt with—not avoiding or ignoring any integral aspect— not only do we generate power (the ability and willingness to act) but, because of the synergy that wholeness allows, we are able to generate enormous power. Without integrity, we lose that synergy and its enormous potential.

Whenever we act with integrity, we immediately feel more expansive and more certain. *In fact, integrity is the necessary foundation for personal empowerment.* The resulting wholeness gives our life depth, dimension, expanded choice, and greater elegance and richness.

Every time we compromise our integrity, we sacrifice a bit of ourselves. We shave off a piece of the wholeness of who we are. The cost is huge: we become less present, less spontaneous, less able to respond, and therefore less powerful. We feel smaller and less confident. We are less willing to reach into the unknown. Innovation or change of any kind becomes increasingly threatening. We suffer, feeling dishonest, empty, separate, and alone as we play games in a plastic reality that has little purpose.

Struggling to fill that void, we place increasingly higher demands on ourselves and in addition project those demands onto others. The resulting performances and so-called successes are never enough. We wind up feeling even more inadequate and unfulfilled, regardless of social, political, or financial achievements. Without a sense of wholeness, there is a sense of chronic separation and alienation. *As long as we act without integrity, we can never feel complete, truly content, satisfied, or happy with ourselves, our relationships, our environment, or with life.*

People who lack integrity often try to compensate with false power. They attempt to intimidate and manipulate in order to have power over someone or something, which is always destructive no matter how justified.

Acting with integrity always has a positive, expansive, and constructive impact. Lack of integrity always has a negative, contracting, and destructive impact. Realize, however, that that impact, positive or negative, by contemporary social standards, may not be immediately obvious. Nevertheless, the impact is inevitable.

There is one thing alone that stands the brunt of life throughout its length: a quiet conscience.
—Euripides

INTEGRITY IS PERSONAL

Integrity is not something anyone else can give to us or take from us. It has nothing to do with popularity or doing that which we deem politically or socially correct. It is based in essence values and principles that we consciously own—not because someone or something imposes it on us from the outside. It's something we have to discover within ourselves.

Anything that has real and lasting value is always a gift from within.
—Franz Kafka

Integrity and morals are often confused. Morals are social codes of acceptable behavior within a particular group. What is considered moral and immoral can vary significantly among groups. These differences are often the basis of many "righteous" judgments.

Even though an individual acts with integrity, if those actions violate the codes of the group to which he or she belongs, that individual may be judged and labeled immoral by that group.

What is morality in any given time or place? It is what a majority then and there happen to like, and immorality is what they dislike.
—Alfred North Whitehead

Integrity is about each of us personally standing tall, acting on essence values. In a world that frequently lacks integrity, acting with integrity can mean standing alone and can result in being ostracized.

Fear of being alone is a fundamental human fear. Real integrity is rare in a world full of insecure, self-centered people doing things in order to be liked or accepted. Therefore, acting with integrity demands and develops courage. *Real courage means facing our fears and still acting responsibly.*

Group conditions require an extra level of awareness. Sometimes individuals who have personal integrity go along with a situation because they assume someone else knows more about it than they do and has the situation handled. When that is not the case, major problems can arise. As General Chain stressed to his general staff, "It is vitally important for the integrity of the organization and its mission that we create and maintain an environment where concerns are freely expressed—where individuals are secure enough to say, 'I don't understand,' where assumptions are checked out, and where open dialogue is the norm. It is only in such an environment that invalid assumptions are likely to be quickly spotted and corrected."

Conversation would be vastly improved by the use of four simple words: I do not know.

—Andre Maurois

INTEGRITY IS THE FOUNDATION OF VISION, PRINCIPLES, AND CHARACTER

Integrity is the bedrock and the cement of our purpose, principles, and character. It is the willingness and ability to responsibly face whatever is before us. It is from this foundation that we develop our sense of value.

Out of that develops our sense of purpose and *vision* of what can be. In living our values and moving toward this ideal vision, we become more of who we truly are. Focusing on vision helps us to see possibilities and enables us to plan with purpose and intention. Without the cement of integrity, we are left distracted, unclear about what to do, ineffective in action, and weighed down by negativity.

Our values, purpose, and vision shape our principles. *Principles*, in this sense, are our self-chosen boundaries of behavior—of what we will and will not do in living our values, maintaining our integrity, and moving toward our vision. They provide the framework for our actions.

In matters of style, swim with the current; in matters of principle, stand like a rock.

—Thomas Jefferson

Our *character* is the degree to which we adhere to our principles. When we are clear about our values and principles, we can respond rather than react to any situation, including a hostile or manipulative one. We can play the game without being caught in it. If we are not clear about our values and principles, we tend to react rather than respond. We wind up feeling controlled by external sources and we become a victim of the game rather than a causative creator of the game.

Our character is our destiny.

—Socrates

Men of genius are admired; men of wealth are envied; men of power are feared; but only men of character are trusted.

—Author unknown

Expediency is often used as justification for violating or ignoring our principles. We may talk of ideals and principles, but if we are not true to them and do not act on them, no matter how much we talk about them, we are not individuals of principle or character. Consequently, we will not move forward in realizing our vision.

There is no substitute for integrity. Without integrity as our bedrock, we have little or no substantive sense of purpose, noble vision, clear principles of behavior, or character. Without integrity, only pretenses of those exist. Without integrity, we feel a void of insufficiency and inadequacy. We attempt to fill that void with substitute status symbols, e.g., money, possessions, position, and/or power. This hunger is insatiable. No matter how much we accrue, it will never be enough to fill that void. Episodes of frustration, confusion, pretense, and denial increase. Integrity is the mortar that keeps our ideals, principles, and character in balanced alignment.

What doth it profit a man if he gains the whole world and loses his own soul?
—Jesus of Nazareth

INTEGRITY IS A CHOICE

Our character is our destiny; not because it is predetermined but because of how we choose to lead our lives, and what qualities we choose to adopt.
—Senator John McCain

Every situation in which we find ourselves involves choice of some kind. Will we embrace or resist change? Will we face or withdraw from a confrontation? Will we celebrate a colleague's achievement, even though he or she may not celebrate ours? Will we ask the advice of a coworker if it means admitting we don't know the answer? Whether we actively participate in and contribute to a specific situation is our individual choice. Living and acting with integrity is a conscious choice—*our* conscious choice.

Even when confronted with difficult situations not of our own making, we can choose how to respond. We may try to convince the world and ourselves otherwise, but at some level we recognize the truth: Only we are responsible for our words and actions. Acting with integrity or acting with a lack of integrity are conscious choices. Beneath all the excuses and denials, we know when we have violated our integrity.

We make choices either reactively (fear-based and stagnating) or responsively (growth-generating). Insecure people have not faced their fears. Consequently they are stuck in them and therefore continue to make more fear-based choices. Those choices always lack integrity and are inevitably limiting, no matter how much we try to justify them.

Secure, mature people face their fear, listen to its message, and positively utilize its energy. By confronting their fear, they are able to move through it and make growth choices.

When making any choice, ask yourself, "Am I making this choice because I'm afraid to choose something else? Avoiding choosing is a choice. If your choice is fear-based, take several deep breaths and look again. You will find you are attempting to avoid confronting some self-perceived weakness and ignoring or discounting some strength. Before committing to a fear-based option, find the strength to reevaluate.

With integrity, we responsibly look at how we created, contributed to, or allowed a situation—positive or negative—to occur. We honestly own our part of it and do what we can to improve a situation without blame, self-pity, or regret.

I know of no more energizing fact than the unquestioned ability of a man to elevate his life by conscious endeavour.
—Henry David Thoreau

Although we can model this quality and encourage others to take responsibility for themselves, at the same time, we cannot take responsibility for others. Taking responsibility for another capable adult creates codependency, which manifests and prolongs a victim stance that always generates self-pity and resentment within both parties. When we live with integrity, we recognize that we are responsible for our own words and actions, and we respect the right of others to make different choices.

People with integrity have positive control over creating and responding to events in their lives. They have a clarity and certainty about what they want and will allow. They do not see life as happening to them, but rather, they make life happen.

When we are not true to ourselves, we are open to being controlled or manipulated by others. Without integrity, control (the ability to start, change or continue, and stop things under one's own determination) becomes a huge issue, and its distorted form becomes a compulsive need to manipulate people, things, or situations, either overtly or covertly.

True integrity is spontaneously choosing to act on our values and, without hesitation, taking responsibility for the consequences of those choices. We do not live in a static universe. Either we choose to grow and become more of who we are, or we choose to contract and diminish our potential.

Every choice we make either contributes to our growth or our decline; toward fulfillment and happiness or toward self-defeat and despair. One choice can instantaneously change our life.

Destiny is not a matter of chance; it is a matter of choice.
—William Jennings Bryan

INTEGRITY IS AT THE CORE OF WHO WE ARE

Integrity, or its lack, is the basis of the image we have of ourselves. We cannot create a sustainable reality that exceeds the fundamental image we have of ourselves. In other words, we make choices that naturally resonate with what we believe about ourselves. If we see ourselves as unimportant and incapable, it is impossible for us to make constructive, expansive decisions with any confidence. Alternately, if we have a healthy, positive sense of self, our decisions, actions, and results naturally reflect this self-image. When we try to make decisions that are at odds with our actual self-image, the outcome will usually be short-lived, reflecting this dissonance. We will unconsciously create or allow circumstances that force our reality to align with our core self-image.

If our desired achievement is beyond our core self-image, we will do something to sabotage it. This is often the reason so many people who appear to be on the verge of success somehow muck it up. It is also why many who have achieved success end up destroying their creation. Despite bluster to the contrary, without integrity we cannot have a positive self-image.

The mind is master over every kind of fortune; itself acts in both ways, being the cause of its own happiness and misery.
—Lucius Annaeus Seneca

QUALITIES THAT DISTINGUISH PEOPLE OF INTEGRITY

Qualities that accompany integrity include presence, honesty, humility, and discernment, to name just a few. Let's explore some of these qualities in greater detail.

People of integrity exude presence. They are able to be attentive and in the moment rather than distant and distracted. They are willing to look at each moment afresh, without the filters of preconceived notions. That presence allows them to discern, evaluate, and reach conclusions relatively free of bias or prejudice. Without presence, we cannot make responsible choices spontaneously. We cannot be spontaneous without being in the moment.

When you act out of present-moment awareness, what you do becomes imbued with a sense of quality, care, and love—even the most simple action.

—Eckhart Tolle

People of integrity add value and have a sense of fair exchange. They consistently contribute to the well being of their environment. They ensure that those who add value, as well as those who do not, are correspondingly and appropriately acknowledged and rewarded.

An honest man is one who knows he can't consume more than he produces.

—Ayn Rand

People of integrity are honest, authentic, and trustworthy. They are willing to look at themselves honestly. They recognize and own both their shortcomings and their strengths. The authenticity of their communication inspires confidence and trust. Authenticity is the basis of trust.

By a lie, a man annihilates his dignity as a man.
—Immanuel Kant

People of integrity act and live with dignity. As such, people of integrity truly respect others and themselves. They respect others while at the same time refusing to tolerate dysfunctional or hurtful behavior. Lack of respect for individual human dignity breeds indifference, intolerance, contempt, abuse, and injustice. People lacking integrity not only have a lack of respect for others but also for themselves. Low self-worth, low self-esteem, and the various manifestations of arrogance all lack dignity and indicate the absence of integrity.

Dignity comes from claiming what is innately ours and letting it grow.
—Sakyong Mipham Rinpoche

People of integrity have keen discernment. They regularly exercise the ability to distinguish and prioritize clearly without prejudice or bias. Because they exhibit presence, humility, honesty, and respect for themselves and others, they optimize their ability to be discerning in any situation.

A wise man learns by the experience of others. An ordinary man learns by his own experience. A fool learns by nobody's experience.
—Author unknown

People of integrity have a wisdom that goes beyond mere knowledge. Wisdom is the presence, awareness and ability to see and responsibly act from the perspective of the big picture without loosing sight of, and being compassionate about, the current situation. It includes but transcends logic and reason. From that awareness, people of integrity realize they are not isolated individuals but rather are part of a larger community, and that whatever they put out, positive or negative, will, directly or indirectly, impact their lives and those with whom they associate. Wise people are thus relatively free of the destructive patterns of greed and prejudice typical of those who are less aware. Consequently, they have a larger perspective, can see and confront more, and are able to provide insights that help bring the world more into balance.

Compassion grows out of our willingness to meet pain rather than flee from it. It listens to the cries of the world, and we are part of the world.
—Christina Feldman

People of integrity are compassionate. Compassion is more than kindness, it is awareness. People of integrity are sensitive to the needs, wants, and desires both of themselves and others. Because they have the courage to face and responsibly address their own fears and suffering, they can recognize, understand, and be compassionate about the suffering of others, while at the same time refraining from rewarding victimhood or creating dependencies, which would not be compassionate at all.

Be kind, for everyone you meet is fighting a hard battle.

—Plato

People of integrity are generous. They are secure enough that they do not have to hang onto things or viewpoints, and so they can easily share—thoughts, feelings, ideas, and concerns, as well as material things. The willingness to share initiates a flow that not only tends to be reciprocated but also opens the sharer to innovation and change. That ability and willingness to share not only facilitates authentic communication but also creates a spaciousness that allows for even more: more relationships; more connection; more intimacy; more willingness to be, do, and have more happiness; more peace; more caring; and more love. These, in turn, build more self-confidence, self-esteem, and self-respect.

The open hand holds more friends than a closed fist.

—Author unknown

People of integrity have power. As pointed out in chapter 1, "Increased responsibility always generates increased power." Since integrity is spontaneous responsibility, it is also spontaneous power. Act with integrity and you instantaneously have power. You only need to recognize that you can be responsible—and then be responsible—to have all the real power you will ever need.

People who live with integrity experience dominion. Dominion is power and the ability to share that power with respect and honor. It also means absolute ownership of responsibility. Its opposite is domination or power over others.

A man of integrity lives in dominion and cannot be dominated by anyone or anything.
—Author unknown

People of integrity are able to fully enjoy life. They are able to appreciate and enjoy what is—savoring the humor in life and appreciating its aesthetics and nuances. Having integrity means being able to be responsible without being dour—being able to spontaneously have fun. People of integrity have a passion for life.

We could hardly wait to get up in the morning!
—Wilber and Orville Wright

People of integrity are loving. Love is about caring, responding to, and respecting ourselves and others with honesty and a depth of passion and compassion. Love without integrity manifests as shallow, codependent relationships rife with dishonesty, deceit, invalidation, broken agreements, and generally abusive behavior. *Without integrity, there is no real love, only pretenses of it.*

One word frees us of all the weight and pain of life. That word is love.
—Sophocles

Note that the qualities of people with integrity are also the characteristics of the emotionally wise leader noted in chapter 2, page 44. In fact, one will not—and cannot—be emotionally mature or wise if integrity is lacking.

Because integrity is about wholeness, anytime our behavior does not align with, and support, any one of the essence qualities, we lose touch with all essence qualities. Our life correspondingly dramatizes their absence in the form of problems and unhappiness. *Our personal integrity defines the limits of what we allow ourselves to be.*

INTEGRITY AND GREATNESS

Gandhi, Hitler, Martin Luther King, Jr., Lincoln, Pol Pot, Stalin all were leaders who motivated others to do things they normally would not do. All shared some common characteristics: all had a vision; all were determined, persistent, and successful in overcoming many obstacles; all had a big impact that dramatically changed the world in their lifetime.

Yet today, the world acknowledges Gandhi, King, and Lincoln as models of great leadership, while vilifying Hitler, Pol Pot, and Stalin as extreme abusers of power. Momentary popularity is seldom a measure of greatness. There was a time when millions revered Hitler and a period when many despised Lincoln. What is the fundamental difference?

Those readily acknowledged as great—Lincoln, Gandhi, and King—lived and acted from essence values; love, caring, compassion, authenticity, responsibility, allowance, inclusion, and so on. Hitler, Stalin, and Pol Pot violated them all, reacting instead out of self-centered fear and rage. For Lincoln, Gandhi, and King, essence values were their starting point; they responded from a position of caring and compassion. That foundation and perspective allowed them to stand tall against considerable social pressure as well as their own human foibles.

Today's and tomorrow's leaders may want to bear this in mind when they find themselves reacting to momentary pressures such as stock prices and popularity polls rather than responding to fundamental needs. Doing so skews priorities, misallocates resources, and is always limiting and rationalized.

Using ends to justify questionable means is a sure sign of a narrowed, frightened perspective and a corresponding lack of integrity. Former Commander in Chief of the Strategic Air Command General Jack Chain said it with bottom-line clarity, "When integrity is lacking, bad things happen!" *When we ignore essence values, we inevitably invite their opposites: hatred, indifference, pretense, dishonesty, irresponsibility, and exclusion.* We cannot and do not create happy conclusions using means that lack integrity. Ends and means must be in alignment. Only by using responsible means will we achieve responsible ends. The irresponsible use of power (ignoring essence values), no matter how rationalized, is inevitably abusive. *Power used responsibly is the essence of greatness.* (See "What Makes Leadership Positive?" chapter 8, page 276.)

Greatness emerges from living essence values. Great leadership motivates others to be increasingly present, authentic, compassionate, generous—in other words to live and model essence values. That is Integrity with a capital I. That is Leadership with a capital L.

Greatness is not found in possessions, power, position, or prestige. It is discovered in goodness, humility, service, and character.

—Author unknown

Happiness is a by-product.

—Robert Tracy

ASSESSING THE STRENGTH OF OUR INTEGRITY

How do we assess our integrity? We need to first look at what we are actually doing and assess whether it is responsible action that positively contributes to our desired ideal. The steps to getting there are the same as the qualities of being there. If we want our environment to be a more responsible one, we need to be more responsible in the moment. If we want more love in our life, we need to be more loving. If we want to be heard more, we need to listen more. In other words, how are we at doing what we say we want?

Life is an energy exchange of giving and receiving. The way to have what you want is to give what you need—emotionally and spiritually.

—Oprah Winfrey

To the degree we wait for someone else to do what we want done, we complain either overtly or covertly. What are your chronic complaints? Complaining without responsible contribution is a lack of integrity. Look where your complaints lie and confront how you have been passing the buck. You will find two patterns that you follow virtually automatically. The first is how you pass the buck. The second is how you rationalize doing so.

Next, we need to assess our follow-through. Integrity means following through with intention on our stated or implied promises. It means not promising what we do not intend to follow up on or deliver. It means putting an end to excuses, rationalizations, and justifications. It means choosing honesty over expediency.

Integrity is about honoring agreements; with ourselves, with others, with nature.
—Author unknown

Points to consider:
- **How often do you find yourself complaining?**
- **What is your most common and repeating complaint?**
- **Who or what do you most often blame?**
- **How frequently do you not keep promises and commitments?**
- **Can you spot your pattern of justification?**
- **What responsibility can you take in relieving or eliminating the sources of your complaints?**

Let honor be as strong an obligation to us as necessity is to others.
—Pliny the Elder

WHEN INTEGRITY IS ABSENT: RECOGNIZING THE SIGNS

It is essential not to confuse the qualities of integrity with charisma, eloquence, charm, or even bottom-line performance. Those qualities and that performance may be very important, sometimes critical, but they are secondary to the fundamental importance of integrity.

Without integrity, other qualities or achievements will be corrupted and abused. When integrity is not a primary standard for all behaviors, is not highly valued for its own sake, or is considered impractical or unimportant or made into a joke or a nonissue, we can observe the following well-rationalized manifestations:

- Authenticity and candor are lacking, or when present, are often criticized as unrealistic or naive.

- Looking good becomes more important than being authentic.

- Charisma, showmanship, and public relations gimmicks are substituted for leadership.

- Different perspective, viewpoints or beliefs are "righteously" invalidated and made wrong.

- Short-term performance increasingly becomes more important than long-term growth and sustainability.

- Ability to manipulate people, situations, and stock prices is rewarded over creating honest communication, sincere relationships, and substantive value.

- Competition becomes redefined as "beating the other guy," rather than a mechanism to bring forth our best.

- Respect for human dignity is ignored and reduced to "taking care of me and only me."

- Vitality and productivity are replaced with pretense and busywork.

- Compromise degenerates into mediocrity rather than flourishing as a synergy of expanded viewpoints.

- Striving for excellence is replaced with insatiable demands for perfection.

- Vision and leadership wither to a focus on how to have control over bureaucracy and issues.

- Compassion becomes too expensive, impractical, or "not our business."

- Polls are used to pander for votes rather than to understand viewpoints and the need to communicate or educate.

- Loyalty becomes undiscerning agreement and support rather than forthright devil's advocacy.

- Agreements and commitments are honored only when convenient or enforced.

- The letter of the law is used to subvert justice rather than to aid it.

Without integrity, our self-image and self-esteem become dependent on what other people think. When that happens, we inevitably feel inadequate. We expend enormous amounts of energy trying to compensate for that feeling of inadequacy but pretend otherwise. Decisions and actions become limited, mechanical and trite. We wind up deceiving ourselves as well as others. Our self-confidence degenerates into arrogance or apathy, and our self-respect evaporates.

Without integrity, our character is replaced with political expedience. Concerns about money, power and status dominate and control our actions and life. We lose balance and perspective. Our compassion for and appreciation of the dignity of every human being deteriorates into insincere, self-centered, closed and unloving attitudes and behaviors. Without integrity, our dreams and vision lose their compelling energy. Our goals become mere mechanical objectives without juice. Our passion for life disintegrates into a compulsive, anxiety-ridden, insatiable need for success at any cost or simply deteriorates and dies.

As we view contemporary society, how often do we observe examples of jealousy, envy and greed accompanied by pretense, denial and dishonesty? These are dysfunctional compensations for underlying feelings of insecurity and powerlessness. Alcohol, drugs and overwork are often used to numb those feelings. We see how lack of integrity precludes authenticity and consequently destroys credibility and trust and devastates relationships and security.

We notice that many of our contemporaries are chronically angry, confused, afraid, defensive, depressed, despairing, apathetic, shallow, work-obsessed, burned out, or wanting to drop out. We see too many who are "leading lives of quiet desperation," and do not have the slightest idea of what to do about it. In fact, these are all symptoms of a lack of integrity. Without integrity, we are unhappy and far, far less than we could be.

When integrity ceases to be a primary standard, the true costs are beyond measure. *Developing social skills and bottom-line abilities can be an important adjunct to, but never a replacement for, acting with integrity.*

The impression forces itself upon one that men measure by false standards, that everyone seeks power, success, riches for himself, and admires others who attain them, while undervaluing the truly precious things in life.

—Sigmund Freud

FUEL FOR POWERFUL CHANGE

Whenever we feel powerless, we need to find where we have violated our sense of personal integrity and correct it. If we feel caught in the game, or that there is nothing we can do about it, or we have to stoop to their level to survive, we must realize that all of those feelings are additional symptoms and messages indicating a lack of integrity.

In this condition, our ability to view other possibilities is severely restricted. We feel powerless. Correspondingly, we will blame, deny, lie, manipulate, feel self-pity and act victimized. We will be irresponsible. We will justify, rationalize, or attempt to explain away even our most blatant irresponsibilities and self-imposed limitations.

People with integrity have a clear, unshakable presence. They have determination and do what responsibly needs to be done. They do not succumb to playing manipulative games because "that's the game out there." They do not whine, justify, or say they had no other choice. If they leave a position, they do so because they choose to, not because of anger, frustration, fear, grief, or apathy, but because of a preference based on recognition of what is responsible. They often have strong opinions and are willing to express them when it is helpful to do so. They have a certainty and self-confidence that is neither self-righteous nor arrogant. Self-righteousness and arrogance, like false power, are compensations born of fear, and they are always used to make ourselves right and others wrong.

When we act with integrity, the resulting level of poised certainty transcends any and all current consensus games and standards. Integrity itself, even without any apparent action, is power and creates positive change. For example, Gandhi's integrity so empowered him that he had far greater impact than all the powerful politicians of his time. That influence even transcended the hatred of vastly different cultural and religious persuasions. Likewise, leaders are poised to have far greater impact on others and their organizations when they are motivated by and act out of integrity. Integrity provides powerful fuel for appropriate and responsible change.

Hold yourself responsible for a higher standard than anyone expects of you. Never excuse yourself.
—Henry Ward Beecher

PUTTING INTEGRITY INTO PRACTICE

To regain our integrity and really change anything, we first must be willing to honestly face and recognize when we are not living with integrity. This can be hard! We may struggle with self-pity. We may be inclined to blame others as a way of projecting our own denials. Blame precludes real assessment of responsibility. It closes the door on constructive decisions and actions.

The first step of putting integrity into practice is to recognize when integrity is missing. Where in our life are we fearful, anxious, angry, or blaming? Where do we feel out of balance? These feelings are indicators of some struggle with doing the right thing and acting with integrity. Continuing upsets and problems are messages that there is still something sticking around, which we have not yet been willing to recognize and take responsibility for.

Acknowledgement of what has happened is the first step to overcoming the consequences of any misfortune.
—William James

Secondly, we need to own that we, and only we, are responsible for our choices, decisions and actions. We need to own fully our part, no matter how big or small, of how we created, allowed, or contributed to the condition (problem, upset) in which we find ourselves.

You have got to do your own growing, no matter how tall your grandfather was.
—Irish proverb

Thirdly, we need to either (a) honestly acknowledge and honor our accomplishments, or (b) forgive ourselves for having messed up. When we have done something positive, it is important to acknowledge it. By acknowledging it, we can let it go when it's time to change. If we don't acknowledge it, we tend to inappropriately hang on even when we need to let it go.

On the other side of the coin, maybe we could have done something better, more elegantly, more lovingly, more honestly, or with more courage, but we did not. Wallowing in self-pity and regret never does anything except keep us stuck in the muck. We need to let recriminations go and realize we did the best we could with the awareness and resources we had at the time. We need to drop the guilt and self-pity (see chapter 4), fully feel the remorse make appropriate amends as best we honestly can, and forgive ourselves. If we do not appropriately acknowledge and forgive ourselves, we will not move on to the fourth step.

Self-pity is our worst enemy, and if we yield to it we never do anything wise in the world.

—Helen Keller

Forgiveness is the scent that the rose leaves on the heel that crushes it.

—Author unknown

Fourthly, we need to do something truly different. Real change means *doing something different.* Such change may be difficult to see now, but if we honestly and thoughtfully work through the first three steps, then we will be much closer to knowing what to do to bring about true change with integrity.

No longer talk about the kind of man that a good man ought to be, but be such.

—Marcus Aurelius

The undertaking of a new action brings new strength.

—Evenius

INTEGRITY AND EMOTIONAL MATURITY

Acting with integrity is both a vehicle for developing our maturity and the very expression of that maturity. If we are honestly willing to confront our confusion, doubt, and fear, and if we are willing to take action, make mistakes, and view those mistakes as learning opportunities, then progress is not only possible but assured. In this sense, practice does make perfect. Once we recognize and own that we alone are responsible for our choices, forgive ourselves for our mistakes, and start acting responsibly, then we can assume the mantle of true maturity.

Who then is free? The wise man who can govern himself.
—Horace

INTEGRITY AND THE GAMES OF LIFE

We can perhaps gain a better understanding of putting integrity and emotional maturity into practice through allegory. Viewing life's challenges and opportunities as games reveals a line-up of fundamental truths and common sense guidelines.

- Life consists of games.
- The anatomy of a game is a barrier to be overcome, with the outcome unpredictable.
- If the outcome is predictable, it is not a game.
- Games provide the challenges that can develop talents and offer a sense of contribution and accomplishment.
- We all need games—everyone plays them.
- The anatomy of a problem is similar to the anatomy of a game. The difference is that a problem includes some denial of responsibility. That's what makes it a problem.

- Responsibility is the ability to appropriately and constructively respond (versus react) to what is.
- If we think playing the game (or having the problem) is up to someone else, we are playing the role of victim.
- There are no victims, only volunteers.
- When we are lacking in games, we will create problems in their stead (if we are being irresponsible and blaming) and act like a victim.
- No one can solve anyone else's problem.
- If we try to solve someone else's problem, the person will resist our solution and resent us.
- There are all kinds and sizes of games (and problems).
- Growth is about shifting from old games to bigger and more productive games.
- Each game has its own rules.
- If we want to play a game, we need to learn or create the rules of that game.
- Wanting the benefits of the game without a willingness to play by its rules is arrogant, alienating, frustrating to all parties, and always unproductive.
- If we don't like the rules or the game, we need to responsibly change them, or find or create another game.
- We, and no one else, choose whether or not we play.
- Not making a choice is a choice.
- Control is the ability to start, change or continue, and stop or complete the game (or problem) under one's own determination.

- Power is both the ability and the willingness to act.
- We can't be truly powerful without being responsible.
- Integrity is the spontaneous assumption of responsibility.
- Without integrity, we have neither control nor power and, as compensation, will attempt to have control over and power over others, overtly or covertly, or be the victim of someone else's games.
- Games lacking integrity are always destructive—there are no exceptions.
- Integrity trumps contemporary social mores and political considerations.
- Sometimes, acts of integrity are interpreted as threats to current values, vested interests or the competition. Consequently, they may be subject to rejection and/or attack.
- A key aspect of integrity is courage—the willingness to face one's fears and still play responsibly.
- At any moment, either we have integrity or we do not; there is no middle ground. We either hit a home run or strike out.
- The measure of our integrity is the measure of who and what we are—greats or wannabes.
- With integrity, we are whole—world champions. Without integrity, we are significantly less than we can be.
- There is nothing more important than playing the game of life with integrity.

When the one great scorer comes to write your name, he marks not that you won or lost, but how you played the game.

—Grantland Rice

Points to consider:

- **What games are we playing?**
- **How are they really contributing beyond ego gratification?**
- **Are they hurting anyone?**
- **How do we rationalize that hurt?**
- **What games do we truly want to play?**
- **What games don't we want to play?**
- **What games are we willing to start, change or continue, or stop and do so with integrity, courage and intention?**

SUMMARY
INTEGRITY—THE KEY TO A FULFILLED LIFE

Integrity is the spontaneous, conscious assumption of personal responsibility. It is the willingness to include the wholeness of what is that gives us depth and breadth. It provides us with a sense of substance. It is a frequency of energy that creates a positive, transforming resonance. Integrity is sensitive to, but transcends, moral codes and considerations of limitations. It precludes blame, regret, denial and self-pity. It creates and demands in us an appreciation of and passion for human dignity. Integrity is the basis of our dignity, grace and sense of personal value and self-esteem. It manifests profound presence. It assures our honesty, our authenticity and our trustworthiness.

Integrity puts us in touch with our true power and our unlimited potential. It gives us an awareness of possibilities that would otherwise seem unfathomable. It generates our ideals and principles and produces our character. It provides calm, certainty, self-confidence; courage to face our confusion, doubt, and fear; and willingness to do what is right. Integrity is what focuses and develops our attention, intention, actions, and a self-image that aligns with and supports our ideals and principles. It allows us to enjoy love and happiness. Integrity gives meaning to life.

Without integrity, we are not whole. With it, we are responsible, loving, caring, creative, courageous and empowered. Our integrity is our bottom line. *There is nothing more important than our integrity.* Integrity is more than an important factor. *Integrity is the vital factor!*

Suggested reading—*Cases In Leadership, Ethics and Organizational Integrity: A Strategic Perspective* by Lynn S. Paine, Ph.D.

The remainder of this book is dedicated to clarifying how we can proactively facilitate a culture and environment of integrity.

THE DNA OF HUMAN DIGNITY

4

EMOTIONAL INTELLIGENCE AND BEYOND

> *If a person is to get the meaning of life he must learn to like the facts about himself—ugly as they may seem to his sentimental vanity—before he can learn the truth behind the facts. And the truth is never ugly.*
>
> —Eugene O'Neill

MOVING TOWARD GREATER INTEGRITY

From a developmental perspective, questions arise about how to facilitate integrity in oneself and others. The key is to recognize the relationship of integrity and emotional maturity. Integrity and emotional maturity are inextricably intertwined. If an individual is emotionally mature, that individual acts with integrity. Conversely, if a person lacks integrity, we know that person is not emotionally mature, despite any pretenses or protests to the contrary. Therefore, because of this correspondence, *if we can facilitate emotional maturity, we have a means to facilitate increased integrity.*

Fortunately, emotional maturity is something we can look at in stages of development. Before we do so, however, we will first look at emotions themselves. This chapter is intended as an emotional intelligence primer. It provides a foundational understanding of emotions, their associated behaviors, and the dynamics involved in developing emotional maturity.

If we want to effectively communicate with, relate to, persuade, lead and motivate others, it is a gross understatement to say it is helpful to understand what makes people tick. It's not simply helpful—it's crucial. And to understand others, we need first to understand ourselves.

He who knows others is learned. He who knows himself is wise.
—Lao Tzu

We need to know more about the dynamics that motivate our behaviors and intentions. We need to understand what influences our perception of ourselves, of others, and of the world. Until we become more aware of how human emotional dynamics function, we tend to flounder in a world of uncertainty and insecurity—not a great foundation for leadership or anything else. We need to grow in emotional intelligence.

The life which is unexamined is not worth living.
—Plato

EMOTIONAL INTELLIGENCE

You may have heard the statement, "Emotional intelligence is the ability to manage your emotions." Sounds reasonable, but what exactly does it mean? How do we go about managing our emotions? Some may say, "Hey, I do that all the time," meaning, "I just stuff the uncomfortable or socially unacceptable emotions." Unfortunately, that's how many people "manage" their emotions. They repress them. Rather than repress our emotions, we need to be more effective in using them to responsibly deal with the ups and downs of life.

How people respond or react to any situation; their responsiveness to new ideas, their flexibility to change, and their willingness to support a plan or action depends on and varies with their emotional state. For example, people who are angry perceive life and how they need to go through it differently than people who are cheerful or people who are grieving. *Each person's interpretation of the same circumstance, his or her sense of priority, as well as the type of communication that will be meaningful and effective for that person, will vary with the individual's emotional state.* When we are reactive rather than responsive, emotions seem to run our life and we are at a loss about what to do.

In order to address adequately the influence of emotions in our life, we need to take a closer look at what constitutes emotional intelligence. Emotional intelligence is having an awareness of:

- What emotions are
- Their purpose, meaning and what they can tell us (if we listen)
- The relationships among emotions
- The different behaviors and attitudes associated with each emotion
- How we tend to misuse emotions
- How can we use emotions to better understand ourselves and more effectively communicate and relate with others

In part, emotional intelligence is gaining clarity about how we have been intimidated, controlled, and limited, and importantly, how we allowed that to happen. We did so by blindly adhering to our fear-based negative ego patterns. As we recognize and assume ownership of our self-generated and self-sustaining patterns—positive and negative—we begin to more consciously exercise greater choice in either working with them or letting them go. Expanding the number of aware choices we make about our patterns of behavior is a positive sign that we're becoming more responsible; we're maturing and owning more of our inherent power.

There can be no transforming of darkness into light, and of apathy into movement, without emotion.

—Carl Jung

WHAT ARE EMOTIONS?

Emotions (energy in motion) are frequencies of energy. They are messages from our subconscious providing us environmental information. They act as filters through which we interpret life, directing us where to focus our attention in order to optimize our survival potential. Each discrete emotion has its own frequency, or rate of vibration, and conveys a specific message that indicates the relative degree of security or potential threat perceived to be present. Having various emotions provides a means to discern subtleties and nuances, providing greater depth and richness to our perceptions and experiences. *The more access we have to our emotions, the greater our ability to discern the richness and subtleties of life.*

Emotions have a specific order and relationship to one another, a hierarchy. Our emotional position in this hierarchy (acutely and chronically) indicates our level of stress (momentarily or accumulatively over time). Different predictable behaviors, attitudes and forms of communication correspond to each of the various levels of security or stress (dis-ease). This concept is developed in detail in chapter 6. Importantly, where we are on this scale emotionally indicates the degree to which we are capable acutely and, over time, chronically of creating positive change. Understanding this hierarchy can be extremely helpful in assessing emotional maturity and, correspondingly, people's ability to contribute to themselves, to others, to an organization and to society.

It is important to recognize that *emotions are not inherently good or bad, positive or negative. They are simply messages.* Issues can arise when we make judgments that some emotions are better than others. We usually do that because we are more comfortable with the "nice" emotions, such as cheerfulness and enthusiasm. We tend to label those emotions as good and the others, such as anger, fear, and grief, as bad. Assignments of good and bad are subjective evaluations. They are opinions, not facts.

Emotions themselves are not problems nor do they create problems. Rather, problems arise out of our unwillingness to confront the messages our emotions are trying to deliver. To repress an emotion is to know we have it but not express it. To suppress an emotion is to pretend to ourselves we do not have it when we do. To harbor an emotion is to have and express it repeatedly but never let it go. When we do these things, we lose access to the feedback and information that would otherwise contribute to our ability to responsibly adapt, prosper and be happy.

When we ignore an emotional message because we don't want to confront it, the emotion does not just go away. Its energy only accumulates, becomes louder and eventually turns into a "shout." Too often, we still do not listen, because at that stage it is not only inconvenient but also uncomfortable. When that shout eventually turns into a "scream" of crisis, we usually react rather than respond.

This cumulative process of *avoiding the uncomfortable and unfamiliar is why much of all needed change, by individuals and organizations, builds to a crisis.* Far too often, it takes a tragedy before we institute needed reforms.

There comes a time for the rosebud when it becomes more painful to remain tight in the bud than to blossom.
—Anais Nin

People also often repress "nice" emotions and their accompanying messages, with the same limiting result. Someone who is feeling enthusiasm but represses it because of a hostile environment is being as inhibited and reactive as one who represses anger or grief. For example, Joe is enthusiastic about being hired to work on what he considers an exciting project. However, the organization he joined places a very high value on being professional, which it interprets as being proper and serious. It regards excitement and enthusiasm as frivolous and childish and therefore frowns upon such a display of emotion as unprofessional. So rather than risk being considered inappropriate, Joe plays it cool and acts appropriately serious—and with those accommodations, his enthusiasm and excitement wane and eventually evaporate. Joe moves from being a motivated producer to being a mediocre performer. Such adaptations may be socially or politically correct, but the emotional and behavioral consequences are always limiting.

Additionally, it is faulty reasoning to assume we can stifle any one emotion without affecting others. When we repress any emotion, we also repress our ability to access, feel, use and appropriately express our entire span of emotions. For instance, we cannot stifle our anger or fear without also stifling our enthusiasm and joy. This is one of the reasons why many people seem to have a limited emotional range or appear mono-emotional, that is, always angry or sad or despairing or even cheerful (which is a cover). In addition, the lack of emotion appropriate to a circumstance, e.g., feeling no grief at the passing of a loved one, is as much an indication of heavy repression as is an explosive, out-of-proportion, reaction to some minor incident.

As we allow ourselves to feel more of our emotions, we become more present. We have greater access to more of our untapped talents and strengths. The more we are in touch with our emotions, the greater our ability to differentiate and add subtlety, nuance, depth and richness to our perceptions. We gain more timely information and greater sophistication in differentiating the nuances of the messages, enabling us to respond quickly, precisely and appropriately. *Our willingness and ability to face more of our emotions correspond directly to our potential effectiveness in all areas of interpersonal interaction.* In summary, expanding access to more of our emotions and their messages is a key to increasing our emotional intelligence and overall effectiveness.

Cherish your own emotions and never undervalue them.
—Robert Henri

AUTHENTIC VERSUS ARTIFICIAL EMOTIONS

Emotionally mature individuals appropriately feel anger in the face of irresponsibility, injustice, or manipulative behavior. The anger is their message that some responsible action needs to be taken. They convert the anger into an energy that will have a positive, corrective effect.

Fear can paralyze, but it can also focus a person's attention in the now, generating the adrenaline needed for quick action and surviving an attack. Grief can help to develop sensitivity and compassion. If an emotion does not possess both positive and negative potential, it is not an authentic emotion but an artificial emotion.

Humankind creates artificial or synthetic emotions as an attempt to avoid dealing with real underlying emotions—most often anger, fear, shame, or hurt. Authentic, or real emotions—such as anger, fear, and grief—possess both positive and negative potential. Unlike authentic emotions, artificial emotions have no redeeming qualities or aspects, only negative ones.

When someone employs an artificial emotion, realize that that person is feeling overwhelmed to some degree and is attempting to avoid dealing with what is really going on. Guilt, martyrdom, and victimhood are examples of artificial emotional states.

Guilt

Guilt is an artificial emotion used to suppress and deny our anger, fear, shame, or hurt. It is a mechanism to pretend we are attempting to take some semblance of responsibility when we are not. It is an attempt to gain some form of manipulative control to compensate for a sense of being out of control. It possesses no positive aspects or potential. We use guilt to misdirect our repressed underlying emotion and to beat up on ourselves and others rather than feel the depth of our caring and love for someone or the sadness of an opportunity lost.

A person using guilt to distract and avoid responsibility may say things like, "I obviously feel guilty. Isn't that enough? You should feel sorry for me because I feel so guilty." Another example of using guilt to manipulate is some statement to the effect of, "After all I did for you, and you can't do this for me?"

Guilt is not the same as remorse. Remorse is a real emotion of feeling truly sorry for the hurt we caused or allowed but which cannot be corrected. Remorse needs to be felt—fully. Only when fully allowed, owned and felt can it resolve the depth of our pain. Its positive potential, similar to that of grief, is the expansion of our sensitivity, compassion and empathy. Fully felt remorse helps to cultivate an increased awareness of, sensitivity to, and responsibility for how our actions impact life. Guilt, however, has no redeeming aspect or potential.

Indulging in guilt is always destructive. Allowing remorse is liberating. If you feel caught in guilt, ask yourself, "What emotion—anger, hurt, fear, or shame—am I attempting to cover by using guilt?"

The more guilty a person tends to feel, the less chance there is that he will be a happy, healthy, or law-abiding citizen.

—Albert Ellis

Martyrdom

Martyrdom is an emotional state characterized by attitudes and feelings of being: unappreciated, misunderstood, hopeless, burdened with impossible demands, innocent of all wrongdoing, mistreated and misjudged.

Martyrs seldom directly express their anger, fear, shame, or hurt or the reasons for it. Instead, they exhibit the following behavioral patterns:

- Self-righteousness
- Refusal to acknowledge any wrongdoing
- Inability to feel or accept gratitude
- Covertly seeking revenge
- Lying
- Expecting noble exoneration in the future

Martyrs create circumstances that will justify their feelings of being unappreciated and misunderstood. The energy of a martyr is based in unconfronted fear and is always hostile. Despite the denials, pretenses and often sophisticated facades, the behavior of a martyr is vicious and destructive.

Victimhood

Victims have the same characteristics as martyrs, only their expression is less sophisticated. The difference is victims, unlike martyrs, are overt and expressive of their anger, hurt, fear, or shame and why they feel that way. Behavior common to victims is that they want others to do things for them because of their sad condition but are never satisfied with whatever is done.

Both victim and martyr roles are subtle combinations of self-pity and self-importance. Alone, those characteristics are more obvious. Combined, the self-pity and self-importance cover each other, are much harder to spot, and are more destructive.

There are few human emotions as warm, comforting, and enveloping as self-pity. And nothing is more corrosive and destructive.

—Megan Reik

FEAR AND ANXIETY

Fear and anxiety are authentic emotions, with both positive and negative potential. Both provide messages to us without which we could be vulnerable. However, fear and anxiety are different, and it is important to distinguish between the two.

Fear

Fear is the automatic response to anything that is different from what was. It is about the threat of potential future loss (real or imagined) and is related to a specific incident or event. Fear is useful in certain circumstances but detrimental in others.

Benefits of fear:

- Fear is a whisper (a warning) that tells us to watch out, that there may be some threat present.

- Fear tells us where there is a lack of trust in a person or situation.

- Fear can slow us down enough to provide the opportunity to change directions.

- Fear tells us we have a belief that is contra-survival and directs us as to where we need to be more responsible.

Liabilities of fear:

- Fear can lead to feelings that we are no longer in control. We can allow it to disempower us by our avoidance of or exaggerated reaction to it.

- Fear always accompanies change and, therefore, acts to slow or prevent it. A little bit of fear gives us pause; too much paralyzes us.

- Fear of repeating errors of the past can prevent us from accurately assessing the present.

- Fear can become the rationalization for manipulations of power playing, "If I am not on top, someone must be on top of me. Therefore, whatever I do is justified."

- Fear can be addictive.

Our fears are more numerous than our dangers, and we suffer more in our imagination than in reality.

—Lucius Annaeus Seneca

Courage is not the absence of fear. Rather, it is the willingness to face our fear, listen to its message, act accordingly, and move beyond it. *A major key to personal growth and emotional maturity is in facing the fear we do have.*

When we fail to confront our fear, authenticity, sincerity, and honesty disappear, and effective communication becomes impossible. Any time we notice people, including ourselves, lacking in those qualities—authenticity, sincerity, and honesty— we can assume they have fears they are not confronting. All dysfunctional behavior originates from some form of an unwillingness to face fear (real or imagined). When that happens fear winds up controlling us. We experience a sense of being out of control, unable to take self-determined action. Therefore, issues concerning control—whether we feel always controlled, never in control, must be in control or won't be controlled— wind up dominating our life.

In our reactive attempts to compensate and regain control, human beings have developed a considerable range of behaviors that attempt to manipulate, intimidate and/or dominate others, overtly or covertly. Some examples are the overcautious naysayer, the domineering tyrant, the workaholic over-achiever, the entitled snob, the passive-aggressive procrastinator, the helpful martyr, and the guilt-producing victim. All are behaviors to compensate for non-confronted fears but ultimately only compound the fear and sense of being out of control. All are inevitably hurtful and destructive.

The way out is the way through. The real treasures lie on the other side of our fear. When we truly confront our fears, we see things we did not see before. It is that clarity that miraculously transmutes the fearful or anxious energy into constructive survival action. When integrated, fear transmutes to sensitivity, aliveness and excitement. As we confront our fear, listen to its message, and take responsible action, limitations begin to dissolve and our entire universe expands.

You gain strength, courage and confidence by every experience in which you really stop to look fear in the face.
—Eleanor Roosevelt

Anxiety

Anxiety is different from fear in that it is not associated with a specific event or a specific time. It is a lack of a sense of a positive future. Anxiety is free-floating and usually results from one or more of the following:

- Undefined pain, anger, hurt, or fear
- Expectation of error, e.g., "I will be less than perfect"
- Anticipated rejection or humiliation
- Disbelief in a positive future
- Trust erroneously placed in a situation, another person, or ourselves if we are untrustworthy

Anxiety is more insidious than fear because it is harder to define. Neither fear nor anxiety can be resolved without being defined. The first step in dealing with either is to get as focused and as specific as possible in determining exactly what we are fearful of or anxious about.

Often asking repetitively, "And what's under that?" will help get us closer to the specifics of the cause of our anxiety. Clarity itself helps dissipate the anxiety. (See "Going Deeper—Getting to the Core" at the end of this chapter.)

ARROGANCE

No one would describe Robert as arrogant. He was professional, well-mannered and gracious. In executing the sale of his company, he felt confident that he had handled the negotiation very well. Just like an experienced negotiator should, he had set high, but not ridiculous, goals and stuck to them. He had established good rapport, determined the other party's needs, met them, and positioned himself well. They, not he, had made the first offer, and he had conceded slowly in small amounts.

Finally, with only a few details left to resolve, the deal was about to close. Then he made his fatal mistake: the other side was making some comments and, feeling the deal was in the bag, Robert only listened casually. They noticed his detachment. In that instant, they felt discounted and lost trust in the sincerity of his claims. His casual inattention was a form of "subtle arrogance," and it cost him a multimillion-dollar deal.

Defining Subtle Arrogance

Arrogance is sometimes obvious to the onlooker. No one likes the know-it-all who flaunts his or her self-importance. We often condemn such a person. However, subtle arrogance comes in many forms and can be just as much if not more dangerous. Consider the following situations:

- An interviewer takes several phone calls during your interview
- Someone interrupts you to make his point
- Your boss ignores your input
- Someone only pretends to listen to you

In each situation the person is effectively communicating, "I and my needs are more important than you and your needs." These behaviors, which we all occasionally exhibit, are subtle forms of arrogance.

Subtle or blatant, arrogance in any form is always destructive to any relationship, regardless of the circumstances and no matter how justified. If we lack presence and display any form of inattention or disinterest, we run the risk of making the other person feel discounted, which immediately breaks rapport. As Robert discovered, it doesn't take blatant arrogance to destroy a negotiation—subtle arrogance does just as much damage.

Being Right at the Cost of Being Effective

Arrogance is often a choice of being right at the cost of being effective. We need to be aware of the potential liability of being caught in thinking, "Well, I am right!" We may be right, but how often have we observed people so arrogantly caught in being right that they stifle relationships and limit their effectiveness?

Old patterns based in insecurities of the past urge us to insist on being right. *We need to ask ourselves, "How am I insisting on being right?"* For example, when another person objects to our viewpoint, do we really listen to the objection, or do we react by stressing our point even harder? This reaction is frustrating to both parties—and it never works.

If we are willing to honestly address that question, perhaps then we can recognize and acknowledge that sometimes we do insist on being right—arrogantly and closed-mindedly—often when we are most unsure of our rightness. Perhaps then we will stop our insistence and actually hear another person's viewpoint. We don't have to agree with it, but we do need to view it without immediately depreciating it. We need to discipline ourselves to listen. We may be amazed at what we hear—and what we have been missing.

The Root of Arrogance

The basis of arrogance, subtle or not, lies in our own insecurities and fears. Fundamentally, we all strive for growth, expansion, and awareness. Unfortunately, pressure from parents and society to be better can be twisted into attitudes of "better than." Acting better than is a compensation and facade for an underlying insecurity, that is, some sense or feeling of being "less than."

That facade is the face of arrogance. When we exhibit it, it keeps us distant from others. It protects us from looking at our fears. The more fearful we are, the more we must defend and maintain that facade at all costs. To do this we must, to some extent, blind ourselves to other viewpoints and put boundaries around our own.

We often attempt to do so by belittling others. Any time we discount another person, it is a put-down. And a put-down is never a small thing! Far too often, it has huge consequences—which are always negative.

When you diminish another person, you lose their ability to contribute to you.
—Michael Naumer

Handling the Cause

We're human and, as such, we're not perfect. On occasion, we all can be arrogant. If we truly want to be more effective, we must limit not only the destructive impact of that arrogance but also the arrogance itself. Fortunately, we can choose to correct arrogant behavior.

As a start, we must have an honest willingness to examine our behavior and look at what is causing the arrogance. Start by looking at what you do to discount other people. Ask yourself, "When and how was I insensitive? When and how did I act better than?" If you don't come up with something, you're probably lying. Find something. Find a whole bunch. Note how you automatically want to justify your behavior. If you feel a bit embarrassed—good. It's an indication you may be actually recognizing and willing to be responsible for the consequences of your arrogance. This is usually a necessary precondition to having the courage to confront the underlying fear that the discounting and devaluating behaviors were attempting to cover. Once you honestly address these questions, you may be ready to ask yourself, "What do I get to avoid by pretending to be better than," or "What am I afraid I'd have to face if didn't have the facade of better than?" These can be tough questions. The fear of facing them is what arrogant behavior attempts to hide. However, when we're ready to face our underlying fears honestly and do so, the pretenses and pressures to maintain them evaporate. The effects can be incredibly liberating.

When we do not confront our fears, we not only force ourselves into very restricted ways of behaving and relating. but we make ourselves susceptible to being controlled and manipulated.

Con artists and manipulators love arrogant people. Because arrogant people have not confronted their fears, they can be easily manipulated. For example, during negotiations, manipulators find and focus on the person's fears and in-securities. Rather than face those fears, many individuals would rather lower their expectations, back off, and make concessions. If we do not face our fears, we will not handle our arrogance, and the bottom-line costs can be significant. However, *if we have faced our fears, no one can use them to manipulate us.*

The steps of addressing arrogance are as follows:

1. Forthrightly admit, "Sometimes I am arrogant."
2. Look for and own the specific ways you discount or belittle others.
3. Find your pattern of excuses, rationalizations, and justifications.
4. Under that pattern, look for the fear(s) it has been covering.

5. Face that fear by choosing to confront and fully feel it. Feel the fear in your body. Stay with it and simply observe what comes up until it dissolves. Feel the expansiveness and sense of freedom when you do so.

6. Acknowledge yourself for your courage and determination. Celebrate!

7. Take appropriate corrective action, which will likely include acknowledging our arrogance to those it may have hurt and asking what we can do to make amends for it.

If we do this whenever we are having difficulties or are upset with others, we may soon find both our arrogance and people problems significantly lessen.

ANGER

Anger is an authentic emotion. As a positive message, it tells us that there is some irresponsibility or injustice that needs addressing. When integrated, anger transmutes to power. By responsibly acting on that message, we transform the energy behind the anger into productive action.

Anger in and of itself is not destructive, but repressed, suppressed, or harbored anger is. Anger is an active emotion and its energy is always processed one way or another; when repressed, anger does not lie dormant within us until we are ready to work with it. Even though we may feel we are effectively repressing our anger, it actively, if silently, becomes a destructive force rather than the liberating force it could be.

Pretending we are not angry, when we are, forces the energy to be processed either in the form of problems or failures or through our body as discomfort or disease. It is not a choice of whether we process anger; we do and we will. Rather, it is a question of how we do so.

Confronting Why We Repress, Suppress, or Harbor Anger

All repressed, suppressed, or harbored anger (or any emotion) is a refusal to confront and take responsibility for some aspect of our behavior. If we find ourselves continually upset and angry (no matter how justified we may think it is), we need to address the following questions:

- What am I avoiding?
- Whom am I punishing?
- What are my control issues?
- Why do I want to feel righteous?
- What do I fear I will lose if I give up my anger?
- How does remaining angry contribute to my feeling of self-importance?
- Do I enjoy self-pity enough to suffocate opportunities for more gratifying interactions?

Anger's Place in Relationships

"Clean" anger never hurt anyone. It is dishonesty that hurts. If we are afraid of losing a relationship if we honestly express our feelings, it's time to look at that relationship and assess it in terms of how we want it to be.

Anger is an emotion. However, the constructive expression of anger is a process that draws upon self-reflection, creative thinking, and effective communication skills. We need to first reflect about why we are angry and where our anger is coming from. Before speaking directly with someone we associate with our anger, we need to think about what we want to say, about what could be specific solutions to our anger. We want to voice our concerns without overwhelming or being accusative toward the other person.

Expressing anger honestly and thoughtfully vitalizes our growth and improves the environment around us. We also need to keep in mind that immediate confrontation while either party is still upset often precludes constructive processing. We need to be responsible and arrange a mutually convenient time and place to speak with the other person about the impact of the interaction—particularly if the other person is taken by surprise or has not thought through his or her own anger. For example, if the other person lashes back or seems unwilling to talk, we need to be responsible and indicate that we want to work things out—even at a future time. Resolution may require an ongoing dialogue.

Getting in touch with one's anger means we are less hidden to ourselves, more present, more aware of information that could help us respond in ways that could end our suffering.
—The Dalai Lama

INTEGRATING THINKING AND FEELING

Emotional intelligence requires more than intellectual knowledge of emotional dynamics. To respond effectively to life situations, we must integrate both cognitive and emotional awareness. Thinking and feeling are meant to work together, to support and add clarity to each other. Emotional intelligence and cognitive intelligence go hand in hand. *We cannot think without feeling, and we cannot feel without thinking.* One without the other is insufficient. It lacks wholeness. It lacks integrity. Together, they create a synergy of greater awareness, producing more responsible, fulfilling choices and actions. When either thinking or feeling is repressed, this synergy of expanded awareness evaporates. The more we responsibly integrate and use our thoughts and feelings in dealing with life situations, the more we move toward emotional maturity.

We know too much and feel too little. At least, we feel too little of those creative emotions from which a good life springs.
—Bertrand Russell

WHY LIFE SEEMS A STRUGGLE

Why is it so few people seem to relish life? Why is it that so many people act weak and disempowered? Why is it that so many are abusive and indifferent? The fact is that emotional maturity and its qualities are not the norm in contemporary society; nor have they been historically. Simply witness man's inhumanity to man across the millennia to the present day.

Constant attention to survival considerations creates the perception of a difficult, even hostile, world where life seems more of a struggle than a joyous event. That notion is a major part of why the paradigm of "no pain, no gain" is so embedded in the current consensus reality. However, living with such a paradigm keeps us reactive and limits our power and potential.

Fear-based, self-centered survival patterns are so familiar that many people feel they are natural and normal. Observing this, psychologist Abraham Maslow defined normal as "the average of an abberated society." Integrity and emotional maturity are often much less familiar to us and, as a result, feel relatively unnatural or abnormal. It is a reason why many people feel disempowered and become chronically angry, anxious, sad, or depressed. It is a major reason why so many resort to drugs—legal or otherwise—to numb the resulting physical, mental, and/or emotional pain.

Is life so wretched? Isn't it rather your vision which is muddled? You are the one who must grow up.

—Dag Hammarskjöld

FEELING EMOTIONS VERSUS EMOTIONALITY

Emotionality, or acting emotional, is the dramatization of repressed feelings; an exaggerated reaction used to deny, cover up, and/or avoid listening to, feeling and expressing real emotions such as hurt, pain, shame, anger and fear.

When we allow emotional drama, we contribute to a world of socially acceptable deceit and limited expression of authentic emotions. For example, a small boy is rejected from some activity by his peer group. He feels hurt and sad and wants to cry. But he has learned that only girls cry—boys do not, boys are tough! At home, he angrily hits his younger brother and then accuses him of being a crybaby. He numbs himself to both the hurt he felt and the hurt he has caused. Repeated enough, it becomes an automatic, chronic pattern of anger, separation and lack of empathy and compassion. Years later, this person is likely to be emotionally and/or physically abusive and have only superficial relationships or deeply codependent relationships.

Allowing self-centered emotionality rather than feeling our real emotions severely restricts our access to the survival information real emotions provide. Repressing feelings limits honest communication and understanding. It keeps us from being empathetic to other people and closes them off to us.

In fact, any repression of feeling depletes our energy and limits our perception of what is possible. It increases our insecurities and self-centeredness, constricts our passions and dreams, and limits our choices and actions. *By repressing emotions, we effectively cut off a significant source of our power,* limiting our potential to positively act and accomplish what we want.

Encouraging the feeling and expression of emotions does not mean encouraging the dumping of hostile feelings on others. "Dumping" behavior is simply another way of avoiding by blaming others for feelings/thoughts we don't want to own.

Often we observe emotional misrepresentation in forms that are not only socially acceptable but also expected. For example, how often are we encouraged to not show anger, anxiety, grief, or depression and instead act pleasant and cheerful even when those attitudes are not remotely close to the truth? How easily we ignore the fact that emotional misrepresentation is a deception, to others and to ourselves. That sort of socially acceptable pretence contributes to the rationalization that it is better to repress emotions than to express our true feelings. If we can learn to differentiate between benign social expectations and repressive ones, we can learn volumes about the level of authentic communication and corresponding sense of security actually present.

When we are dishonest about our feelings, we contribute to a world of pretence and its inevitable dysfunctional consequence. We provide a myriad of social reasons why those pretences are needed or acceptable, but it is our own dishonesty, based in some fear that we are unwilling to confront, that restricts our choices, actions, results and relationships.

It is acknowledging and *responsibly* expressing actual feelings, not some dramatized or sugary surrogate, that generates our sense of aliveness, passion, compassion and depth of connection. All of that, along with our trustworthiness, dies a lonely death when we are no longer authentic about our actual feelings. We wind up feeling isolated, alone, powerless, afraid and full of unacknowledged rage.

He that would be superior to external influences must first become superior to his own passions.

—Samuel Johnson

WHAT IS RAGE?

Rage is the emotional expression of feeling powerless. Rage is not just extreme anger. That is just one possible manifestation. Rage has to do with boundary issues, where either too much or too little of something is occurring. When boundaries are too permeable we feel violated. When they are too rigid we feel restricted or excluded. If those conditions persist, the result is we feel powerless to do anything about our situation. When we feel powerless we have rage.

More often than not, our rage is not out in the open but lies hidden, covered by all our self-deceiving pretenses. Any time we have repressed something or allowed ourselves to be repressed, we have accumulated rage. When we repress our emotions—any emotion, "good" or "bad"—we cannot hear and cannot respond to its message. We instead react, feel ineffective and powerless, and accumulate rage. Unless enlightened, everyone has some rage, and we continue to see its manifestations in the world, ranging from simple inconsideration, constant blaming, and child and spouse abuse, all the way to terrorism, mass murder, and genocide. Repress anyone or any population long enough and the rage will explode in irrational, unloving and destructive ways. Witness 9/11 and the Middle East.

Rage is associated with a sense of excessive loss of value or self-worth and an intense sorrow or abject denial of shame and pain. Shame is the sense of being defective. Pain is a synergy of separation from and longing for something: emotional pain—belonging; mental pain—understanding; physical pain—control. Rather than confront all that, we repress the shame, the pain and the rage—and we settle.

HOW WE SETTLE

We often settle for doing the same old things, simply because those things are familiar to us and familiarity makes them easier. We settle for using a few skills rather than capitalizing on the depth of our real talents. We settle for being busy rather than truly productive and lose the excitement and joy that a full sense of real productivity brings. We settle for mediocrity rather than excellence. We falsely believe it is easier to settle into a pattern of blame and exaggeration than to accept responsibility for and ownership of how we contributed to the situation. We become expert at justifying or denying the resultant boredom, frustration, anxiety and sense of powerlessness.

Sometimes I worry about being a success in a mediocre world.
—Lily Tomlin

Too many of us settle for pretense, feel like phonies, and would not dare act out our claims of what we are going to do, for fear we might expose the self-perceived inadequacies we try so hard to hide. The result is that we miss out on many of our dreams and desires, which we otherwise are fully capable of living.

If unchecked, appearance rather than substance becomes our emphasis and way of life. We become insincere actors expending energy that provides little real satisfaction, regardless of our claims to the contrary. Concern for others becomes little more than lip service. Self-centeredness reigns and is rationalized as individual initiative. Skill at one-upmanship is admired and emulated. Character and integrity are given little real weight. Material and political success becomes the measure of the person. Underneath it all, the sense of powerlessness builds.

We wind up leading soap-opera lives, acting out someone else's script rather than authoring and directing our own story. Many become "empty suits" who occupy a desk, draw a salary, make little or no real contribution and have emotionally dropped out.

There are an enormous number of managers who have retired on the job.
—Peter Drucker

Sometimes our rage bursts through in overtly destructive ways. One such way is being judgemental. Judgements, in this sense, are reactive, hostile conclusions that are asserted based on previously formed ideas devoid of present-time discernment or evaluation. These judgements are usually projections of aspects of ourselves we reject.

One way to cope with feelings of being overwhelmed is to go numb. Going numb is a way of avoiding. It is a defense mechanism to dodge facing some real or imagined pain. Addictions and addictive behaviors are compulsive ways of trying to anesthetize the pain of feeling what we are afraid to face.

The stoic, unfeeling, numbed-out individual is a person who no longer has access to the whole range of emotions and to the information those emotions provide. That individual has limited survival and success potential. *Greater differentiation and discernment, increased clarity of communication, enhanced survival potential, and expanded enjoyment of life all come with the healthy use of more emotions, not fewer.*

High regard and a positive public image is a natural human preference. However, we will not feel satisfied or fulfilled unless we ground that image in honesty, authenticity and real contribution—essence values. When we are dishonest about our feelings, we lose the richness that different feelings were intended to provide. We lose integrity. Rather than being in control of our life, the "stuff out there" controls us. We increasingly become more afraid, self-centered and defensive. To "protect" ourselves, we increasingly react, withdraw and build higher walls. The rage builds.

When we end our repression, we regain our willingness and ability to respond to what exists. We become more responsible and empowered. We regain the perspective, confidence, passion and compassion that result from owning our power. We replace our rage with a sense of calm.

The growth of wisdom may be gauged exactly by the diminution of ill temper.

—Friedrich Nietzsche

Individuals whose chronic behavior is hurtful, limiting, or unloving to themselves and others have lost touch with the core of their real power—essence values. In reacting to the perceived loss, they substitute a whole set of compensating values, beliefs, strategies, behaviors and rationalizations that only serve to limit them further. This perceived loss is a delusion, for we cannot lose essence qualities because they are core to our very being—but we can lose touch with them. They are there in our shadow.

THE SHADOW

The shadow is the part of ourselves that is the reservoir for all those things for which we are not willing or able to take responsibility. In effect, a part of us says, "I'll store this thing that seems too much for you to deal with now until you are able to take responsibility for this aspect of yourself." In effect, it is a friend helping to keep us from being completely overwhelmed.

Our shadow is the sum total of all the denied aspects, positive or negative, that help make up who we are. It is what we are capable of but will not confront. It is all those bad things we insist we could not do and those bad things we did do but will not own. It is all the repressed and denied rage, anger, pain, hurt and shame.

Importantly, the shadow is also the storehouse of all our unacknowledged or denied greatness—those strengths, gifts and talents we have not owned. It is where our repressed desire, passion, compassion, creativity, and joy reside. It is where all our unacknowledged potential lies hidden.

Some call these negative and positive aspects the dark and light shadows. Whatever we call it, or however we compartmentalize it, all aspects—the light as well as the dark—must be confronted and owned before we can fully integrate them, be empowered and more fully enjoy life.

By looking at our patterns—all of them, including our dark ones—we're able to see how we run and hide and keep ourselves busy so that we never have to let our hearts be penetrated.

—Pema Chodron

THE EGO

Although often confused with the shadow, the ego is different. As humans developed the capacity to think, our animal instincts significantly diminished or became dormant. The ego is a survival mechanism created by humankind to replace many of those animal instincts. Its function is to be an information gatherer of what is going on around us. It is then our responsibility to use our ability to think for the purpose of evaluating that data and taking appropriate survival action.

However, when we become stressed, due to trauma or other events, we increasingly avoid doing what we need to do, including evaluating data input. So, in our stressed state and corresponding irresponsibility, we dump the job of evaluating on our ego.

But our ego is not equipped to evaluate and make decisions. It is only able to gather data. When we demand of our ego to do something of which it is incapable, it becomes overwhelmed. Under extreme stress dormant animal instincts can be reactively restimulated. Just as we do when we feel overwhelmed and afraid, and in the interest of survival, our oppressed ego fights the perceived oppressor—in this case, ourselves.

By being irresponsible and not facing our fears, we create a negative ego. Our ego, instead of being a helpful servant, is now out to get us. We have given away our power of choice to our ego and wind up falsely believing that we really have no choice about many things.

Although we do not want a negative ego, we need a healthy ego. In fact, a well-functioning ego is necessary for emotional maturity to develop (see "Stages of Ego Development," Table 5.1, page 159).

The process of owning our shadow diminishes the negative ego and builds the healthy one. As an example, someone asked Mother Teresa how she was able to have such a powerful impact. Her immediate response was that she had to own the potential Hitler in herself. Her willingness to face her negative potential transmuted, integrated and used that energy positively. Added to her existing positive energy, it synergistically manifested a power and effectiveness that amazed the world.

Creating the future at the leading edge is dependent on each one of us waking up and transcending our attachment to the fears of the ego.
—Andrew Cohen

A CRY FOR LOVE

All dysfunctional behavior—no matter how despicable, hurtful, or destructive—*is, at its very foundation, a cry for love.* The key to being responsible in the face of dysfunctional behavior is to realize that although someone else's actions may be unacceptable, that person is in pain. The more hurtful the behavior someone exhibits, the more that person is hurting. He or she is projecting that hurt as a defense. In that reactive and irrational state, the person is behaving in ways that produce the opposite of what he or she needs and truly wants. *The more dysfunctional the behavior, the more the person needs and is craving love.*

Creating and maintaining appropriate boundaries around dysfunctional behavior is a key indicator of and testimony to mature responsiveness. Boundaries can be too weak or too strong. An example of a too-weak boundary is an individual having difficulty saying no to additional assignments when already overloaded. Another example is an unwillingness to define, set and maintain standards of acceptable behavior. Boundaries that are too strong are just as dysfunctional. In this scenario, individuals say no too often and do not say yes enough. They exclude things, activities and people that could contribute to their well-being. We all need boundaries. Otherwise, we would be overwhelmed. However, we need to keep them in perspective and balance.

When dealing with dysfunctional behavior, it is important to remain empathetic and compassionate to the underlying cry for love while also maintaining responsible boundaries. Integrating and balancing both is a measure of our ability to be truly responsive versus reactive. That facility is an indication of our emotional maturity and is a critical component of effective, powerful and compassionate leadership.

Love alone is capable of uniting living beings in such a way as to complete and fulfill them, for it alone takes them and joins them to what is deepest within themselves.
—Pierre Teilhard de Chardin

SO YOU WANT TO BE HAPPY

If you want to be happy, stop doing the things that are bad for you and start doing the things that are good for you.
—The Dalai Lama

Happiness can be defined as getting our needs met, and joy as getting our preferences met. What do we really want in our life?

What are our needs? What are our preferences? What are the qualities and characteristics of those needs and preferences? Do we know the difference? How do we get there?

The steps to getting there and the qualities of being there are the same. If we want more honesty and love in our life, we need to be more honest and loving. It can be that simple. *If we are not experiencing the qualities we say we want, it behooves us to look honestly at our willingness to truly be and have those qualities in our life.*

Many of us, if not most, have an automatic tendency to look outside of ourselves, outside of the here and now, to find happiness. It appears that many of us do not realize we already have the capacity and enough conditions present to be happy right now. We have created a limiting attitude based on a false belief that happiness is not possible now; that it is out there, not in here. We need to recognize that it is only a belief and that it is our belief. Since it is ours, we do have the potential to change it if we choose. Happiness is only a choice away. What keeps us from making that choice?

We can't be happy when we're not present. *Unhappiness or discontent has, at its core, an unwillingness to be present with something.* It simply means there is something we do not want to deal with, something we do not want to face. We lack presence.

Why do we avoid facing what is? Because there is something present that restimulates some false sense of insufficiency—some sense of not being up to the task of dealing with it. However, by not confronting that lie, it sticks, and we wind up believing it and spend our life trying to compensate for it.

What you resist, persists.

—Carl Jung

That basic lie—that a better something, e.g., happiness, connection, and fulfillment, is out there, separate from ourselves —traps us in a chronic sense of not being enough. It is what keeps us stuck in our compulsive compensations. As long as we believe better is out there, not in here, it will remain so, and we will never have a sense of attaining it—no matter how hard we try. As long as we spend our efforts trying to perfect our compensations, grasping for what we feel is missing, we will always feel inadequate and unhappy.

Grasping is the source of all our problems. Learning to live is learning to let go.

—Sogyal Rinpoche

No matter how skillful our compensations, how much we gain through them, or how much they are acknowledged and admired by the outside world, they never will be enough. We will experience pain and suffering, in the form of disconnection and separation, and we will perpetuate a limiting, impoverished perspective.

When we recognize that what we want and must deal with is within, not out there, and when we accept that we are responsible for our own condition, then we can let go of the limiting and misdirected compensations. Only then are we fully capable of owning our power, being empowered, and being happy more of the time.

To the degree that we are willing to feel our feelings and appropriately express them, we open the door to increasing responsibility for what transpires in our life. Doing so is a choice away.

Winning and losing are about attitudes and perceptions. We choose them. Being happy or unhappy is a choice, *our* choice. *When we own that it is our choice and only our choice, we no longer feel controlled and victimized by the stuff out there.* We increasingly expand our ability to responsibly make needed change. Only then can true happiness and joy be a continuing part of our life.

We deem those happy who from experience of life have learned to bear its ills without being overcome by them.

—Carl Jung

GOING DEEPER—GETTING TO THE CORE

Sometimes we have emotions that act as a cover of a deeper feeling that, consciously or unconsciously, we are not willing or able to deal with in the moment. For example, expressions of hostility often cover underlying fear, grief, shame, despair, or even a deeper level of anger of which we are currently unaware. *As long as the underlying emotions and their messages are not brought to light, the problems they represent do not resolve, and we repeat endlessly their more superficial manifestations.*

"What's under That?" is a simple but potentially empowering process that can help individuals get unstuck from a persisting negative emotional state.

What's under That?

1. Ask the individual,, "What emotion are you experiencing?" (Response)

2. Ask, "Where do you feel it in your body?" (Response) (Note: All emotions can be physically located in the body.)

3. Ask, "What emotion is under that emotion?" (Response)

4. Ask, "And what emotion is under that?" (Response)

Keep repeating the question after each response until the answer is repeatedly the same emotion. This is likely to be or be close to the core emotion underlying the presenting issue. Often, simply getting in touch with a new depth of feeling previously repressed or suppressed is all that is needed to provide relief sometimes accompanied by some new awareness. If this does not occur, proceed with step 5.

5. Ask the individual to describe the emotion in physical terms, e.g., shape, size, weight, color, and so on.

6. Ask the individual, under your direction, to change the physical dimensions one by one. For example, say, "Change the shape to a sphere," or "Double its size," or "Have it weigh three pounds," or "Change its color to green." Ask the person to make approximately a half dozen changes; acknowledging them each time they

do so. Then suggest they make the choices and tell you what changes they made. Acknowledge them for doing so. Continue until relief and recognition occur.

5. Have the person acknowledge his or her accomplishment and celebrate.

Doing all steps except 3 and 4 can also be quite effective, as can doing all steps except 5 and 6. Allow yourself to be creative in the way you combine steps 3, 4, 5, and 6. As long as you are present and your intention is to be of help, trusting and acting on your intuition will stand you in good stead.

Note: This simple process can be very effective in helping individuals recognize that they have more choice than they were acknowledging they had. Unless there is some chemical/hormonal imbalance, remaining stuck in a dysfunctional emotional state is, ultimately, an active choice we make to avoid dealing with whatever we consider may or will be even worse. When we do so we lose presence—the ability and willingness (power) to be with and respond versus react to what is. *Staying stuck in any emotional state simply means we have not yet been willing or able to listen, hear and respond to its message.* Accordingly, its energy does not transmute and positively integrate.

Being able and willing to more fully view the multiple aspects of any emotional state (or situation) helps provide a more objective perspective. This allows us to see the emotion simply for what it is—a message of how we are doing, not something we need to avoid. That clarity helps to dissipate the controlling and stifling influence we allowed it to have. That is why going deeper, in a safe but increasingly self-causative way, can be so therapeutically empowering. It rekindles our power of choice.

MAKING THE TOUGH CALL

In a world of imperfect information and unlimited viewpoints, we seldom, if ever, have certainty about our assessments, choices, or decisions. Nevertheless, leaders are continually required to make them. "It's a tough call but it's mine to make," is the hallmark of a courageous, proactive decision-maker, but only if it comes from a responsive, non-reactive perspective. Arrogant people often attempt to hide their fears with similar sounding macho statements but then promised results are unlikely.

All men should strive to learn before they die what they are running from, and to, and why.

—James Thurber

The very things we wish to avoid, neglect, and flee from turn out to be the prima materiá from which all real growth comes from.

—Andrew Harvey

Only when decisions are made from a responsive, i.e., mature perspective will constructive, contributing results be forthcoming. *Raise emotional maturity and needed tough decisions start being made in a more timely, efficient and effective manner.*

In the following chapter, we take a deeper look at emotional maturity as a foundation for personal happiness and effective leadership.

5

EMOTIONAL MATURITY

For all of man's evolution and considerable technological accomplishments, psychologically he is still very, very immature.
—J. Krishnamurti

DEFINING EMOTIONAL MATURITY

Emotional maturity is a balance between a healthy ego identity (a sense of being an autonomous individual) and an ability and willingness to relate to others in an authentic and meaningful way. It means being willing and able to integrate independence with interdependence and to responsibly confront and deal with all the issues of life—the bad as well as the good. It is about ending the blame and owning the stuff for which we avoid responsibility. It is living essence values and doing so spontaneously. Emotionally mature people see their lives as a sequence of personal choices for which they are singularly responsible. In other words, *emotional maturity is acting with integrity.*

The development of emotional maturity relates directly to the stages of ego development. Each stage's respective focus of attention is as follows:

Stage 1: Infant/Young Child—"Am I getting enough?"

Stage 2: Child/Young Adolescent—"Am I good enough?"

Stage 3: Adolescent/Young Adult—"Am I being, doing, having, learning, and growing enough?"

Stage 4: Mature Adult—"I am enough."

We all need to experience these stages. Each stage provides a necessary learning experience that needs integration as part of the growing up/maturing process. It is the process of going from being totally dependent (Stage 1), to the gradual breaking of that dependency (Stage 2), to a sense of autonomous independence (Stage 3), to inclusive interdependence (Stage 4).

The self is not something ready-made, but something in continuous formation through choice of action.

—John Dewey

If any stage is not allowed to develop fully, the needed learning is not integrated, and an individual tends to become emotionally stuck in that stage. For example, sometimes parents expect or demand (for their own immature ego needs) that their child act like an adult before the child is ready. One common resulting manifestation is that later in life the child, who is now an adult, has little sense of play and often feels that he has not yet grown up but needs to pretend that he is, making him feel like a phony in the process. Another common result of a child having missed his or her play years is, that, as an adult, the person attempts to compensate for that loss by acting childish in present time. In fact, many adults are stuck in one of the earlier stages of ego development. These people can spend a great deal of energy concerned about fixing something they sense is not as it should be, yet they are unclear about exactly what that something is. This, too, adds to an uncomfortable sense of a lack of authenticity.

Stifled ego development offers a partial explanation for why we observe so much dysfunctional, self-serving behavior. The behaviors we generally see, and those that are so often rewarded, are not those of honesty, authenticity, and collaboration but their opposites. Collaborative behavior, a characteristic of a mature ego, seems to be a rarity too often given little more than lip service. Instead, we place an overly heavy emphasis on competition and the accumulation of material possessions, typical of an adolescent perception of needs and priorities. Achievement in competition and material accumulation appears to be the primary measure of success in much of society.

There is nothing inherently wrong with competition or the accumulation of material possessions. Their impact, positive or negative, depends on whether we interpret and act upon them from a mature perspective. Competition among individuals functioning from a mature adult ego stimulates creativity and produces a challenging learning environment that tends to manifest as an innovative, dynamic expansion of possibilities. Competition among people in any other stage is predictably self-serving and problematic. It is often destructive and always rationalized. This is simply another reason why *it is imperative that raising the emotional maturity of the organization be a senior management priority.*

Maslow's Hierarchy of Needs describes the needs of human beings in dealing with the issues they must confront in both growing up and life in general. It corresponds to the stages of ego development (see Table 5.1). As physical beings, we have survival and security needs. As relational beings, we have belonging needs. As contributing beings, we have esteem needs. As evolving, growing beings, we have actualizing needs. All those needs are continually present; only their emphasis changes. They are all human needs, but keeping them in balance and perspective is a must.

Our perceptions of needs change with time and context. Those perceptions are primarily based on the messages we receive from our emotions. Various aspects and nuances of those needs (survival, security, belonging, and so forth) continue to recycle throughout life. Part of the learning, developing, and maturing process is to gain experience in what works and what does not work in getting those needs met. Each time any one of those needs becomes a particular focus of attention, it provides another opportunity to expand our awareness and ability in that arena.

A fundamental truth about development is that each stage has lessons that need to be learned and integrated before we can fully move on. Those grown-ups we observe acting like children or adolescents much of the time have not confronted some needed lesson(s) and thus remain stuck in one of the earlier stages.

When we confront the fears around those lessons, we can integrate their meaning and value. We are then able to move on to the next stage. By doing so responsibly, we grow and begin meeting our needs in an increasingly efficient (maximum effect for the least amount of effort) manner.

TABLE 5.1

Correlation of the Stages of Ego Development and Maslow's Hierarchy of Needs

Stages of Ego Development	Maslow's Hierarchy of Needs
Mature Adult "I am enough."	**Self-Actualization**
Adolescent/ Young Adult "Am I learning, doing, growing, being enough?"	**Esteem**
Child/ Young Adolescent "Am I good enough?"	**Belonging**
	Security
Infant/ Young Child "Am I getting enough?"	
	Survival

The further along people are in the stages of ego development, the more easily and elegantly they can handle the needs of the lower stages (survival, security, belonging) as those needs arise or resurface in the give-and-take of life. The mature adult deals with those reoccurring needs as a part of life but doesn't become stuck in them. An overemphasis on any one of those needs, to the exclusion or minimization of the others, creates an imbalance in dealing with the wholeness of life. Integrity is lost.

A workaholic, for instance, is chronically out of balance, using work to avoid, deny, or repress something. The resulting workaholic behavior is little more than a compulsive compensation. Until we confront our denials and repressions, we will not advance to the next ego stage, regardless of financial, social, or political success.

Observe how many people are chronically irritable or depressed, and how many focus much of their attention on losses or regrets of the past and/or fears about the future. Notice how few have the courage to live their dreams in the present. These people have not attained adult ego maturity. This is not about judgments of good or bad, right or wrong. Rather, it is an observation about people who are less happy, less passionate, and less fulfilled by the life they are living than they could be.

When survival, security, belonging, or esteem issues remanifest, as they do in our never ending growth process, mature people use each experience as a learning and growth opportunity, regardless of the label of good or bad placed on it, and consistently demonstrate a responsive ability to restore a positive balance to their environment. On the other hand, someone stuck in an immature ego state will be reactionary, have difficulty learning from their experience, and be resistant to constructive change.

Society's emphasis on appearance, at the expense of substance, and the pretenses and facades that such emphasis encourages, often makes it difficult to grasp an individual's actual level of emotional maturity and stage of ego development. One way to make an assessment is simply to observe what ego behavior the person reverts to when under stress. The person will manifest the behaviors and attitudes of one of the four stages described above. In current society, the Mature Adult Stage is the least likely to be present. Most often, we observe that the type of need an individual reveals (such as security or belonging) will correspond to its parallel ego stage as indicated in Table 5.1.

Dr. Frederick Herzberg studied the factors involved in getting people to accomplish tasks. He found two main categories, one of which he called motivational factors—factors that propelled people toward accomplishment. The second he called hygiene or maintenance factors—factors needed to keep people on the job. For example, a salary must be sufficient to meet an individual's survival needs. Once those needs are met, other things become more important.

According to Herzberg, personal growth is a much higher motivational factor than salary or working conditions. However, just as with the stages of ego development and Maslow's Hierarchy of Needs, lower-order needs must be met sufficiently before higher-order considerations can even come into play. Herzberg's factors appear to correspond closely with both the stages of ego development and Maslow's Hierarchy of Needs (see Table 5.2).

TABLE 5.2

Correlation of the Stages of Ego Development, Maslow's Hierarchy of Needs, and Herzberg's Two-Factor Job Model

Stages of Ego Development	Maslow's Hierarchy of Needs	Herzberg's Two-Factor Job-Model
Mature Adult "I am enough."	**Self-Actualization**	**Motivational Factors** Growth Potential Responsibility Achievement Recognition Advancement
Adolescent/ Young Adult "Am I learning, doing, growing, being enough?"	**Esteem**	**Maintenance Factors** Interpersonal Relations— Peers, Supervisors, Subordinates
Child/ Young Adolescent "Am I good enough?"	**Belonging**	Company Policy
	Security	Job Security
Infant/ Young Child "Am I getting enough?"		Work Conditions
	Survival	Salary

For many people, the process of ego development is stunted. In fact, unfortunately most adults, regardless of outward measures of success, are not emotionally secure. Many are still emotionally children or adolescents only occupying older bodies. How many adults do you know, who when under a little stress, revert to the reactive, self-centered behavior of a spoiled child or adolescent? When that occurs, which may be often, decisions made and actions taken are on a correspondingly immature level.

As we move from emotional naivete and immaturity toward being more emotionally intelligent and mature, we correspondingly develop a greater sense of security. This manifests in behaviors that are less self-centered, and more honest, authentic, and responsible more of the time. Communication and interpersonal effectiveness significantly expand. This dramatically affects organizational effectiveness as well as personal happiness. The maturation process is a learning, growing, sometimes exciting and sometimes frustrating experience. If not repressed, the process can be transformative and enormously fulfilling.

THE MATURITY PARADOX

Ever hear the phrase, "It's not about you!" or "Not everything is about you!" usually meaning, "Get out of your selfish self-centeredness!" You may also have heard, "It is all about you!" meaning everything you do has an impact. Both are true and at first glance may initially appear paradoxical. However, they are not. They simply represent different ego/maturity stages or levels. The former two statements represent frustration and communication that self-centered childish or adolescent attitudes are becoming tiresome and unacceptable. The latter is a statement about our willingness and ability to take responsible action for whatever situation in which we find ourselves (maturity). That does not mean doing anything perfectly, but it does mean doing the very best we can with the resources we have to make the situation better.

THE GENESIS OF LIMITATION

Man is made by his beliefs. As he believes, so he is.
—Bhagavad Gita

Limiting behaviors originate from limiting beliefs. Our beliefs form the basis of our experiences and how we perceive ourselves and the world around us. When those beliefs are limited, we limit our perception and experience of what is possible. It doesn't matter if those beliefs are false. As long as we believe them, they will accordingly impact and mold our perception of experience. The more limiting our beliefs, the less powerful we feel. Actually, any beliefs, even the noble ones, narrow our focus and are limiting and restrictive.

The universal core delusion that drives our limiting beliefs and behaviors is one of insignificance, in other words, not feeling enough. Some form of trauma—physical, mental, emotional, or spiritual—during which we feel overwhelmed and helpless often triggers this delusion. A trauma is usually an event so overwhelming that we can't/won't allow in what is happening. It is anything that keeps a person from fully experiencing, integrating, and responding to what is occurring in the moment. The result of trauma is that we severely narrow and limit our focus to defensive survival behaviors. We react rather than respond.

With each trauma, we narrow our focus further, often until we believe ourselves to be helpless and insignificant. Each of us tries in our own unique way to compensate for that feeling of insignificance. We develop sophisticated strategies to deal with our sense of not being good enough. We create masks (personality traits) to hide a stressful feeling of insignificance from ourselves as well as others.

Initially, those strategies were survival mechanisms that appeared to deal with the situation or provide some stress relief. When that stress reappeared, we again used what seemed to work in the past. Eventually, those strategies become the unconscious, automatic defense patterns we use reactively when anything even resembling the original trauma or stress reappears. We start to identify with the pattern: "That's who I am. Doing anything different just wouldn't be me." Letting go of that pattern, of that identification, feels like losing or abandoning a part of ourselves. Hence, we have an understandable reluctance to give it up. All beliefs, limiting or otherwise, are self-sustained.

The major problem is that this unconscious, reactive behavior shuts out discernment of the actual present-time situation, limiting, if not eliminating, an appropriate response. However, because our limiting considerations are a delusion, in trying to compensate for that delusion, we are trying to solve a problem that fundamentally does not exist. Therefore, any compensating behavior(s), no matter how brilliantly achieved and acknowledged, will never be sufficient. Our fixation on the delusion demands increasingly more energy and attention, depleting us—physically, mentally, and emotionally. This process of deterioration increasingly impairs our ability to communicate authentically and be happy.

THE SPIRAL OF DETERIORATION

As stress increases, our compensations become more intense and irrational. Being able to see the big picture and experience abundance, ease, happiness, and joy progressively deteriorates, first into a somewhat more conservative and narrower outlook. If the stress continues, so does the deterioration. We become combative, exhibiting antagonism, anger, and blame. As our fear increases, we regress to covert hostility and passive-aggressive behavior. The spiral of deterioration continues from fear to a sense of loss, to despair, and finally, to apathy.

As we deteriorate, our perspectives become narrower and more fixated. Our sense of being able to cope with life diminishes. We become increasingly self-centered and selfish. More and more, we perceive the world as hostile, to be defended against or avoided. Our desperation intensifies. We wind up feeling out of control and powerless and attempt to compensate by assuming control and power over others. We increasingly replace responsibility, honesty, trustworthiness, and happiness with their opposites. Our behaviors become more irrational, dysfunctional, unworkable, and destructive. The results of these behaviors are the opposite of what we actually need.

As we honestly recognize where we are in our deterioration and face our immature behaviors, we are then—and only then—in a position to reverse the process.

THE MATURATION PROCESS

The maturation process (growing up) is the reverse of the deterioration process described above. It includes an increasing willingness to face our fears and take responsibility for our current and previously disowned behaviors. It means becoming less self-centered. It also includes an increasing willingness to recognize, acknowledge, and start using more of our inherent strengths, gifts, and talents. *Ultimately, maturity is our willingness and ability to recognize and take responsibility for the impact of all our attitudes and behaviors.*

Paradoxically, it is when we reject something that our attention becomes fixated on it. When we are willing to view and own what we have been denying, we release the fixated attention. We feel lighter and more open. We can then see and own a fuller range of capabilities, including those from our dark as well as from our light shadow, and thus have all those energies synergistically available. *Listening to the message of our emotions and responsibly confronting our denials provides us a quantum leap in potential.*

EMOTIONAL MATURITY IS A CONSCIOUS CHOICE

Human beings, by changing the inner attitudes of their minds, can change the outer aspects of their lives.
—William James

As helpful as understanding emotional dynamics can be, that knowledge does not automatically make a person emotionally mature. Likewise, emotional maturity does not happen because we reach a certain age, have a job, get married, have children, make lots of money, or attain a high social or political position. Genes and hormones drive children and adolescents. However, beyond adolescence, we have to consciously choose maturity. *Emotional maturity is a result of conscious choice—our conscious choice to be responsible for our impact.* If we do not make this choice, we will not move beyond the emotional immaturity of an adolescent, despite any trappings of material success. Once past adolescence, we can choose to be emotionally mature, with all the power and freedom that maturity provides.

Every individual has a place to fill in the world, and it is important whether he chooses to do so or not.
—Nathaniel Hawthorne

Self-centeredness and self-importance are characteristics of children and adolescents, who expect to be taken care of, demand special treatment, and complain that life is not meeting their demands. This does not make them bad. It is simply part of the maturation process intended to help them to learn what works in contributing to a happier environment for all. However, when these behaviors manifest chronically in a grown-up, they are indications that that person has not integrated the needed lessons and is not a mature, responsive adult. Rather, he or she is still reacting out of the behavioral patterns of the self-centered child or self-important adolescent.

There are a great many people who look grown up and appear to be successful by contemporary standards, but who are emotionally still children or adolescents. Perhaps they had dysfunctional parents who had no idea how to model responsible mature behavior. If the only adult models they experienced were reactive ones, it is likely that they would model similar behavior or its reactive counterpart. Regardless of the reason, they are people caught in reactive behavior who erroneously view maturity and responsibility as burdens to be avoided.

Reactive behavior is inappropriate in dealing with any circumstance. Reactive patterns often originate early in childhood, when the individual had little experience or guidance in developing adequate defense mechanisms. Unless a person's childhood environment was unusually mature and appropriately supportive and nurturing, the person usually lacks a fundamental sense of security. The common result is that the individual grows up with a compensatory need for what often becomes an insatiable fixation on substitute symbols for security, such as money, status, power, prestige, approval, or acceptance.

Grounded in a fundamental sense of security, personal empowerment, and self-esteem, the emotionally mature adult does not need compensatory symbols of success. He or she may prefer them and often has them but does not need them. He or she may prefer to be accepted but does not need to be accepted.

Therapists speak of the need for letting go of the past and interrupting habituated, dysfunctional patterns. By interrupting dysfunctional patterns of the past and breaking their grip on us, we are more available to be present, to discern, evaluate, and choose actions that optimize and empower us. In order to let go of our dysfunctional patterns, we first need to recognize them.

However, because change generates confusion, doubt and fear, we often resist even seeing anything that would cause us to give up our familiar patterns—even when they are blatantly ruining our life. So we keep doing what is familiar—choosing "the devil we know over the devil we don't"—hoping that it will somehow create a different result. This is why change, individually or organizationally, is usually so difficult and is resisted even when obviously needed.

I tell you the past is a bucket of ashes.
—Carl Sandburg

Truly growing up, becoming emotionally mature, is about letting go of the past, being in the now, and responding, not reacting, to what is. Hanging onto the past becomes a convenient way to scapegoat and blame parents, others, and life situations for our problems and relationship issues. We use scapegoats to avoid facing our own irresponsible, immature behaviors. Instead of being responsive to what is, we are reactive to what was and are thereby less able to appropriately deal with what is.

A fundamental part of the route from adolescence to adult maturity is letting go of blaming others for our pain. Blame is about hanging onto unresolved grievances and irresponsibilities of the past. We need to learn to forgive ourselves as well as others before we can take charge of our life in the present.

Our parents may not have been exemplary, and they did have a significant impact on us. Some of that impact was less than ideal. Some may have been very hurtful and destructive. However, that was then and this is now! Is hanging on to upsets and resentments of the past worth the cost we are paying physically, mentally and emotionally? *We have to ask honestly, who is recreating the issue now?*

Alas, after a certain age, every man is responsible for his own face.
—Albert Camus

We ought not to look back unless it is to derive useful lessons from past errors, and for the purpose of profiting by dearly bought experience.
—George Washington

BLAME

Blame has nothing to do with honest assessment of cause. It is a reactive denial and an exaggerated projection of cause. When people blame others they are in effect saying, "I'm not responsible—someone else is." Blame implies a victim: "I'm innocent and have been abused." The behavior, being reactive versus responsive, is disproportionate to the problem and accusatory in tone. With blame, there is no constructive action, only complaining, whining, or aggressive behavior.

It may be true that we have been unjustly treated in a situation. However, *far too often we use another person's irresponsible behavior as a distraction and excuse from looking at our part in allowing or creating the situation.* A blaming reaction to someone else's behavior is often an attempt to deny—to ourselves as well as to others—how we have contributed to or allowed some unacceptable behavior. Blaming is using other people to deny and distract us from aspects of ourselves for which we have not yet owned responsibility.

Whenever we blame, we disown something, lose our integrity and give away our power. It is the intensity of the blaming reaction, versus constructive responding, that hints at the degree of denial present. This reactive behavior, denying any ownership of responsibility, severely limits the blamer's potential for making any real change: "You can't sell it if you don't own it." That is why people who blame others will often stay upset and angry, sometimes for years. Their denial of any ownership of responsibility precludes constructive change and keeps their anger intact.

One ought to examine himself for a very long time before thinking of condemning others.
—Molière (Jean-Baptiste Poquelin)

FROM BLAME TO RESPONSIBILITY—THE KEY TO POWER AND EMPOWERMENT

We should every night call ourselves to an account. Our vices will abate of themselves if they are brought every day to the shaft.
—Lucius Annaeus Seneca

A powerful exercise is to look at what and how we blame. The faults we find in others are often indicators of what we need to look at in ourselves. If we are willing, we can use what we are upset about as a reflection to help us identify and own some aspect of ourselves that we are denying or have not recognized before.

We are responsible for our impact. Others are responsible for their impact. The more of our impact we recognize and take responsibility for, the more empowered we become. When we realize we are blaming and/or defending (symptoms of an unwillingness to confront something), we need to find and own what responsibility we've been avoiding and/or denying. If we are willing to use what upsets us as a mirror to look deeper and to take more responsibility for our impact, we open the door to expanded awareness, growth and empowerment.

We need to recognize and own our piece of a situation—no more, no less. *Denying any of our impact, no matter how large or small, positive or negative, is disempowering to ourselves.* Our willingness to observe, confront and own our part is where the opportunities for growth, maturity and personal empowerment lie.

Facing it, always facing it, that's the way to get through. Face it.
—Joseph Conrad

The Gulp Stage

If we are upset and are, in effect, judging what some person did or did not do, we need to ask how we have done some form of that ourselves. There is something of a similar nature, or mirror image, that we have not recognized or owned before. When we are misemotional about someone else's behavior, inevitably we are hiding something from ourselves. For example, if we find ourselves feeling upset with and blaming someone because he or she did not follow through as promised, it is an opportunity to look closer at how we have not been fully responsible for our own promised or implied follow-through. This is often the "gulp" stage, for it is here that we finally recognize how irresponsible we have been.

What isn't part of ourselves doesn't disturb us.

—Herman Hess

It may very well be true that another person was irresponsible and didn't deliver as promised—and that may need to be dealt with—but *the opportunity and the empowering aspect is our increased willingness to recognize and take more ownership of the impact of our own behavior.*

When we shift our attention from how the other person is upsetting us (placing responsibility out there) to how we are doing something similar and have been denying it (placing responsibility within), three things immediately occur:

- We are less upset (our attention has shifted from blame to being more responsible)

- We have more positive control—we shifted our focus and intention from where we had little control (the other person) to where we have greater control (ourselves)

- We feel lighter and more empowered (the inevitable result of taking increased responsibility for our own behavior)

Going deeper is an opportunity not only to observe an aspect of our impact for which we have not been taking responsibility, but also to recognize the pattern of how we have been avoiding responsibility. By doing so we keep hidden from ourselves our real power and greatness. When we are able to recognize and own our pattern are we able to drop the victim attitude. Only then are we willing to be personally responsible, own our inherent power, expand our options and choices and empower ourselves to manifest constructive change.

The elegance of this process is that it is not dependent on the rightness or wrongness of either party. It is dependent solely on our willingness to observe and take responsibility for our own part in creating or allowing the upsetting situation to occur.

When you see a man of the highest caliber, give thought to obtaining his stature. When you see one who is not, go home and conduct a self-examination.

—Confucius

He who has so little knowledge of human nature as to seek happiness by changing anything other than his own disposition will waste his life in fruitless efforts and multiply the grief he intends to remove.

—Samuel Johnson

WILLINGNESS—THE DETERMINING FACTOR

Willingness is the determining factor of our empowerment, success, abundance and happiness. Our willingness or lack thereof sets the boundaries of our reality. To expand those boundaries, we need to review our willingness.

Power is the ability and willingness to act. Both must be present. When you have no power to get something accomplished, sometimes it is simply a lack of ability, but more often than not, it's a lack of willingness. In most cases, if we're truly willing, we can develop the necessary abilities or resources.

Often, we base our sense of deservability or worthiness on what we do or have. We make judgements about who is deserving enough or worthy enough, including ourselves. Such judgements not only indicate our biases but also are simply not valid, for *on a fundamental level, we all deserve and we all are worthy. No matter how hard we try or how much we achieve, nothing we accomplish will ever make us any more worthy or deserving than we already are.*

Our sense of personal empowerment and happiness is based on our willingness to recognize and acknowledge our inherent deservability and worth.

What Are We Willing to Be, Do and Have?

What are we willing to be? What are we willing to do? What are we willing to have? What are we *not* willing to be, do and have? Are we willing to do what is necessary to develop the skills and resources to be, do and have what we say we want? Part of emotional maturity is honestly looking at the answers to these questions. Are we willing to do the following?

- Be attentive to whatever our present reality is, including our fears
- Be authentic and honest (with ourselves and others); own our personal shadow
- Recognize and respect the fact that others are entitled to their own viewpoint, attitude and position, even if it differs from ours
- Own our power; give ourselves permission to act
- Do the right thing just because it is the right thing
- Persist through the inevitable resistance to changes (act with commitment, determination and resolve)

- Recognize and be responsible for our impact
- Face the confusion, doubt and fear inherent in any real change
- Reconsider our cultural bias, which emphasizes appearance over substance; own how we're contributing to that bias
- Face and persist through the awkward phase of learning how to do something different
- Recognize and act on our inherent strengths; put concepts and ideas into action
- Choose to be, do and have what we truly want

Since patterns of behavior are largely unconscious and automatic, we tend to see and hear primarily within that automatic framework. Consequently, we fail to hear when other people try to tell us, nicely or otherwise, that perhaps we are causing some harm by our actions or ways of relating. As we become more willing to hear, face and move through our fears, we are often surprised, even astounded, to realize how blind we have been to the harm we have caused, allowed, or to which we have contributed to. This is the "gulp" stage (described earlier on page 173). This is what we would rather not face, but it is exactly what we must see and accept if we are to change and grow.

The worst thing we can do to ourselves is let our fears control our willingness to look at ourselves honestly. The more we disown, the more we give away our power. The more we become victims, the more we need to create justifications and rationalizations, such as, "There's nothing I can do about it—that's the way it is. That's reality."

I realized the problem was me and nobody could change me except myself.
—John Petworth

We cannot get to where we really want to go without being aware of our own habits and patterns. *Growth is a process of being increasingly willing to peel back, expose and take responsibility for the layers of our own self-deception.* If we are not willing to face our fears and persist through the inevitable resistance, fear and resistance will control our life. We become confused about what we think we want. As a result, no matter how much we accumulate, it is never enough. We remain unsatisfied with what we have, frustrated and unhappy.

The trick to life is not getting what you want, but wanting what you get.
—Katherine Hepburn

If we are willing to face all of our patterns, including the less-than-desirable ones, we can then see how we deceive ourselves and others and limit our happiness and possibilities. Recognizing other people's patterns is helpful. *Recognizing our own patterns is vital.* The willingness to be present in our current reality—be with both the good and the bad—is the crucial starting point. It enables us to be more consciously aware of what we are actually creating, allowing and/or contributing to, in the midst of everyday activities. That awareness is the first step toward retaking control of our life.

The bottom-line question is, how willing are we to be honest with ourselves? When we are willing to face and own our patterns, they can no longer run our life; we are less judgmental and are clearer on what else will contribute to our growth and happiness. Our universe of choice expands.

I do myself a greater injury in lying than I do him of whom I tell a lie.
—Michel Eyquem de Montaigne

Starting the Flow

We have to bridge the gap between our capacity to appreciate the problem and our willingness to actually become the solution ourselves as truly enlightened human beings.
—Andrew Cohen

Anyone who wants or needs to get things done that require the assistance of others knows that one of our most valuable assets is the willingness of other people to help. It is important to be able to distinguish the willing person from the unwilling person. Temporary upset can be confused with unwillingness. Willingness is measured by observable contributions. No contribution equals little or no willingness.

Beyond being able to differentiate the willing from the unwilling, the ability to create, develop and preserve willingness in others is foundational to generating an attitude and culture of service. In order to develop willingness in others, we must first be willing to help them with their needs.

(See "In-Depth Probing," chapter 7, page 246 and "The Value of Competent Coaching," chapter 8, page 291.)

Far too often, we don't think about the needs of others and only communicate when we want something from them. We expect, and sometimes demand, a flow of willingness when we have done little or nothing to earn it. How willing have we been and how willing are we to be helpful? Without some ulterior motive, how often do we ask and mean, "How can I help you?" How often do we observe someone needing something and just provide it? How often have we been thanked for our helpfulness?

Willingness creates willingness. If we are willing to help others, they tend to be willing to help us. Therefore, we need to take the initiative. We need to start the flow. Being interested in and listening to the viewpoints, feelings, needs and aspirations of others is key. By doing so, we help create and preserve people's sense of importance and value. This, in turn, creates the foundation of willingness.

We establish the communication. We find out what others need and provide it to the best of our ability and resources. Our emphasis should be on others' needs, not our own. It should be on outflow rather than inflow, on giving not receiving.

Such a simple thing as the giving of yourself—giving thoughtfulness, time, help, of understanding—will trigger the cycle of abundance.
—Norman Vincent Peale

Occasionally, we will experience people who just take and never give, but for the most part, our willingness to help will generate a reciprocal behavior in others. If we are honestly willing to be present and interested, to listen, to evaluate and to responsibly help satisfy other people's needs, we will start the process of developing a willingness in others to do the same. Are you willing to start the flow? Reading *Robert K. Greenleaf: A Life of Servant Leadership* by Don M. Frick is a helpful starting point.

Maturity begins to grow when you can sense your concern for others outweighing your concern for yourself.
—John McNaughton

EMOTIONALLY HEALTHY AND EMOTIONALLY UNHEALTHY —THE DIFFERENCE

If you are distressed by anything external, the pain is not due to the thing itself, but to your estimate of it; and thus you have the power to revoke it at any minute.
—Marcus Aurelius

A measure of an individual's emotional health and maturity is not that the person always feels good, but rather that he or she has the ability and willingness to recognize, confront and own the emotion he or she is experiencing, including the "not so nice" emotions.

Becoming more emotionally mature is about becoming more consciously aware of and taking greater personal responsibility for the choices we make and the impact of those choices. Emotions are the communication that provides the basis for differentiation and discernment of what that impact is. Our emotional health reflects our ability to be authentically responsive to the entire hierarchy of emotions. Real feelings, when not repressed, expedite greater clarity, certainty and focus. They help us take greater responsibility for ourselves and our environment.

The healthier a person, the greater is his or her ability and flexibility in feeling and appropriately expressing the entire span of emotions, from apathy and despair to enthusiasm and bliss. Healthy, emotionally mature people are more able to face and deal with whatever is present in the moment. The healthy person feels joy at a friend's success, fear when a bull charges, anger at injustice, and grief over the loss of a loved one. Healthy people feel the feeling, get its message, and convert the emotional energy into positive action. They are able and willing to respond to the situation at hand. They are aware of and accountable for the impact they create. They are correspondingly more resilient, reliable and trustworthy in dealing with all situations, including negative ones. Communication between emotionally mature people is much more honest and effective. Therefore, contribution and real productivity expand. Increased morale follows when people feel they are contributing and productive.

Do emotionally mature people get angry? Of course. They get angry at incompetence, irresponsibility, injustice, and destructive, manipulative behavior. However, they are not reactive in their anger. They do not identify with the emotion. Rather, they acknowledge it and are responsive to it (they realize the anger is a message that something is wrong in the environment, and they responsibly act on it). The energy of their anger is quickly transformed into constructive, appropriately forceful corrective action.

Do emotionally mature individuals feel grief? Again, of course. But they don't try to repress it. They let themselves experience the sadness and the emptiness it represents. They are honest with themselves about their feelings. This honesty is what allows them to move beyond their grief. They may always miss the object of their loss, but they are not consumed by it. Their experience helps them develop greater sensitivity, empathy and compassion toward themselves as well as others. They can move on and see life as full of opportunities for learning and growth.

Similarly, emotionally mature people face their fears. They recognize that fear is a message that they need to be particularly present, observant and discerning. As we become increasingly more willing and able to face our fears, we find a whole expanded universe of possibility and opportunity previously hidden. We become more aware. In fact, by facing our fears, we dramatically expand our ability to confront and learn from all our emotions—from apathy and despair through anger and antagonism to happiness and joy. The willingness to face our fears is what real courage is all about.

The fact that you are not yet dead is not sufficient proof that you are alive. Aliveness is measured by degrees of awareness.
—Brother David Steindl-Rast

Immature people do not listen to the messages. They are less willing to experience the entire span of emotions. They repress the uncomfortable emotions, often projecting those very feelings onto others, or they arrogantly rationalize ignoring them by labeling them as inappropriate. Since they are relatively unwilling to deal with what is, their *lack of responsiveness translates into a correspondingly reduced awareness and resiliency to recover from any stressful situation.* To compensate, they further project responsibility onto and blame others. *Consequently, they remain in an overwhelmed and dysfunctional state much longer.*

As this spiral of irresponsibility continues, immature people limit their ability to learn, change and grow. Their chronic emotional state stays negative and limiting. They tend to perceive life as a series of frustrations and limitations. Authentic communication is replaced with glibness and lies. Real productivity is replaced with busywork and pretense.

We all have our ups and downs in dealing with life. We acutely experience (unless we repress) the entire range of emotions and their associated behaviors. However, the emotionally mature person is responsive rather than reactive. For this reason, the mature person deals with their own occasional dysfunctional attitudes and behaviors expeditiously.

The degree to which an individual is chronically reactive rather than responsive is the degree, regardless of social appearances, of that person's emotional immaturity. To most of life's pressures, the average person tends to be more reactive than responsive. In this reactivity, insecurity rules. This creates jealousy, envy and rage. The accompanying manifestations are self-centeredness, defensiveness, lack of authenticity, social pretense, sabotaging behavior, greed, restricted choice and unhappiness. Indications of immaturity are the degree to which those factors chronically dominate a person's attitudes and behaviors. To the degree they do, that person treats others as either threats or needed sources of approval or gratification. An emotionally mature adult is not controlled by such factors.

The mature person is one who recognizes that challenges encountered in life are part of the continuing learning and growing process. He or she is both willing and able to deal with those challenges responsibly. Emotionally healthy people do not always feel good, but their overall outlook on life is positive. They enjoy themselves and others while recognizing their own and others' foibles. They deal with problem situations directly, take responsibility for their mistakes, learn from them and move on to a higher, more productive and contributing manner of living.

Part of being mature is recognizing what needs to be done and doing it. It is being able to appreciate and enjoy the nuances of the process even when the process is not ideal. Mature people do not demand instant gratification, as would a child, or only see things as adolescents tend to, as black or white, good or bad, pleasure or pain. Mature people face and deal with all of life, including the problems, responsibly. *They learn from experience— and don't get stuck in any particular experience.*

The art of living lies not in eliminating but in growing with troubles.
—Bernard M. Baruch

When we confront and own what makes us tick—including our darker side—the things we were afraid to face usually turn out to be less threatening than we believed them to be. However, if we do not confront those things, they can become dangerous liabilities.

The more we are willing to face, the more we recognize our inherent power. We see more of our potential. As we do so, we see that we have greater choice in everything we do and have. We also become more aware of the real power that greater choice gives us. We begin to honor ourselves and our values, principles and commitments more.

Our sense of self-respect and self-esteem grows as well as our appreciation and respect for the dignity of others. Our self-image expands as we start recognizing and using more of our inherent strengths and talents. As this expansion occurs, we no longer need to create problems just to avoid looking at what is really there. We can stop our unique form of compulsiveness, whether it is overeating, overworking, or over or under-doing anything. In other words, we stop harming and sabotaging ourselves and others.

Things are no longer as upsetting as they used to be. When issues do arise, we deal with them much more directly and expeditiously. We see much more humor in the circumstances of life. A sense of balanced perspective is more easily a larger part of our life. We begin living life with more passion and compassion. We have more vitality. We become emotionally mature beings of character and integrity.

What a wonderful life I've had! I only wish I'd realized it sooner!
—Sidonie Gabrielle Collette

REVIEW

We live in a dynamic, continually evolving universe where change is the sole constant. Change creates challenges. Depending on our perspective, those challenges will be regarded as either opportunities or problems. How effective we are in dealing with change directly impacts our sense of well-being and happiness.

Which perspective we assume is largely determined by our level of emotional maturity which, in turn, is a measure of our real power. It mirrors our ability and willingness to be fully responsible and accountable for everything we say and do, including our attitudes.

Growing in emotional maturity is about becoming more consciously aware of and taking personal responsibility for the choices we make and the impact those choices have. It is about understanding how we unnecessarily continue to restrict ourselves and how, by choice, we can face and end those limitations. It is about increasing recognition, acceptance and ownership of what we deny or reject about ourselves and our behavior. It is about being willing and able to be responsibly present and deal with what is.

An organization's ability to adapt, innovate and implement change is significantly impacted by the emotional maturity of its members. An organization's approach to developing its people; its contribution to society, public reputation, profitability, viability and sustainability; as well as employee attitudes, morale and turnover, are all significantly impacted by the emotional maturity and integrity of its members. Economic and political factors, technical expertise, product uniqueness, personal charisma and the like all have influence and can be important. However, they are secondary to the profoundly fundamental impact of emotional maturity and integrity.

As we move from emotional naivete and immaturity toward being more emotionally intelligent and mature, behaviors manifest that are correspondingly less self-centered, more present, and more honest, authentic and responsible more of the time. Authentic communication and interpersonal effectiveness dramatically expand. This always positively impacts managerial and leadership capabilities as well as personal happiness. That maturation process is sometimes scary and confusing, but when not hindered or repressed, it is an enormously fulfilling experience and adventure.

Raise emotional maturity and we have those who are more secure, discerning, responsible, productive and happy. From that foundation knowing what's right and acting on it becomes an effortless, natural occurrence.

The DNA of Enlightenment

6

SIX LEVELS OF MATURITY

The world is a looking glass, and gives back to every man the reflection of his own face.

—William Thackeray

How individuals deal with change and their effectiveness in contributing to themselves, their loved ones, an organization, or to society directly relate to their emotional state and emotional maturity. Although integrity is not highlighted in this chapter, keep in mind that *integrity and emotional maturity are inextricably intertwined.* Integrity and all its qualities are the essence of emotional maturity.

In reviewing the range of emotions from positive, loving, contributing and happy, to negative, unloving, selfish and depressed, we observe six fairly distinct behavioral levels, each composed of a number of discrete emotions. Each level represents a different way of perceiving and responding or reacting to life situations.

DIFFERENT PERCEPTIONS, DIFFERENT REALITIES

Reality is what we perceive it to be. The more people who agree with a particular viewpoint, the more convincing or real that viewpoint becomes. *Our perceptions and viewpoints depend on our emotional state at the time.* Those perceptions vary as our emotions change, acutely and chronically. If we are angry, we interpret data or circumstances differently than when we are grieving or when we are feeling happy, bored or despairing. Our emotions act as filters through which we interpret and respond or react. *Essence values remain, but as the filters (emotions) through which we view them change, so does the perception and interpretation of their meaning, importance and priority.*

Each level has its own different set of filters. Attitudes correspond to our emotional state and, therefore, vary with each level. This in turn influences how we think, choose and act. Because of the filters, individuals perceive things differently at different emotional levels. Correspondingly, though the specifics vary, individuals at the same emotional level tend to have generally similar beliefs and attitudes and likely experience the world in quite similar ways. Conversely, individuals at different levels view and interpret the same life situations differently.

Happiness does not depend on outward things but on the way we see them.

—Leo Tolstoy

Knowing the characteristics of each level provides us with invaluable information to potentially understand, predict and effectively deal with the entire range of human behavior. The levels are a primary and foundational platform from which we can more effectively access, relate, communicate, motivate and lead. How to do so is developed in chapter 8.

Although the expression of each level always has cultural and personality nuances and variations, the emotions and emotional levels themselves retain their relationship to each other and their underlying messages. This emotional hierarchy applies to all human beings, regardless of culture, gender or personality differences. The principles and dynamics are fundamental, universal and cross-cultural. Not understanding them is, and has been, incredibly costly throughout human history.

THE LEVELS AS INDICATORS

The levels of emotional maturity are a scale of how well we are actually being responsibly causative and effective in dealing with the ups and downs of life. They are a reliable reflection of our intentions, attitudes, perspectives and behaviors. The higher our level, the greater our sense of security, the broader our perspective and the more responsive (resilient) versus reactive we are.

Each level indicates the relative presence of and potential for the following attributes:

- Love/compassion/generosity
- Values/principles/character
- Presence/awareness/discernment
- Honesty/authenticity/trustworthiness
- Allowance /appreciation/gratitude/respect
- Emotional health/sanity
- Courage/responsibility/accountability

- Resilience/flexibility/adaptability
- Self-worth/self-esteem
- Self-confidence/self-respect
- Communication/dialogue
- Collaboration/teamwork
- Purpose/vision/vitality
- Willingness/intention
- Power/empowerment
- Leadership potential
- Creativity/innovation
- Determination/perseverance
- Contribution/productivity
- Viability/sustainability
- Happiness/morale

The higher the level, the more the positive aspects manifest. The lower the level, the greater the sense of being overwhelmed and the more the negative counterparts come into play. This applies to individuals, families, groups, organizations, governments, countries and cultures. *The level at which a person functions (acutely and chronically) is a reflection of that person's sense of who she or he is.*

DOING WHAT'S RIGHT—FINDING AN OBJECTIVE MEASURE

What is the right thing? By whose standard? By whose interpretation? From what perspective? Judgments of right or wrong, good or bad, ugly or beautiful are subjective. They are opinions, not facts. To reiterate, at each emotional level, individuals have different subjective, but generally predictable, sets of associated attitudes and behaviors. By knowing these sets, we can assess a person's corresponding level of emotional maturity. Similarly, by knowing the emotional level at which the person is functioning, we can reliably describe that person's basic attitudes and perspectives as well as predict likely behavior.

At any level, individuals are able to provide arguments as to the rightness of their perspectives. How persuasive they are depends on how closely those arguments align or resonate with the perspectives of their audience, which, in turn, depend on the audience's emotional level. At any level, behavior is cross-context; that is, behavior in one arena of life will be seen in other arenas. For example, individuals who violate/honor agreements with their spouse will likely violate/honor agreements in business.

The levels of emotional maturity represent the degree to which essence qualities and values are being actualized. Those qualities, mentioned in chapter 3, include love, authenticity, honesty, allowance, forgiveness, presence, generosity and compassion, among others. *The degree to which those qualities are allowed, encouraged, supported, and actually present is a measure of a person's or an organization's emotional maturity.*

The more these essence qualities are present, the higher the level of emotional maturity. The higher the level, the broader and more inclusive the viewpoint; the greater the discernment, the less the influence of biases; and, the more objective and trustworthy any resultant perspective is likely to be. Therefore, the levels of emotional maturity provide a vehicle for better *understanding a person's subjective perspective.* This, in turn, *allows a more objective evaluation* of that person's potential for both knowing what's right and doing it.

Make us choose the harder right instead of the easier wrong and never be content with a half truth when the whole can be won.
—West Point Cadet Prayer

THE SIX LEVELS OF EMOTIONAL MATURITY

The individual levels of emotional maturity are named as follows:

- Level 6 — Leader
- Level 5 — Doer
- Level 4 — Coper
- Level 3 — Opposer
- Level 2 — Manipulator
- Level 1 — Victim

Level 6 represents the essence of emotional maturity. At this level, an individual communicates and performs with integrity. Levels 5 through 1 reflect varying degrees of emotional immaturity and a corresponding lack of integrity, with Level 5 being the least immature. As we move down the levels, manifestations of responsible, mature behavior exponentially decline (See Figure 6.1). Below Level 1 is the arena of psychosis (extreme emotional dysfunction). Be cognizant that each level has a range within itself. As we move higher or lower within a level, we begin to see more characteristics common to the next higher or lower level.

True empowerment, with all its positive aspects, only barely begins at Level 4. Positive impact increases exponentially as

FIGURE 6.1

Levels of Emotional Maturity and Net Impact on Self and Others

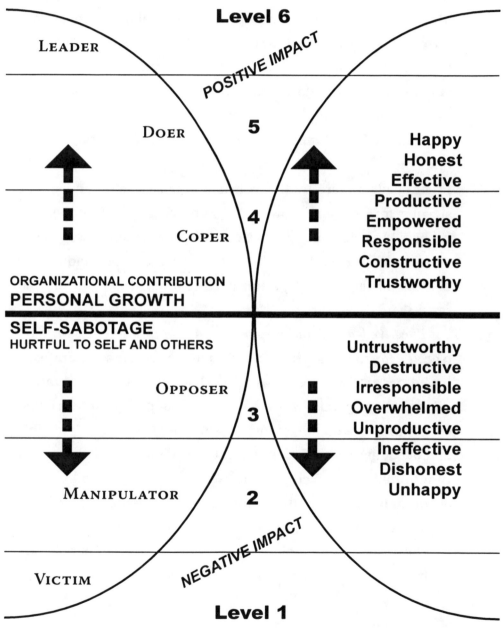

we move up the levels. The higher the level, the greater the fundamental sense of security. This corresponds to a positive willingness and ability to create—to learn, grow and contribute. The higher the level, the greater a person's ability to deal with change constructively. Conversely, at the lower levels, individuals predictably are overwhelmed and dysfunctional in the face of change. The farther down the levels a person is, the more they perceive life situations as problematic.

Being a good leader is inseparable from being emotionally mature (see "What Makes Leadership Positive," page 276). Emotionally mature leaders consistently insist upon and model striving for personal growth and excellence. They neither cut corners nor demand perfection (an unattainable state in a dynamic universe). Rather, they strive for excellence and ensure delivery of quality and performance consistent with promised results.

Effective leaders and responsible associates function at Level 6 or at a high Level 5. These individuals, with their comparatively broad perspective, are aware of and sensitive to others and to different viewpoints. They have an expanded awareness that everything they do has an impact, and that they are responsible and accountable for that impact. For the marginal contributor functioning at Level 4, this sense of responsibility and accountability is rapidly diminishing. For people chronically functioning at Level 3 and below, responsibility is not part of their repertoire, only pretenses of it. These people are dysfunctional and a liability to themselves and others.

Preceding the following descriptions of each of the six levels is a set of Haiku verses. Haiku is a popular form of Japanese verse written in 17 (5-7-5) syllables, employing evocative allusions or comparisons. The verses are intended to provide a sense of the flavor that characterizes each level.

 ## LEVEL 6 - Leaders

To help others grow
A passionate delight as
Others stretch their might

Despite resistance,
As leader, he breaks new ground
Courageous is he

She is a winner
Respects human dignity
Has integrity!

Strategic thinker
Great presence that sees the best
That mankind can be

He thinks, feels, loves
He balances life forces
Honors you and me

Integrity—yes!
Presence and respect galore!
What more could one ask?

The qualities of integrity are what define this level. At Level 6, individuals live and demonstrate emotional maturity and integrity and therefore have a positive, expansive effect on their environment. They know and are secure in their values and thus have a strong sense of self-respect and self-confidence. Only at Level 6 do individuals fully perceive *the primary importance* of living essence values. At all other levels, social values tend to take precedence over essence values by relative degree; the lower the level, the less priority given to essence values.

Leaders are responsible and compassionate mentors. They are ethical motivators who consistently deliver what they promise. In their own unique way, they are responsibly proactive. Whatever the personality, social demeanor, or human foibles of Leaders, honesty, authenticity and integrity are at their core. Their social styles may vary widely, from blunt to diplomatic, from "out there" to subdued, but Leaders consciously do the best job they can with the resources they have to make the world a better place.

Because Leaders respect themselves, they respect the dignity of others. Their self-confidence allows them to candidly confront their limitations and problems and learn from them. They will confront and communicate concerns that their more timid associates tend to couch in social niceties and political correctness. This willingness and ability to face what needs confronting establishes and confirms the maturity of Leaders. As a result, Leaders have the ability to see the big picture without losing sight of the current picture. They have a wisdom that goes beyond logic and reason without losing sight of them. This is often called intuition, and Leaders are willing to act on it.

In a world unaccustomed to candor, Level 6 Leaders' forthright, honest communication and authenticity are refreshing to some people but can be uncomfortable for others. Regardless, their presence and authenticity establishes credibility and trust. In fact, natural, authentic presence is one of Leaders' most immediately noticeable qualities. When Leaders are with you, they're totally with you—present and attentive. That presence helps them create a trusting space, establish rapport, evaluate priorities, make objective decisions, gain support, ensure quality and timely execution, and manifest constructive results.

Leaders have a great sense of personal certainty (not arrogance—subtle or overt—which is a defensive manifestation of Level 2 or Level 3). Therefore, they are able to make quick, solid decisions. This ability sometimes befuddles their more conservative associates, who are more dependent on external factors and are less willing to honor their intuitive, inner knowing.

Leaders have a predisposition and drive for excellence but are not caught in insatiable demands for perfection. They seek and honestly consider differing viewpoints. They demonstrate, demand and reward authenticity and responsibility as well as high performance. Compassionate and caring to their core, these people are empowered and will not tolerate or ignore irresponsibility for any reason, including political expedience.

Level 6 is where the ideal win-win relationship has the greatest chance of occurring. This integral environment is the residence of the emotionally wise leader referred to in Chapter 2. Leadership at this level creates a viable and sustainable foundation based in presence and, consequently, the ability to respond to the entirety of what is. This ability is only fully available to and capable of being optimized by a person at Level 6. When this occurs, there is almost an ethereal quality to that person's presence.

The best and most beautiful things in the world cannot be seen or even touched. They must be felt with the heart.
—Helen Keller

 **LEVEL 5 - Doers**

*Progressive we are
But let's check it out before
Starting something new*

*We can follow through
We do strive for excellence
Sometimes falling short*

*Good people we are
Still, we have some fears to face
To attain greatness*

*Able manager
But to be a great leader,
More boldness needed*

Doers have many of the positive qualities and characteristics of Leaders. They are generally responsible and conscientious. However, they do not quite have the full sense of "I am enough" that characterizes Leaders. As a result, they're still relatively insecure, narrower in perspective, and more influenced by outside social and political pressures and standards. In a sense, they're still "trying to make it." Social image concerns, therefore, are still disproportionately important.

We are very near to greatness; one step and we are safe. Can we not take the leap?

—Ralph Waldo Emerson

Doers tend to be more conservative than the relatively expansive, proactive people of Level 6. Doers are open to positive ideas, provided the actions or changes do not disrupt what has been shown to be workable. They are interested enough in positive ideas to check them out. Though they are progressive and will move forward, they like things substantiated first. Once enough data and documentation are provided, they will make a decision. If the decision is positive, they will tend to want to pilot the idea first before committing further. In spite of these conservative approaches, the emotional maturity of people functioning at level 5 is above society's norm which, on average. appears to fluctuate between levels 3 and 4. Consequently, as doers they are the primary producer group in current society. Nevertheless, these people show some signs of emotional immaturity. Therefore, they still manifest less of their potential than they are capable.

If one advances confidently in the direction of his dreams and endeavors to live the life he imagined, he will meet with a success unexpected in common hours.

—Henry David Thoreau

 **LEVEL 4 - Copers**

First priority—
To find the easiest way
To do the least work

Least effort, their goal
To keep their job, they just do
Enough to get by

Make their life easy
But don't expect a return
They can't be bothered

Contentment is nice,
But if stuck too long, it may
Be complacency

They observe and wait
Action is too much bother,
So they do little

Vacant they can be
Shallow they too often are
Much more depth needed

Copers are just responsible and motivated enough to do those things necessary to keep their job but not much more.

They want life to be easy, so they expend as little effort as possible into anything, including growth. They tend to be observers rather than participants. Their attention and interest are mainly on making life easier for themselves. Although not particularly dependable, they are generally likable because they try to avoid disagreements and do little to upset the status quo.

Copers are often described as being mellow. They are likely to be somewhat nonchalant about details and commitments. At Level 4, few things are given "big deal" status. Being only marginally responsible, they simply go along. To them, life seems okay—not particularly good but not particularly bad. However, unless Copers move toward growth and become more proactive, their contentment inevitably turns to complacency and eventually to contraction, where they can easily drop into the antagonism of Level 3 and become testy. Copers, in particular, need to realize that we live in a dynamic, nonstatic universe where we are either expanding or contracting. They need to be consciously more responsibly proactive if they are to enjoy more of life's wonders.

People functioning at Levels 5 and 6 are assets to an organization or group. Copers, however, are marginal employees. Unless they are willing and able to grow, Copers will be only marginally responsible. Promoting them to positions of responsibility because of seniority or for political reasons will likely create additional management problems. However, sometimes the increased responsibility helps inspire Copers to be more responsible. It will do so rather quickly or not at all. If not, the increased responsibility will tend to be overwhelming for the Coper and predictably lead to lower-level behavior.

Indolence is a delightful but distressing state; we must be doing something to be happy. Action is no less necessary than thought to the instinctive tendencies of the human frame.

—Mahatma Gandhi

BEHAVIOR BELOW LEVEL 4

Between Level 3 and Level 4 is an important dividing line. Above that line, individuals are more secure than insecure and become increasingly more secure as they move up the levels. Below that line, the opposite is true. People operating on the lower three levels have a sense of being overwhelmed by their environment and are insecure and afraid.

The greater the sense of being overwhelmed, the more unhappy and needy people are, regardless of social appearances. Overwhelmed people's perspective is decidedly narrow and restricted. Their decisions and actions are correspondingly more self-centered, defensive, irresponsible and destructive. Their behaviors are a reaction to fear and a mask to hide it. Their sense of self-worth, regardless of their social facade, is low. They are reacting in a very limited way to deal with what they perceive as a threat to their survival and even to their very existence. Unfortunately, their reactive behavior is inevitably negative and destructive to themselves and others.

Individuals who are functioning on the lower levels have lost sight of their inherent strengths and power. Their attention is on their weaknesses and limitations. They feel powerless and out of control. They view the world as being hostile and unloving. Their perspective of what is possible is severely limited. They lash out in attempts to regain some semblance of control. Because they feel powerless, they need others also to feel powerless. This arrangement is the only way they feel they can regain some of the control they feel they are losing. They attempt to achieve control through some form of intimidation (Level 3), covert manipulation (Level 2), or appeasement (Level 1). The lower an individual is on the scale of emotional maturity, the more likely he is to deceive himself as well as others.

It is the nature of ambition to make men liars and cheaters, to hide the truth in their breasts, and show, like jugglers, another thing in their mouths, to cut all friendships and enmities to the measure of their own interests, and to make good countenance without the help of good will.
—Gaius Sallustius Crispus

When people function on the lower levels, they do not conform to high-level rules of justice and fair behavior. They may pretend to do so, but only because they feel it will give them some manipulative advantage. People who operate at more responsible levels sometimes do not understand this and will attempt to be reasonable about putting up with someone's destructive behavior. The higher-level individuals tolerate it because, from their point of view, that sort of irrational behavior does not make sense. Therefore, they assume others "can't be as bad as all that," or should be given the benefit of the doubt. This approach simply does not work when people are consistently operating on the lower levels. Rather, this reasonable behavior is regarded by people operating on the lower levels as foolishly naive, and they will attempt to take advantage of it.

Individuals operating below Level 4, acutely or chronically, are a liability both to themselves and to their environment. As their sense of feeling overwhelmed increases, their outlook, attitudes and behavior become increasingly negative. Too often, organizations tolerate low-level behavior, rationalizing, "He is so good at doing his main task that we can't afford to lose him." That kind of justification often covers an unwillingness or inability to confront and deal with dysfunctional behavior. It is one of the costliest yet most common errors made in dealing with lower-level individuals or organizations.

Lower-level individuals drain energy from everyone around them. They stifle the development of responsibility, creativity, innovation and morale. *Retaining people who chronically function at Level 3 and below depresses the entire environment.* Supervisors who do not correct this behavior or terminate those individuals are failing in their responsibilities. *Recognizing and ending the pattern of chronic lower-level behavior is essential to the development of an emotionally mature environment.* It is vital to optimizing productivity and morale.

The feeling of inferiority rules the mental life and can be clearly recognized in the sense of incompleteness and unfulfillment, and in the uninterrupted struggle both of individuals and humanity.
—Alfred Adler

LEVEL 3 - Opposers

Antagonism—
A sure sign of overwhelm
Testy they sure are

To regain control
They threaten to use such force
To make you give in

Stomp, rage, and bluster
Intimidation their way
To grab your power

Anger they do show—
Under the hostility
Powerless they feel

Level 3 is the first level at which an individual's net impact is more destructive than constructive, both to himself and to his environment. Opposers' certainty and security have gone from positive to negative. Individuals at this level are starting to feel overwhelmed by their environment. As pressures mount, the environment increasingly is viewed as a threat. Their defense is to lash out, attack, or oppose whomever or whatever they perceive to be the problem. This behavior ranges from being testy about specific things to being outright bullies about everything.

Opposers' basic operating mode is to oppose or attack other viewpoints. They do so to compensate for their sense of feeling powerless and out of control. They will exaggerate some element of truth to divert the attention of others from their goals and strengths to their weaknesses. By intimidating others into fear or apathy, Opposers gain a false sense of control and power. Emotionally, Opposers are either antagonistic or angry. They are often effective at using these behaviors to intimidate others into making concessions. If others buy into the intimidation, the

Opposers feel they have won. It is important to recognize that intimidating or invalidating behavior only is effective when the receiving party goes into agreement with some aspect of the threat or put-down.

For Copers (Level 4), honoring truth and agreements is a casual affair, dependent on what is convenient. Much more forceful, Opposers (Level 3) attack agreements and exaggerate the facts and circumstances to their advantage. Responsibility for their own actions rapidly disappears and in its place is blame—it is someone else's fault. *As the level of emotional maturity declines, individuals accept less and less responsibility for their actions and increasingly project blame onto others for suboptimal situations or results.*

In the upper range of Level 3, Opposers display overt hostility and focused opposition. They feel the environment is hostile to their survival, but they think they have some idea who or what is doing them wrong. They resort to antagonistic types of statements such as, "Bookkeeping messed up my account four times!" or "Terry's two mistakes cost me a raise!" The Opposer's focused attacks are based on some exaggerated grievance and blindness to his or her part in contributing to the situation.

In the lower range of this level, an individual's hostility moves from focused and specific to dispersed and generalized. At the generalized anger level, the antagonistic statement, "Bookkeeping messed up my account four times!" becomes "The organization is always screwing up!" or "They never do it right." Universal, non-specific terms such as, "always," "never," and "they" are often heard in the angry Opposer's statements, such as, "You always do that to me!" or "They never give me the benefit of the doubt!"

However, the social unacceptability of overt hostility can create problems for Opposers. As a defense, sometimes they repress the overt expression of hostility. With that repression, the individual deteriorates to Level 2, the Manipulator. The hostility is still present, only now it is hidden. The skewing of truth and a decreased ability to communicate honestly and productively gets progressively worse as we move down the levels.

He took over anger to intimidate subordinates, and in time, anger took over him.

—Saint Albertus Magnus

 LEVEL 2 - Manipulators

Deniers of fault	*Deception they do*
Masters of misdirection	*With lies and put-downs their tools*
Stealers of credit	*To cover their fears*
Great heights they do want—	*By subtle deceits,*
Never a concern for whom	*Riding the backs of others*
They often do hurt	*Great heights they may gain*
Void of compassion	*Vicious they sure are!*
Not loyal or trustworthy	*Those who ignore this warning*
A friend they are not	*Will pay a big price*

Manipulators are hostile and insecure. They are afraid to openly express their fears and hostility. Rather, they rely on subtle put-downs, misdirection, denials, invalidations and skillful lying.

They hide their hostility and destructive intention with artful deceit and covert manipulation. Individuals at this level are very dangerous. Their underlying hostility is vicious and directed outward. They are expert at hiding their true intentions and thus are difficult to identify and deal with. Individuals at all the other levels are relatively overt in their behaviors and, once you understand their characteristics, comparatively easy to observe. Not so with this level.

Manipulators have no sense of responsibility—only pretenses of it. They can appear to be socially graceful, real charmers. They are the masters of deception. They can rise to high levels in organizations, usually by subtly manipulating their way into receiving undeserved credit and skillfully misdirecting the blame for their irresponsibility onto others.

Manipulators need to win at any cost. Their purpose is to get others to doubt their own abilities so they, the Manipulator, can gain some advantage. Their intention is to manipulate others to focus on their weaknesses. They do so by the skillful use of partial truths, subtle put-downs and invalidations. Manipulators ultimately want others to drop into fear or apathy—to believe that if they do not concede to what the Manipulator wants, the consequences will be even worse.

Manipulators have little concept of exchange or sense of fairness. Mutual benefit is not their intention. No matter how much they may talk win-win, that talk is only a manipulative ploy. They regard others as their enemies and thereby justify any means necessary to do others in. Their self-centered attitude is that they are only doing what they need to do to survive in this (to them) obviously hostile world.

At this level, the use of manipulation may be quite sophisticated. Manipulators often are able to assume any social level that will meet their hostile and unscrupulous ends. This is the level of the con man, whose intent is to exploit others but not give them the slightest hint of what is actually happening until its too late. Manipulators view people who act with compassion, honesty and integrity as simpletons who deserve to be taken advantage of. Using charm and fine manners, they convince Grandma to invest her life savings in a nonexistent venture. They justify such acts as giving trusting people a much-needed learning experience in how the "real world" operates. They can be the ultimate subtle cynic and manifest many sociopathic characteristics.

We can destroy ourselves by cynicism and disillusion, just as effectively as by bombs.
—Lord Clark

Although Manipulators can appear charming, sincere and sophisticated, their actual perception and understanding is quite limited. They are seldom aware enough to realize or acknowledge how destructive their behavior is to themselves, much less to others. What can appear to be intelligent, compassionate behavior is not that at all. Do not confuse shrewd manipulation with intelligence. The shrewdness observed at this level is based in fear, entirely self-centered and always limiting and hurtful. That behavior is neither intelligent nor compassionate. Manipulators have a social facade that will seldom give even a hint that they are, in fact, very insecure, frightened individuals.

No passion so effectively robs the mind of its powers of acting and reasoning as fear.

—Edmund Burke

Manipulators identify with the hostility of the Opposer but are afraid to express it. They silently admire the bravery exhibited by Level 3 Opposer behavior (that is, the willingness to express hostility overtly). This is why displays of strength and willingness to use overt force have an influencing and persuasive effect on people at this level.

Manipulators are compulsive liars and invariably do not deliver what they promise (none of the lower levels do). They tend to have well-justified excuses as to why the important report was late, why they could not keep the meeting, why the something-that-went-wrong was someone else's responsibility. Manipulators do not assume responsibility but instead point fingers. Everything they say or do will always appear to have justifications, including the Manipulator's subtle put-downs. For example, when we find ourselves feeling upset with a particular interaction but have difficulty pinpointing why, often it's an indication of the presence of a Manipulator's passive-aggressive behavior.

Remember, no one can make you feel inferior, or anything else, without your consent.

—Eleanor Roosevelt

When this happens, we can ask ourselves, "Who said what just prior to my feeling upset?" Often, we will find some form of subtle invalidation. If we point it out or object, the originator will likely deny it, saying it was only a joke or we misunderstood or we are taking it out of context or suggest we are being overly sensitive. Perhaps we did misunderstand or were overly sensitive. We must be willing to look at that. And—their behavior may also be passive-aggressive, with which lies and denials go hand-in-hand. We all can be covertly hostile at times. It is an indication that we are angry about something but too afraid to be candid about it. We want to determine if that behavior is momentary but not typical of the individual or if it is a hint of a chronic passive-aggressive state. Observe that person over time. Beyond the socially acceptable behavior, does a chronic pattern of subtle hostility emerge?

Don't think there are no crocodiles because the water is calm.
—Mayan proverb

 **LEVEL 1 - Victims**

I'm just a victim
Of unfair circumstances
Innocent of fault

Overwhelmed I am
What possibly can I do
But whine or appease

One way to control
Be a pathetic victim
To get what I want

Make others guilty
For my life's poor condition—
Suckers they sure are

The Manipulator is afraid that a hostile environment is about to do them in. The Victim-level individual feels he or she already has been done in, and has an overwhelming sense of powerlessness. They cry, whine, or attempt to appease. Emotional states include self-pity, grief, despair, hopelessness and apathy. Victims have a very narrow, self-centered and selfish viewpoint. They have little, if any, sense of responsibility for anything, and truth has little meaning.

Victims may try to gain some feeble semblance of control by getting others to feel sympathetic toward them. They are experts at creating a very sad story. They attempt to make others feel guilty and uncaring if they do not buy into their victim condition. No matter how much you give or try to help Victims, it is never enough. Eventually, they will accuse and blame you for at least some of their woes.

Another form a Victim's behavior may take is in constantly giving, not out of caring or exchange, but as attempts to buy off or appease their imagined oppressor. One form of Victim is the yes-man.

Victims' attitudes tend to take some form of, "What's the use? Why bother? I'll never get out of this mess," or "Poor me, look at what they've done to me." Victims will, subtly or otherwise, always let you know they are somehow suffering and that none of their struggle is their responsibility—it's always someone else's fault.

As long as we feel victimized, we give up our power to change.
—Author unknown

I hate a fellow whom pride, or cowardice, or laziness drives into a corner, and who does nothing when he is there but sit and growl; let him come out as I do, and bark.
—Samuel Johnson

At Level 1, an individual has little, if any, sense of having control of or impact on anything but rather a sense of being affected by everything. People who chronically function at the victim level always will have unsolvable problems. Victims do not see solutions, only problems. If offered a solution, Victims will have myriad excuses for how the solution cannot or will not work. In fact, Victims often get upset with people who solve their problems. Since they only know how to operate when their world is full of problems, solving their problems takes away the little sense of control they have and makes them feel more confused.

Victims are usually a problem for only a relatively short period of time because their general ineffectiveness and crybaby behavior is not tolerated for long, except in codependent situations. This codependency is typically most obvious in family situations and businesses. Not confronting the individual and allowing such behavior to continue is not only costly to the business and disruptive to the family, but enables the individual to avoid further what he or she needs to face. Though the individual will resist any change (sometimes insultingly so), under all their moans, that person has a desperate desire to end his or her depressed state and respects the forthright person who won't allow irresponsible behavior to continue.

MOTIVATION AND THE LEVELS

In comparing various motivational models (Table 6.1), we observe that only at the highest level of emotional maturity is the person motivated by growth and responsible action. A true adult (emotionally mature) has a well-developed ego, acts responsibly, and experiences inclusive growth and self-actualization.

TABLE 6.1

Correlation of the Levels of Emotional Maturity with Three Models of Motivation

Levels of Emotional Maturity	Stages of Ego Development	Maslow's Hierarchy of Needs	Herzberg's Two-Factor Job Model
Leader	Mature Adult "I am enough."	Self-Actualization	**Motivational Factors** Growth Potential Responsibility Achievement
Doer	Adolescent/ Young Adult "Am I learning, doing, growing, being enough?"	Esteem	Recognition Advancement
Coper			**Maintenance Factors** Interpersonal Relations— Peers,
Opposer	Child/ Young Adolescent "Am I good enough?"	Belonging	Supervisors, Subordinates Company Policy
Manipulator		Security	Job Security
	Infant/ Young Child "Am I getting enough?"		Work Conditions
Victim		Survival	Salary

SELF-ESTEEM VERSUS OTHER-ESTEEM

Self-esteem is our personal (self) evaluation of how responsible we are. People with low self-esteem are simply telling the world that, in their own opinion, they have not been responsible in living essence values. As we assume more responsibility, our personal esteem rises and we begin to make the break from being dependent on others for everything, including our sense of esteem.

We may like and appreciate the esteem of others as an addition to, not a substitute for, our own esteem. We need to see beyond external social praise and look inward to assess honestly our internal sense of self. If that self-assessment is positive, our esteem will be positive regardless of how contemporary society views us.

At the level of Esteem needs in Maslow's Hierarchy of Needs, people often become confused. While dealing with the lower order needs (Survival, Security, Belonging), we often create reliance, and even dependency, on others to meet those needs. Addressing the issues of esteem needs offers an opportunity to move from dependence on others to assuming greater personal responsibility—a vital and necessary learning in our maturation process. However, if we do not integrate the lessons of the lower-level needs, we cannot make the jump to the next level (Esteem) and we do not learn to evaluate ourselves (self-esteem).

Instead, we compensate by continuing to look outside of ourselves to others for our esteem. We become preoccupied with other people's opinions and other external symbols of success to convince ourselves that we are good enough. When anyone is dependent on outside esteem, rather than simply preferring it, that behavior is indicative of emotional maturity only slightly above Level 3—Opposer (corresponding to Belonging on Maslow's Hierarchy of Needs, see Table 6.1, page 215), and often lower.

If we remain stuck in the lower levels, we whine about regrets of the past, are overly fearful or anxious about the future, complain about what we don't have (overtly or covertly), project our frustrations often onto those closest to us, and substitute pretense for authenticity in our compulsive striving to get others to esteem us when we don't esteem ourselves. It never works.

Self-esteem, not other-esteem, is a prerequisite to self-actualization. Without real self-esteem, we remain stuck in an insatiable need for and dependency on other people's approval. *Other people's opinions can be an important and valuable source of feedback but not of self-esteem.* That only comes from our own evaluation (self-evaluation) of how well we are living essence values and thus being responsible, respectful of others, and empowering and honoring ourselves.

THE DNA OF SELF-ESTEEM

ABOUT TEAM BUILDING

Two fundamental ingredients are required to create a true team: 1) honest, open communication, and 2) a common, aligned purpose. The higher the level of emotional maturity and integrity present within an organization, the more likely these fundamentals will be present or created and the easier the process of team building will be.

In order to achieve its potential, any true team-building effort must strive to develop both cooperation (involvement with the other to enhance the self) and collaboration (involvement that considers the other's enhancement). Optimum synergy can be attained only when collaboration exists and that only occurs when communication is not repressed. *Competently dealing with repressed communication is fundamental to effective team building.* (See "Dealing with Repressed Communication," chapter 7, page 241)

True collaboration only occurs at Level 6 and high Level 5. Since authentic collaboration is vital to effective team building, *attempts at team building at any other level will be predictably ineffective.*

Results of cooperation at Level 4 will be marginal and usually short-lived. Cooperation below Level 4 is a sham. People functioning below Level 4 have an underlying sense of overwhelm and feelings of hostility which, invariably creates separation and sabotaging behavior. Thus, cooperative efforts at these lower levels are, at minimum, disingenuous and ultimately destructive. When individuals operating at the lower levels (lack of integrity) get together, they may generate personal gain, but it inevitably will be at a significantly greater net cost to the environment. Ensuring organizational members are emotionally mature is the easiest, most efficient, and most effective way to have a truly productive and motivating team development program.

Together we can do so much.

—Helen Keller

THE DNA OF COLLABORATION

The following table (Table 6.2) presents a variety of attitudinal and behavioral characteristics for each level. It has proven useful in 1) assessing an individual's (or group's) emotional level, 2) anticipating behaviors not yet observed, and 3) determining the kind of communication most likely to facilitate movement up the levels.

By observing an individual's behavior and attitude and noting on which level they fall, a pattern will begin to emerge. Most chronic behaviors will be predominantly on one level, with the remainder not more than a level above or below. *Behavioral attitudes observed two or more levels above the predominate level are likely social facades.*

TABLE 6.2 - The Levels of Emotional Maturity

		A Chronic Patterns	B Emotional Stability	C Emotions/ Attitudes
Level 6 **Leader**	Emotional Maturity	High integrity. Comfortable presence. Clear focus. Big picture. Considerate of real needs. Positive action and results. Appreciates and enjoys life. Life is an adventure. Humor.	High emotional stability. Very sane. Expresses and deals with entire range of emotions easily. High emotional resiliency.	Passionate. Joyful. Enthusiastic. Happy. Strong interest.
Level 5 **Doer**		Conscientious. Positive, provided claims are substantiated. Pleasant. Proactive devil's advocate.	Generally stable. Reasonably sane. Can express and deal with most of the emotional range. Fair to good emotional resiliency.	Positive. Progressive. Open. Interested.
Level 4 **Coper**		More an observer than a participant. Casual, mellow. Takes the path of least resistance. Careless.	Marginal stability. Restricted emotional range. Can easily become irritable under minimal stress.	Contentment. Neutral. Disinterest. Boredom.
Level 3 **Opposer**	Emotional Immaturity	Sees world as hostile, threatening. Narrow emotional range. Best defense is an offense. Angry person. The debater.	Unstable. Hostile outbursts. Criticizes. Blames. Threatens. Intimidates.	Irritable. Antagonistic. Overt anger. Resentment.
Level 2 **Manipu-** **lator**		World is so threatening that must hide own fear, hostile intentions and behaviors. Highly Self-absorbed. The con man. The gossip. The martyr. The two-face.	Pretends emotional stability not in fact present. Uses manipulative, subtle invalidations. Often pretends to be operating at Level 5 or 6.	Unexpressed resentment. Unsympathetic. Passive-aggressive. Covert hostility. Fear. Anxiety.
Level 1 **Victim**		Cry-baby. Complainer. Whiner or just numbed out. Poor me. Yes man. The victim.	Minimal emotional stability or resiliency. Can't do anything about it. Emotional basket case.	Regret. Self-pity. Grief. Despair. Apathy. Numb.

D Productivity/ Ability to Execute	E Learning Capacity	F Interest		
Highly productive. Gets positive results fast, effortlessly. Completes cycles of action. Can-do attitude. Excellent follow-through.	Open to new concepts. Evaluation and discernment skills finely tuned. High ability to differentiate relative importances. Quick study.	Broad, far-reaching interests. High sense of the aesthetics of life, people, things. Gets involved with focus and intensity. High enjoyment of many things/activities. Life is an opportunity. Passionate about life.	Willing / Can Do	6
Usually productive. Will try to do it attitude. Completes most things.	Open to concepts supported by experience. Fair to good differentiation abilities.	Narrower scope of interests than Level 6. Enjoys/participates in/ focuses on a relatively limited number of things.		5
Marginal. Will do just enough to get by. Many things left incomplete.	Indifferent. Marginal student.	Neutral about most things. Casual, detached observer rather than a participant. Interested in things that make his/her life easier.	Pretended Willingness / Unwilling / Can't Do	4
Destructive. Will oppose real productivity. Executes by the use of force or threat. Short-term results only. Burns out subordinates.	Rejects new concepts as threatening.	Interested in opposing, attacking, and aggressive defense.		3
Appears to be productive, but actually highly destructive. Will covertly undermine real productivity and positive results. Often sophisticated excuses.	Pretends openness to new concepts, but is threatened by them so covertly invalidates them.	Fascinated by things and tricks that can be used to manipulate or put down others for own selfish interests.		2
Zero.	Learning capacity non-existent. "It's impossible, why bother." Can't do attitude.	Self-absorbed. No real interest in actions or activities outside of themselves. Attention solely on problems for which they refuse to take action or responsibility.		1

	G Trustworthy	H Handling of Truth	I Willingness to Confront
Level 6 **Leader**	Definitely.	Bluntly truthful to self and constructively truthful with others. Honesty, authenticity and forthrightness are hallmarks.	Will confront whatever needs to be dealt with. Observational abilities finely tuned. Willingness to explore other beliefs and reassess one's own. Great presence.
Level 5 **Doer**	Most of the time.	Reasonably truthful to self and socially truthful to others.	Selectively confronts. Fair to good observational abilities. Cautious progress.
Level 4 **Coper**	Marginal	Casual about truth. Careless of facts. Insincere.	Minimally confronts. Observational skills minimal. Difficult situations are avoided or ignored.
Level 3 **Opposer**	No!	Predictably exaggerates negative aspects. Blames others. Angry when own exaggerations or negative impact noted.	Attacks others to avoid confronting own irresponsibility. Tends to back down quickly when threats do not work.
Level 2 **Manipu-lator**	No!!!	Chronic, but artful liar. Subtly twists the truth to confuse and invalidate others. Uses a version of the truth to hurt.	Covertly manipulates and misdirects to avoid confronting and owning any responsibility.
Level 1 **Victim**	You must be kidding!	Will say anything to gain sympathy or appease.	Avoids almost all issues. Too inwardly focused to observe much at all.

Honest / Authentic

Dishonest / Pretense / Deceit

J Ethics/Integrity	K Responsibility	L Real Sense of Self-Esteem and Self-Worth		
Truly walks his/her talk. Responsibly acts on what he/she believes to be correct action, even if in conflict with social/moral/current norms. Principles and character solid. Has courage to act on convictions.	Outstanding. Willing and able to respond appropriately and joyously. Faces and deals with whatever needs to be confronted.	Fully own their worthiness. Honest, positive self-evaluation. Not dependent on others' opinions for their esteem, only for feedback.	Responsible	6
Reasonable ethics, but is influenced by social and moral standards. Walks his/her talk most of the time.	Acceptable. Attention on maintaining and improving what currently works.	Somewhat more dependent on others for sense of esteem and worthiness.		5
Goes along with social and moral conventions if convenient to do so. Convenience and "getting by" of senior importance.	Poor to Marginal. Will demonstrate responsibility to maintain position and little more. Careless.	Marginal.	▼ ▼ ▼	4
Fights social/moral codes as stupid, arcane. The revolutionary. Attacks those with integrity and/or those who point out integrity deficiencies.	Irresponsible. Views responsibility as a burden. Overtly blames others. Attacks and accuses to avoid own responsibility.	Low. Masked by arrogant or macho behavior.	Irresponsible / Blame ▼ ▼	3
Pretends integrity, but definitely lacking. Facade of noble moral platitudes and justifications to the effect that the ends justifies the means. Politically correct. The subversive.	Apparently responsible, but actually highly irresponsible. Covertly misdirects blame to others. Capricious.	Very low. Masked by sophisticated facade, pretense, and lies.	▼	2
Will do anything to fend off the oppressor. All behaviors for which they are continually sorry are justified by their victim condition.	Almost totally irresponsible. "It's not my fault."	Non-existent.	▼	1

		M Sense of Being Able to Handle Life	**N** Concept of Fairness and Exchange	**O** Persistence on a Given Course
Level 6 **Leader**	Rational / Feeling	Definitely! True confidence that they can, at minimum, cope with life's contingencies, no matter what they are.	Outstanding. Gives and demands fair exchange. Strong sense of justice for all concerned. Balanced perspective. Will not tolerate dishonest or unjust behavior.	Strong, creative persistence and direction toward constructive goals. Thorough follow-up. Gets the best results possible under adverse conditions.
Level 5 **Doer**		Generally has sense of being able to handle most situations.	Decent. Generally acceptable.	Fair to good persistence, if obstacles are not too great
Level 4 **Coper**	Misemotional	Marginal. Limited to making personal life easier, more comfortable.	Expects partners to contribute without much consideration to equal exchange. Cheap.	Poor persistence and concentration. Will shift focus in face of obstacles or inconvenience.
Level 3 **Opposer**	Repressed Feeling / Irrational /	Starting to feel overwhelmed. Uses macho behavior as a defensive compensation.	Demands more than worth. Uses threats to get more than otherwise would. Uses blame to avoid owning responsibility.	Destructive persistence. Begins strongly, weakens quickly.
Level 2 **Manipu-** **lator**		Feels overwhelmed. Cool demeanor covers sense of inadequacy. Too afraid to fight back openly, so does so via covert means.	Does not deliver as promised. No real concept of exchange. Selfish, self-centered. Lies about value provided. Wants something for nothing. Creates excuses to avoid fair payment. Criminal.	Vacillation on any given course except to manipulate others. Wants to get even or get something for nothing.
Level 1 **Victim**		Virtually totally overwhelmed. I can't do anything about it. Victim mentality.	Expects to be taken care of with no exchange.	Sporadic persistence toward self-destruction.

P Goals/Time	Q Thought/ Decision-Making Process	R Handling of Agreements		
Focused goals. Very much in the present. Creates time to accomplish many things. Action toward expansive future. Willing to delay gratification for greater future benefit.	Highly attuned observational abilities. Broad perspective and positive attitudes pro- vide basis for fast, decisive, highly rational decisions and choices. Respect and empathy fully integrated in decision-making process.	Delivers what they promise. Will not knowingly violate valid agreements except to meet truly higher ethical imperatives. Does not use the higher imperative as a justification.	Productive	6
Goals shorter term and smaller scale than Level 6. Reasonable present time focus.	Decisions rational, but perspective compared to Level 6 somewhat narrower, resulting in slower, more complicated, and less- sophisticated reasoning.	May justify breaking agreements for practical considerations. May use higher imperative as a justification.		5
Unfocused, minimal goals. Waiting for it to happen. Dispersed, little sense of time.	Barely rational—indecisive. Decisions/ choices are narrow and self-centered.	Often indifferent to agreements. Does what is momentarily convenient.	Unproductive / Destructive	4
Demands instant gratification. No sense of future consequences. Goals are to attack "opposition" now, before it gets worse.	No longer rational or re- sponsible, but opposing. Irresponsible. Destructive decisions and choices.	Openly attacks and fights agreements. Exaggerates and blames others as an excuse.		3
Goals are to misdirect a hostile world's attention away from self and get even covertly for real or imagined wrongs of the past. Subtle, persuasive reasons why doesn't deliver as promised.	Almost totally reactive. Real, constructive analytical abilities gone. Choices and decisions destructive for all concerned. Apparent sophistication is actually a facade based on lies, manipulations.	Pretends to honor agreements, but always has justified reasons for breaking them. Skillful use of the legal system for own selfish ends		2
Zero goals except survival. Attention on past. Major regrets. No time to do anything, so does nothing.	Irrational, no analytic abilities extant. Decisions, or lack of them, destructive. No sense of having a choice in anything.	Whines about imposed agreements that he/she couldn't do anything about.		1

		S Relationships	**T** Handling of Control/Power
Level 6 Leader	Caring	High degree of mutual responsibility and trust. Happy, joyous, cocreator. Long term potential high. Loyalty high. Honors commitments. Vulnerability and real intimacy high. Treats people fairly and with respect.	Very strong sense of being able to positively control all aspects of life. Very secure—helps others empower themselves. Willing to lead or follow as appropriate. Power = ability and willingness to act = ability to get sane, productive results. Execution and follow-up outstanding.
Level 5 Doer		Decent sense of contribution. Satisfied with most relationships. Reasonably happy.	Less of above. Feels generally adequate about controlling most of life's situations. Willing and able to act responsibly and effectively most of the time.
Level 4 Coper	Self-Absorbed / Self-Centered / Selfish / Uncaring	Shallow. Not happy, not unhappy. Casual about commitment. No real intimacy. Multiple short-term relationships or stays with one partner because it's a hassle to move.	Follows orders in a slipshod manner. Respects and wants sane direction and focus. Sense of wasting life away, but not knowing how to be in more positive control. Low-level chronic anxiety. Willingness and ability to act diminishing.
Level 3 Opposer		Demanding, bully, threatening, macho. Potential sadist. Casual shifts in loyalty for selfish gain. Unhappy. Does not honor commitments, but demands others honor theirs. Fights intimacy. Blames partners for its lack. Creates dependencies.	Starting to feel overwhelmed—out of control. Compensates by lashing out. Feels must control others. Will resent and oppose orders from others. Power = "power over" by overt domination. Disempowers others.
Level 2 Manipu- lator		Emotionally suppressive. Terrified of real intimacy. Subtle, continuous put-downs, "make-wrongs" and invalidations. No real concept of relationship. Creates dependencies. Predictably promiscuous.	Underlying fear of losing all—too afraid to lash out. Compulsive need to control others by manipulation, lies, invalidation and misdirection—seeks hidden power. Power = "power over" by covert dominion. Disempowers others.
Level 1 Victim		Demands to be taken care of. Gross codependency. Miserable.	No sense of controlling anything. Feeble attempts to control by getting others to feel guilty or sorry for them. Brings others down to their level through pity. Feels powerless. Underlying rage.

U Attitudes Toward Life	V Form of Communication	W Win-Win Outcome			
Views experiences, including losses, as an opportunity and a challenge to learn and grow. Life is an adventure. Curious about, enjoys life most of the time. "We can do it."	Authentic. Encourages real dialogue. Will not tolerate destructive, dishonest communications. Excellent listener. Acknowledges well.	Outstanding probability. Even "losses" are a learning experience from which to expand and grow.	Secure / Happy		6
Some experiences are opportunities and can be interesting—most are OK. "Life isn't bad."	Reasonable, open to viewpoints that do not stray too far from the status quo. Tolerates social lies. Plays devil's advocate.	Decent probability.			5
"I'm not unhappy." "It's someone else's responsibility." "I can't be bothered."	Casual conversation. Devaluates urgencies. Glib. Superficial. Mundane.	Possible, but remote.			4
Most experiences are threatening. "It's a hostile world." "Must be tough." Angry at most things. Critical of people, situations, and life.	Blames. Attacks. Demands. Opposes or rejects other viewpoints. Sarcastic. Angry or antagonistic. The Debator.	Not possible.	Insecure / Unhappy		3
Most experiences are a lie. "People are out to con you." "Better get them before they get you." Cynical.	Uses subtle forms of invalidation as put-downs. Twists, depreciates positive communication. Expert at creating reasonable excuses for nondelivery of what is promised. Misleading.	Definitely not! (Don't be fooled by the promises—they're invariably exaggerations and lies.)			2
Life is overwhelming. It's sad, or despairing. "There's nothing I can do about it." "I can't."	Expressions of worry, fear. Pleas for sympathy, or attempts at appeasement.	Forget it!			1

	X Typical Eye Contact	Y Has Rapport With	Z Motivated By
Level 6 Leader	Can look at you directly, comfortably with interest. "Real contact." Communicates presence.	Positive, caring, responsible viewpoints, actions, and results. High Integrity.	Demonstrations of authenticity, integrity, compassion, and positive action.
Level 5 Doer	Less of above.	People, things, and communication that supports and enhances a status quo.	Big picture. Expanded possibilities. Personal growth opportunity. Level 6 behavior.
Level 4 Coper	No real eye contact. Casual contact. Just as interested in looking at the paperweight as you.	Being entertained. Laid-back activities. Not being hassled.	Those things that make their job or situation easier.
Level 3 Opposer	Looks at you as a target to attack.	Statements and actions of overt hostility against a perceived common enemy.	Mellow behavior. They need to be heard. Will tend to be persuaded by those with patience and the ability to truly listen.
Level 2 Manipulator	Ranges from apparent, charming interest to fleeting avoidance.	Gossip. Covert, subtle, invalidations of others. Cynicism.	Willingness to use overt force against perceived common threat. Underlying fear causes them to hide their hostility. Will follow those brave enough to be overtly hostile.
Level 1 Victim	Ranges from sad, pleading to unfocused indifference.	Sympathy and agreement with how they've been victimized.	Statements of fear and covert actions against the "enemy."

Courage (Levels 6–5)

Lack Of Courage / Cowardice (Levels 4–1)

SUMMARY OF LEVEL BEHAVIOR

The levels represent actual and potential degrees of all of the following: responsibility, integrity, maturity, security, honesty, authenticity, trustworthiness, compassion, empathy, inclusiveness, balanced perspective, happiness, resiliency, collaboration, reliability, accountability, productivity, and contribution. By knowing from which emotional level a person is functioning, we can reliably assess the relative degree of any or all of the above qualities.

Individuals or organizations operating chronically at Levels 1, 2, and 3 are emotionally challenged and dysfunctional. They will manifest correspondingly limited viewpoints, attitudes, abilities and behaviors. At Level 4 this also will be true, but less so. People operating at Levels 4 and above demonstrate increasing responsibility, trustworthiness and a win-win viewpoint. It is only at sustained Levels 5 and 6 that we find individuals and organizations that are capable of capitalizing on their larger potential.

Individuals and organizations at Levels 1–3 are defensively and reactively hostile to change, no matter how needed. At Level 4, they generally are mildly resistant to change because it is a bother, unless it is to their personal advantage. At Level 5, they are open to and supportive of responsible change. At Level 6, they proactively encourage and embrace responsible change.

Level 6 Leaders offer the broadest perspective and most consistently responsible, mature behavior. They demonstrate authenticity, rational certainty and creativity in proactively expanding and balancing relevant factors. They expect, demand, and model behavior based in essence values, i.e., integrity. These emotionally mature individuals live the qualities that create a sane, healthy environment where win-win situations are, in fact, the norm.

Level 5 Doers are mostly positive, and action and results-oriented, but with a proviso—that their willingness to move, expand and try new things occur after they first thoroughly test, examine and validate what they're learning along the way. They tend to be proactive devil's advocates.

Level 4 Copers are only slightly more positive than negative and are characterized by doing just enough things right to get by.

Level 3 Opposers and the levels below represent a lose-lose situation in which individuals perceive themselves as being overwhelmed by their environment and consequently fight back in the only ways they know how. Level 3 Opposers and those lower on the levels of emotional maturity negatively affect their colleagues and workplace, resulting in compromised honesty, responsibility and meaningful contributions. At Level 3, individuals are still strong enough to overtly lash out at their environment in the form of opposition, attack and intimidation, which are emotionally characterized by antagonism and anger. At this level, people are not only obviously hostile but, despite their bluster, frightened.

Level 2 Manipulators are too frightened even to outwardly express their hostility, so they go undercover. They cover their passive-aggressive hostility with social niceties, deceits and subtle invalidations of others that are always destructive but difficult to spot.

Level 1 Victims feel as though they have already lost. The emotions most characterized by people caught at this level are self-pity, grief, despair, hopelessness and apathy. Victim behavior takes on pathetic forms of helplessness to gain sympathy or gross attempts at appeasement.

A NEGOTIATION APPLICATION

In negotiations, being able to assess the level of the other party is invaluable to optimizing the due diligence process, the give-and-take process, and the follow-up relationship. It is particularly helpful in pinpointing areas that need a deeper look; predicting and dealing with likely responses or reactions, including intimidating and manipulative tactics; and making choices regarding continuing or terminating the relationship.

For example, let us assume that for strategic purposes we want to acquire firm A. We have assessed that the key person with whom we will be negotiating, the CEO, likely functions chronically at levels 2 and 3. Once we have made that determination, we know that though we may need to deal with this individual to accomplish our strategic objective, we do not want a continuing relationship with him. However, he insists as a condition of sale that he be hired as a consultant and member of the management committee. He argues eloquently that this company is near and dear to his heart, that only he knows the nuances of the business, and that he has invaluable personal relationships with key clients. We could easily rationalize that, "Yes, he does know many important nuances, and we certainly would not want any disruptions to key client relationships.

Perhaps we should give him the benefit of the doubt." *However, we know that a person who chronically functions in the lower levels is predictably destructive.* Promises made will not be kept and problems *will* manifest.

It is imperative that in our desire to close the deal and get on with it, we do not rationalize accepting what would be, at best, a problematic relationship (all low-level relationships are). We need to do what it will take to reach an acceptable conclusion, which means for us that we own the company and he is no longer associated with it or us. But, what about all the good relationships he developed? Aren't we risking them by excluding him? Probably not. Why? Because low level relationships are based on manipulation and intimidation, and many clients actually may be relieved that the touted great relationship is no longer present. By the same reasoning, we could also lose clients because we kept him on board. *Understanding the levels of emotional maturity provides a foundation of clarity and certainty that helps us determine the responsible position to maintain, and do so, even under trying circumstances.*

Points to consider:

- **Can you identify individuals whose behaviors/attitudes are examples of each of the six levels of emotional maturity? List their typical behaviors, attitudes, beliefs, values?**

- **At what level do you think your organization chronically operates? List specific attitudes and behaviors.**

- **At what level do you function most of the time?**

7

THE POWER OF
COMMUNICATION

*The reason why so few people are agreeable in conversation is
that each is thinking more about what he intends to say than
what others are saying.*

—Francois, Duc de La Rochefoucauld

The ability to accurately assess levels of emotional maturity
and facilitate individual movement to higher levels of
emotional maturity are *core competencies,* key to optimizing
leadership and organizational effectiveness. They are *foundational
to both interpersonal growth and management development.*

Helping to facilitate others toward greater emotional maturity
requires that the facilitators themselves be emotionally mature;
otherwise, their intentions and actions simply are not productive.
People at Level 3—Opposer (see chapter 6, page 206) or below
are counterproductive. Additionally, a facilitator needs to understand and be able to apply good communication skills, which
include recognizing and dealing with repressed communication.
When those are lacking, facilitating emotional maturity is much
more problematic. How an individual or a group communicates,

233

including how they respond or react to communication, is one of the best indicators of that individuals or group's level of emotional maturity. Unfortunately, effective communication skills—key to competent facilitation—are often lacking. Therefore, before we deal directly with the dynamics of facilitating people up the levels (addressed in chapter 8), we will first briefly review some often forgotten or ignored communication basics.

GOOD LISTENERS—A RARE COMMODITY

Good listeners are a rather rare commodity in a world of busy people trying to get other busy people's attention. We feel we must be "on," say the bright thing, make the great presentation, and look good no matter what. That emphasis on the need to perform has contributed to repressing our willingness and ability to listen and our skill at it. It has created a culture where slick performances based on glib one-liners and sound bites rule the day. The emphasis is on performing at the expense of listening and learning. Let's face it, we're not learning very much when we're doing all the talking. There is nothing wrong with talking or performing, if balanced with appropriate listening and acknowledging.

Rather than putting so much attention on being interesting, it behooves us all to put more emphasis on our ability to listen, to pay real attention to the other person's needs, wants, and aspirations, and to be interested in them and their perspectives.

We often talk of the importance of establishing rapport but too often forget that one of the most powerful and effective ways to do so is simply to be a good listener. Good listening communicates interest in the other person. Attentive listening acts as a validation of the other person. This is always appreciated, whether acknowledged or not, and is usually reciprocated. Besides, we learn a lot more when we listen than when we perform—and we make far fewer mistakes and a lot more friends.

Yet, how often do we break rapport by doing things like minimizing what the other person is saying? How often do we interrupt by sharing similar stories, diagnosing, criticizing, rescuing, advising, or fixing? We would be far better off talking less and consciously being more present and attentive, listening with interest, acknowledging as appropriate, and speaking primarily to verify for clarification and understanding. For more on this topic, read *Listening Leaders* by Steil and Bommelji.

There are two kinds of bores—those who talk too much and those who listen too little.
—Author unknown

You can win more friends with your ears than with your mouth.
—Author unknown

THE VALUE OF ACKNOWLEDGEMENTS

Acknowledgement, like listening, is underrated, misunderstood and under-used. Most of us continually under-acknowledge, over-acknowledge, or (most commonly) do not bother to acknowledge at all.

Understanding what constitutes acknowledgement, as well as its impact, can increase our effectiveness and the esteem in which we are held by others.

An effective acknowledgement communicates to the other person that his or her communication was received and understood. It does not necessarily imply acceptance or rejection, only "Thank you, I understand what you said." Proper use of an acknowledgement keeps the speaker from wondering, "Did they get it or didn't they?" It lets the speaker know that he or she need not repeat. Acknowledgements also act as validations, for it lets the speaker know that his or her communication was valuable enough for the listener to pay attention and respond.

Failure to acknowledge even the simplest of communications is one of the most common and costly errors in day-to-day communication. This leads to more misunderstandings than we can imagine. How many times have you failed to give a simple acknowledgement to a communication that you understood? You probably reasoned that there was no need for acknowledgement, that it was obvious that you got it. But was it? The person trying to communicate with you is not always sure of that. Providing no acknowledgement leaves some doubt, and the other person's attention tends to remain on the communication. As a result, the person may repeat it unnecessarily, which is frustrating to both of you. Another common reaction is that the person feels slighted because she thinks you did not even bother to take the time to say, "I heard you." Whatever rapport there may have been in the beginning can quickly erode, sometimes to the point of a dramatic outburst. You may be baffled and think the other person is a little crazy, or you may be critical of yourself for being ineffective. Most times, neither of those results will occur if you acknowledge the communication.

Cultures can vary, sometimes significantly, in their use of acknowledgements. This can and has created misunderstandings and, in many instances, spurred negative attitudes that are largely unjustified.

For example, Americans and Japanese have traditionally tended to be very different in their understanding and use of acknowledgements. For the Japanese, acknowledgements are a very important communication element in their desire to be polite in all social and business interactions. They continually use acknowledgements as a way to be gracious. Americans, however, tend to be poor acknowledgers, seldom even think about acknowledgments, and far too often don't bother with them at all.

This difference can create unnecessary upsets. For example when an American negotiator says to his Japanese counterpart, "I think you should order X widgets." The Japanese negotiator acknowledges with, "Hai, domo," which literally translated means, "Yes—thanks." If the American is unfamiliar with Japanese etiquette, he may interpret this as agreement and assume he has an order. To the Japanese, however, his acknowledgement simply meant "Thank you—I understand that you would like me to order X widgets." The intention was not to indicate acceptance or agreement but simply a polite acknowledgement of what the American negotiator said.

When the order does not materialize, the American may feel the Japanese negotiator was disingenuous. If that occurs often enough, the American may develop a biased attitude of, "You just can't trust those people." The Japanese, on the other hand, may start to wonder how they should deal with those presumptuous, impolite Americans.

Cultural differences are not part of this book's scope. However, they can be a significant factor of which anyone dealing with other cultures needs to be acutely aware.

> **Points to consider:**
> - **When was the last time you consciously acknowledged another person's communication?**
> - **When was the last time you thanked someone for their communication?**
> - **Who in your group does the best job of acknowledging others? What asset or strength does that provide them?**

FROM DISCUSSION TO DIALOGUE—MOVING TOWARD GREATER UNDERSTANDING

The primary purpose of communication is to expand understanding. More often, however, communication involves one or both parties trying to convince the other of the rightness of their viewpoint. There is little, if any, real listening or acknowledgement from either party.

How often do we observe different viewpoints taken as attacks that need to be defended against rather than simply as different viewpoints? Instead of expanding understanding, these attempts at communication result in upsets, increased intolerance, and diminished understanding. Scientist David Bohm calls this form of counterproductive communication discussion. He suggests we would be much better served by dialogue than by discussion.

In true dialogue, judgements are consciously suspended. There is only the presentation of viewpoints. An opinion is recognized as simply one viewpoint of many possible viewpoints. There are no attempts to convince the other party, defend a position, or obtain specific results. Rather, there is the intention to set aside prejudices, truthfully share viewpoints, and be open and honestly desire to learn about and from the other person's perspective.

The willingness of all parties to learn from each other is an essential quality of dialogue. When that willingness is present, dialogue takes place just by being together. When we are truly open and believe there is something valuable to learn from the other party, we expand awareness—of the other person as well as ourselves. Not only does dialogue expand the breadth of understanding, but it also offers the probability of reaching greater depths within ourselves.

For dialogue to be meaningful, both parties must be open to the positive and the negative aspects of their respective positions. *Both parties must understand that there can be truth outside their current set of truths.* Both parties need to be open to the possibility that by engaging in dialogue their position and viewpoint might change.

Who is not so sure of his own correctness will learn many things.
—Palestinian maxim

By the act of observing and listening with the intention to learn, we are able to appreciate the beauty and value of other viewpoints as well as our own. In fact, the ability and willingness to be present with another person's perspective opens up many new possibilities.

This is freedom—freedom from the limitation of our own self-imposed intolerance and the fear that fuels it. It is also freedom to learn and grow. With real dialogue, we are more receptive to viewpoints previously rejected out of hand. True dialogue helps us develop empathy. It is validating and honoring to all parties. It increases rapport and builds respect. It broadens our consideration of what is possible. It expands our options and choices.

An unwillingness to dialogue is an indication that fear and some sense of overwhelm is at least acutely, if not chronically, present. This must be dealt with before honest communication can take place. If the situation is acute rather than chronic, skillful use of the appropriate *facilitation level* (developed in chapter 8) can often move a person to an emotional state where real dialogue can take place. As long as a sense of overwhelm remains, true dialogue will not be present. A negative situation will not resolve until, at a minimum, the sense of overwhelm is relieved.

True dialogue occurs only at Levels 5 and 6 on the levels of emotional maturity (see chapter 6). By recognizing when we are in a discussion rather than a dialogue, we open the door to improving real communication. By owning how we are creating, allowing, or contributing to an unproductive form of interaction, we are taking responsibility for our impact and thereby empowering ourselves. By consciously and proactively changing from discussion to dialogue, we open the door to a whole new world of expanded awareness. Moving toward authentic dialogue should be our conscious intention in every interaction

Let the next sentence out of your mouth be from your very highest self.
—Quaker prayer

Points to consider:

- **What percentage of your conversations are dialogue versus discussion?**
- **With whom can you dialogue most easily?**
- **What do you notice or appreciate about that exchange?**

DEALING WITH REPRESSED COMMUNICATION

Our lives begin to end the day we become silent about things that matter.
—Reverend Martin Luther King, Jr.

Results are the manifestation of our acting with willingness and intention. Real feelings and honest communication give our willingness and intention juice. When feelings and communication are repressed, willingness wanes, and intention is dispersed. Authenticity, dialogue, collaboration and true teamwork are effectively eliminated. Creativity and innovation wither, and productivity is far less than we are capable of. Disappointment and frustration follow.

What does it take to end repression? Organizationally, it takes a leadership committed to creating a safe, secure environment where people are free to express their opinions, needs and desires. Individually, it takes courage to face the fear of letting go of old, familiar, and perhaps even comfortable but dysfunctional patterns. It takes commitment to persist through the inevitable resistance to any change—our own and that of others—and it takes willingness to communicate honestly and respectfully.

In many cultures, indirectness and social politeness are expected norms of proper behavior. In those cultures, candor is often resisted—sometimes strongly—and the resistance is always rationalized. These norms should not be arrogantly ignored, but rather, appreciated for their original intention of respecting individual human dignity. However, far too often the original intention has been lost and has deteriorated into little more than a justification for lack of honesty, candor and authenticity, which, in turn, is a cover to avoid acknowledging, facing and feeling underlying fears of inadequacy.

Honestly assessing what is respect for and what is fear of honest expression must be done conscientiously and responsibly. Social norms should be considered and, as appropriate, appreciated and honored but never at the expense of honesty. *Ultimately, lack of honesty is always based in fear, no matter how rationalized.*

The following is recommended for addressing repressed communication:

- Require candor and honesty as a fundamental condition of continued employment. (Note how many people, directly or indirectly, regard this requirement as ridiculously impractical—a rather telling indication of the actual level of communication and inefficiencies present.) This may be scary for some people, and for those who are afraid, this requirement just brings the fear that was already there to the surface.

- Initiate programs that clarify and provide an understanding of what real communication and emotional maturity are, how they are to be practiced in the workplace, and what individuals need to do to grow and expand.

- Offer competent, confidential, one-on-one coaching to help selected individuals confront their fears and uncover or express what they have repressed. This coaching is highly personal and tailored to the individual. Ensure the coaches can competently apply the facilitation skills presented in chapter 8. (Also, see "In-Depth Probing to Determine Real Needs", this chapter, page 246, and "The Value of Competent Coaching", chapter 8, page 291.)

- Offer confidential, competently facilitated, small-group sessions in which individuals can feel safe to express themselves and clear upsets or confusion with group members. The intention is to use the group process to help individuals develop the willingness and skills to communicate authentically. An important aspect is to help the participants gain clarity about their own needs. Immature, insecure people often will use these activities as opportunities to dump on others. Therefore, competent emotionally mature facilitation is necessary.

- Implement the above steps with enough people and reinforcement to attain critical mass.

The willingness to candidly share is one of the two fundamental elements of a true team. The other element that develops a potential team into an actual team is a mutual focus for which each member feels ownership and commitment. Without candid communication, attention is dispersed and mutual focus is much harder, if not impossible, to achieve.

With repressed communication present, there is no true team, only a pretense of one. *Repressed communication is, by far, the primary reason team-building attempts fail.* Its chronic presence is a direct indication of immature and dysfunctional leadership. How damaging that is depends largely on its pervasiveness and duration. Effective team development, productivity and morale require and demand that the cause be determined and handled.

Lessening, if not eliminating, repressed communication is a crucial aspect of creating true teams and manifesting the synergy true teams are capable of producing. The process of clearing interpersonal communications may have the important added benefit of clarifying and focusing personal values, which, until elucidated, can confuse and confound organizational values.

When repressed communication is released, an amazing phenomenon occurs. A seemingly disproportionate amount of positive energy comes forth, and a willingness to be open and vulnerable spontaneously occurs. Individuals become more allowing, tolerant, and open to new viewpoints. Rapport increases, along with a willingness to trust and to share thoughts and ideas, even if those ideas are extreme.

Eliminating *repressed communication* results in a significantly greater willingness and ability to look at and own previously unconscious but nonetheless self-imposed and self-limiting considerations. *Doing so is the substance of personal empowerment and growth.*

The higher the emotional maturity of an organization, the less repressed the communication—and visa versa. Imagine for a moment what your family, group or organization would be like and how the world would feel if everyone felt safe enough to be authentic in his or her communication.

FOCUS OF ATTENTION

The truly great performers, presenters and communicators have three things in common: First, their intention is to deliver something of value to someone. Second, they are professionals and know their material. Third, they are in excellent communication with their audience; that is, they have their attention on their audience, not on themselves. The more a person is interested in us, the more we become interested in him or her.

Far too many presenters primarily focus on being interesting. The most effective communicators consciously keep their interest and attention on their audience, being interested in them versus being interesting to them. This simple shift of attention establishes greater presence and rapport and is consequently more power-fully motivating and effective. This dynamic is fundamental and senior to presentation style, which can and should vary to align and support the unique and natural strengths of the presenter.

IN-DEPTH PROBING TO DETERMINE REAL NEEDS

The important thing is to not stop questioning. Curiosity has its own reasoning for existing. Never lose a holy curiosity.
—Albert Einstein

The principles and dynamics of in-depth probing are applicable to any interpersonal interaction. They are particularly useful when the intention is to go deeper in discovering underlying needs and intentions. Graciously applied, in-depth probing is useful in any communication setting. It is especially valuable in sales, negotiation, therapy, and conflict-resolution situations. This section on probing utilizes a sales context as an example.

Sales professionals know that people buy benefits, not features. This is true, but which benefits? Individuals differ considerably in what they value. While there are common fundamentals to human motivation, at any particular time individuals have unique needs, wants and aspirations, which change as emotions and/or circumstances change. Many a sale has been lost because the needed benefit was not offered or an inappropriate one was presented. To discover the benefit or benefits that best meet your prospect's unique needs, in-depth probing can be very useful. The probing must be in-depth for two reasons:

1. The prospect often is not consciously aware of what he or she needs or wants.

2. It may not occur to the prospect to tell you a particular need because he or she has no idea that you could or would be willing to meet it.

Successful in-depth probing depends on the prober applying the following principles:

- Being present
- Having a genuine willingness to listen and understand the other person's unique needs and point of view
- Competently applying in-depth probing principles and appropriate acknowledgments

In-depth probing is a highly individualized process and cannot be conducted in a rote fashion. Understanding and initially matching the other person's emotional level is key. Doing so, in itself, helps to establish rapport.

Engendering confidence by really being present with the other person and taking a sincere interest in him or her is an essential part of the in-depth probing process. Your ability to comfortably maintain presence, listen willingly, and acknowledge appropriately will do more toward selling you and your product than anything else. Technical competence and impressive credentials can be very helpful. Those attributes should not be slighted, but they are of secondary importance to the in-depth probing process.

Remember, you are the purveyor of your product. If people don't buy you, they usually are much less willing to buy what you are selling. They are much less likely to buy you if you are not sincerely interested in them and willing to listen to their needs, wants and aspirations.

Follow-Up

Most people only scratch the surface when they probe. Most do not follow up on their open-ended questions. A typical probing session conducted by an unsophisticated prober consists of the following:

- Asking one open-ended question
- Getting a superficial, automatic response
- Asking a few directive questions
- Asking another, different open-ended question
- Getting another automatic response, and so on

People who make the error of prematurely switching to a different open-ended question or prematurely firing away with directive questions have little idea how superficial the elicited information may be, or how much real and valuable information they might be passing up. Furthermore, the person being interviewed often feels he is either being interrogated or has not really been understood. Good probing does the following:

1. Establishes a solid base for good two-way communication

2. Increases mutual respect and understanding

3. Obtains a wealth of useful data about your prospect's needs—not only objective needs but also subjective needs, attitudes and emotional state—information that may be an invaluable positioning tool and crucial to the negotiating process

The initial effort spent on in-depth probing will save you time in the long run. It not only will give you significantly more information about the other party's needs and underlying concerns, but also will deepen the interpersonal connection. Why? Because in-depth probing demands excellent listening and acknowledgment skills, which act as validations of the other person and are always appreciated.

In many situations, negotiating or otherwise, the canned, automatic, fast responses to probing questions are knowingly or unknowingly superficial. Often, they misrepresent the real situation because they omit more than they disclose. Frequently, your client will be unaware of some aspect of his real needs. If the client had been fully aware of all the aspects of the situation, he/she probably would have already satisfied their needs. Clarity about needs usually leads to rapid solutions and, subsequently, rapid sales.

Skillful in-depth probing cuts through the superficiality and helps determine what the person's real needs and aspirations are. The best follow-up to an open-ended question is a request for more communication on the same question. This approach guides the individual into looking with more depth at aspects he or she may not have previously thought about or noticed.

A common result is that the person achieves some new or deeper realizations concerning his or her needs and, often, insights into how to handle them. The individual feels good because, of course, it was his or her realization, and since you helped arrive at it, the individual likely perceives you as competent and helpful. Furthermore, you now have possible specific solutions that are very real to him or her. Of the, say, twelve benefits your service or product may offer, you now know the one or two that will most closely meet your prospect's perceived needs. Those are the ones you stress. You may be surprised by what ends up being significant. The other benefits may be mentioned, but they are far less important to that individual. Without probing for the individual's perception of need, you may neglect mentioning a benefit that is important to him or her. The important benefit to that person was benefit number eleven out of twelve and, at least to you, it just did not seem important.

In-depth probing adds an important extra dimension and its value should not be underestimated. Just because a person stops talking does not mean that there is not a lot more of importance to be said on a subject, or that you as the prober now know all there is to know.

To be a good prober, you must learn how to follow up. You must learn to think in series. All open-ended questions have series. When conducting in-depth probing, as the responses are given, you know what your next question will be. Simply ask for more on the same question. This is not a rote procedure. Keep to the original subject until you and the other person are satisfied that a complete and accurate picture has been presented. Be sure you have fully heard the person.

Examples of follow-up probes:
Example 1
    "How…?" (Response)
    "How else might…?" (Response)
    "Are there any other ways…?" (Response)

Example 2

"What about...?" (Response)

"Anything else about...?" (Response)

"Are there any other thoughts/feelings/ideas
about...?" (Response)

Example 3

"Tell me about...". (Response)

"Tell me more about...". (Response)

"Can you go into that a little further?" (Response)

The main point here is that you do not stop with the first answer and move on to another question. After each response, you keep asking for a little more—other thoughts, feelings, and considerations. The person will start looking more closely and may come up with things of which even he or she wasn't aware. Remember, keep asking for more. It is easier and more comfortable than you think, once you get the hang of it. The information you obtain often will amaze you. Keep doing it; keep asking for more until your prospect definitively says that's the whole thing or all of a sudden smiles and says something to the effect of, "Gee, I just realized...," or "Very interesting. I now see that the actual situation is...," exhibiting a new awareness of the issue. After all, it may never have been fully explored before! There is always more there than either party may consciously realize or even suspect.

You may be surprised by the number of levels you can reach. Always keep the original question in mind and always come back to it. It even helps to write it down. Do not allow yourself to go off on tangents. Directive questions can be used to terminate a tangent or redirect attention. You may want to ask a few directive questions to get specific information as a point arises or simply to add variety to the communication.

Do not lapse into conversation—you can lose control of the process and forget your purpose and intention. You can ask an open-ended question about a more specific area as it comes up, and follow that to its conclusion. However, always return to the original question and follow it through. If the person continues to talk and show interest, don't interrupt, but do be sure to get your question answered. If the person is answering your question, it's best not to ask directive questions. You can always go back and get those specifics later. Wait for a pause. Do not interrupt unless you are obviously not getting your question answered. When you are getting an answer, listen.

MORE ON ESTABLISHING RAPPORT

Like attracts like. When people are like each other, they tend to like each other. Both the tone of your voice and your body language have a significant impact on how the other party receives your communication. In initially establishing rapport with someone, try to be aware of and match the voice tonality and body language of the other person. If the person is a fast talker and your pace tends to be slow, speed it up. If the other person sits up straight and crosses his or her legs, and you do the same, you create an image of being similar. You might be amazed at how these simple techniques combined with good listening skills help set the foundation for making your probing easier and more fruitful. As with any technique, these can be misused or abused. Always keep in mind that your intention when probing is to better understand and responsibly address all parties' needs.

COMMENTS ON GETTING MORE INFORMATION

In addition to being a good listener, there are some useful techniques for getting and keeping a person talking on a subject or for directing more talk on a subject area:

- Volunteer some information. If you start the flow, the other person usually responds in kind.

- Be silent. Most people continue to talk to fill a void. This, of course, should be handled with discretion.

- Provide partial acknowledgements. This shows interest and indicates that you want the other person to continue.

  - An occasional affirmative nod of the head, a soft "uh-huh" or "right" keeps the person talking.

  - A full acknowledgement ("Good! Thank you.") says, in effect, "I fully understand what you said and you do not have to go on."

  - A premature acknowledgement (acknowledging before the other party has completed his or her communication) also keeps people talking, but only because they believe you could not possibly know all they had to say. It can make them feel frustrated and upset with you. Some people cut others off to save time or because they think they already know what the person is saying.

- A lack of acknowledgement can lead to upsets. This is often the cause of people talking until they are blue in the face. They do so because, since you did not acknowledge what they said, they think you must not have understood. So they continue, hoping to hear an acknowledgement indicating that you have understood.

- Repeat words or phrases. Take a word or phrase from the last answer you got and repeat it in a questioning manner. For example, the person says, "I really enjoyed seeing the pink barn." You say, "Pink barn?" The individual will tend to expand on what you question by some statement like, "You know, the pink barn down by Sutter's Mill. It was up for sale last year, but Mr. Peterson got mad at his real estate agent and took it off the market. And do you know what? Last month they discovered oil."

DEVELOPING A CONSULTATIVE RELATIONSHIP— A SALES EXAMPLE

The typical sales process tends to violate effective communication concepts and principles. With willingness, intention, and practice, however, these violations can be easily redressed. Most selling (especially when there is pressure for volume) consists of the following general steps:

A. Knowing the products or services
B. Obtaining some general information about the prospect
C. Establishing contact
D. Making a presentation of the products or services
E. Asking for an order

Rote application of these steps can degenerate into a hard-sell, used-car-salesman approach and image. A much better sequence of action that facilitates the development of a consultative relationship is as follows:

1. Know your products or services.

2. Establish contact and rapport. Be present and interested.

3. Observe, address, and acknowledge what the prospect's attention is on at that time.

4. Probe in depth. Listen. Acknowledge appropriately. Do not lapse into conversation. Listen. Do not interrupt. Listen. Do not give your pitch. Listen. Determine the prospect's needs, from his or her point of view. When the client stops, ask if there's anything else. Listen. Repeat as necessary.

5. Match the perceived needs of the prospect with the specific benefits of your services that are relevant to the prospect.

6. Close.

7. Ensure that what was promised is delivered to the client's satisfaction. Honor your commitments.

In most sales training and sales supervision the previous A–E sequence is usually emphasized. Any probing that is taught usually focuses on points that can position what the seller wants to sell without a comparable focus on determining what the buyer's perceived needs are from the buyer's viewpoint.

The suggested action sequence (1–7) tends to be mishandled as follows: Although Action 1 is fundamental, its application varies greatly. Action 2 tends to be superficial and social. Action 3 is usually overlooked entirely (this is the foundation for establishing presence, awareness, sensitivity so often glossed over). Action 4 often mainly consists of asking a series of directive questions that the salesperson wants to have answered, which frequently have little relevance to the prospect's perceived needs. Action 5 is often inadequately accomplished because Action 4 was lacking in sufficient probing skills. For example, the probing was not in-depth enough (stopped asking for more before the prospect said there was no more); there were too many interruptions (making a sales pitch or touting some credential before the probing was completed); or there was a lack of appropriate acknowledgement. In order to compensate for the shortcomings mentioned above, Action 6 tends to be manipulative and technique-oriented rather than natural. Action 7 is seldom consistently applied.

Observation tends to verify that when long-term positive relationships have developed, the salesperson has followed the previous 1–7 sequence of actions. This basic sequence, appropriately modified, is applicable to all forms of interpersonal interaction—from customer relations, sales and negotiation to personal development and family relations.

SOME HELPFUL PROCESSES

The following processes, if done with honesty and candor, can be amazingly effective in dissipating conflicts and improving communication.

Communication Clearing Process

The purpose of the communication clearing process is to reduce misunderstandings and upsets and help move the communication toward greater dialogue. The person who is upset usually initiates this, but it can also be used simply to initiate a dialogue to gain more clarity on a topic. If one or both parties are upset, it's prudent to have this process facilitated by a neutral third party.

Willingness and intention on the part of both parties to be open to at least considering the viewpoints and perceptions of the other party are crucial to the effective use of this process. The viewpoints do not have to be accepted, but they must be considered or there is no dialogue, only rigid positions in opposition.

The sequence of dialogue, with only one person speaking at a time and the other person listening, should progress as follows:

1. Be as present as possible.

2. Person A states the facts only.

   a. Person B states what he or she heard stated, without evaluation or discussion (Active Listening). If needed, Person A clarifies for Person B anything missed or misunderstood. If appropriate, Person B is asked to repeat the clarification back to Person A.

3. Person A states his or her feelings (the emotional impact the facts had). Person A uses "I" statements only—"I felt...." He or she does not use "You" statements: "You made me feel...." "You did...." (Person B practices Active Listening).

4. Person A states any conclusions reached or judgements made. (Active Listening)

5. Person A requests what he or she wants, if anything, from Person B. (Active Listening)

6. Person A asks Person B if he or she would care to respond. If the answer is yes, Person A practices Active Listening.

7. If appropriate, Person B may now share his or her interpretation of the event or situation using the same sequence.

Self-Image Process

Our self-image is the platform from which we project into the world. How positive that image is directly affects our ability to communicate with authenticity and confidence.

Most people don't take the time to figure out what their self-image is. Our self-image defines the boundaries of what we are willing to experience and our ability to capitalize on our much larger potential. If we are willing to stretch that image, we can change and grow. This process can create profound change, but it must be done sincerely, without artifice. It is personal and private and requires complete honesty.

To begin the process, write paragraphs and paragraphs in a free flow of thought describing how you see yourself living your life. This is for your own private edification. You are not writing to impress anyone. Do not write only the good stuff or the bad stuff, but all of the stuff. Be willing to look at and own it all. After all, it is the wholeness—the integrity—of your actual self-image about which you are trying to obtain clarity. You cannot change what you will not confront.

Wait 24 hours. Let it integrate. Read what you wrote and condense it into one or two pages. Wait 24 hours. Take the one or two pages and condense them into a paragraph. Wait 24 hours. Take the concept of what that paragraph expresses and condense it into one sentence or phrase. Wait 24 hours. Condense that sentence or phrase to one word that expresses its essence. That is the old image. That is the image you have had of yourself, despite any pretenses or self-deception. It has been the boundary of what you have allowed yourself to be, to do, and to have. Wait 24 hours.

Reverse the process for your new image. Choose one word that expresses what you want your image to be. Wait 24 hours. Expand that word to one sentence. Wait 24 hours. Expand that sentence to one or two paragraphs. Wait 24 hours. Expand those paragraphs into one or two pages. Wait 24 hours. Expand those pages by writing (in the present tense) as many pages with as much vivid detail as possible describing how it is living that image.

Once you have the details of that new image, consciously, proactively, and persistently do your best to start living it.

RECAP OF IMPORTANT POINTS

- Your primary intention in communicating should be to honestly determine and ethically serve the actual needs and aspirations of the other party.

- Establish good rapport. Be present with interest and a willingness to listen. Acknowledge appropriately.

- Don't assume you know—or that the other person's initial remarks have told you—what is actually needed.

- Probe in-depth to determine the other person's actual needs (from his or her point of view).

- As appropriate, align and emphasize benefits that meet specific perceived needs.

- If what you have to offer does not meet the other party's needs, if possible, refer him or her to something or someone who can help. Your helpfulness is often remembered.

Giving is a talent; to know what a person wants, to know when and how to get it, to give it lovingly and well.

—Pamela Glenconner

THE DNA OF DIALOGUE

8

FACILITATING
EMOTIONAL MATURITY

The significant problems we face cannot be solved at the same level of thinking we were at when we created them.
—Albert Einstein

Changes in emotional maturity, as indicated in chapter 6, have exponential effects. Raise a person's emotional maturity and you dramatically raise their energetic vibration and range of perceived possibilities. Add that higher frequency to any system and you raise the resonance and potential of the entire system. Because of its exponential impact, doing so with even a few people can make a huge difference. Raise it for many and the impact toward creating an environment of integrity can be of a significant magnitude. This will only happen when management's intention to do so itself has integrity (chapter 2, Step I, page 52).

Organizationally, we can move toward accomplishing this by: 1) assessing (see chapter 6), adding, and/or removing individuals based on their chronic level of emotional maturity, and 2) facilitating willing individuals to higher emotional levels. Helping to develop skills to do the latter is the purpose of this chapter.

KEEPING A DYNAMIC BALANCE

We live in a dynamic, nonstatic universe. When we align with its energies, we feel in harmony with and gracefully and elegantly responsive to the ebb and flow of life. We feel balanced, centered, fluid, energized and alive. We are empowered, loving and compassionate.

Growing up, or maturing, is not about finding and maintaining a static state, but rather is a continual process of awareness and action toward dynamic balance—and rebalance—in the continuing give-and-take of life. This dynamism offers interest, challenge, adventure, excitement and purpose to our lives. *The purpose of this chapter is to assist you in developing the skills to facilitate others, as well as yourself, to higher levels of emotional maturity*, in which dynamic balance becomes a larger part of all our lives.

Lack of dynamic rebalancing, or no change, equates with boredom, stagnancy, apathy and death. *The levels of emotional maturity provide a relative measure of how aware, dynamically balanced and alive we actually are.* As a reminder, emotions, their order, their relationship to each other, and their underlying messages are the same for all human beings, regardless of personality, gender, or cultural differences. As important as these differences can be, they all function within this universal emotional framework.

What is it we are balancing and rebalancing? We are striving to harmonize the areas that our emotions are telling us are out of balance and therefore causing us stress. Finding dynamic rebalance is about listening to, understanding, and responding (not reacting) to the emotion we are experiencing in the moment (being present).

When we ignore or repress our emotional messages, we lose our ability to respond to that dynamic process. Instead, we react; we stay too far out of balance and feel unstable, insecure and afraid. In defense, our attention narrows. Our universe of perceived possibilities contracts and we increasingly feel overwhelmed, mired in problems, out of control, powerless and alone. We become increasingly self-centered and reactively hostile, fearful, sad, despairing, or apathetic. As the need for rebalancing (change) increases, so does a corresponding resistance to it.

In our reactive state, instead of relishing dynamic rebalancing, we fight it. Mistakenly, we regard change as a threat instead of an opportunity. We yearn for a static "certainty" that only limits options and exaggerates our sense of powerlessness and isolation. Our perception of what we feel we need and want is correspondingly distorted. *Before we can even determine what we truly need and want, we need to move back toward dynamic balance.* Only then will we have the perspective for responsible choice and action.

Understanding emotional dynamics helps us to see more easily though social facades and differentiate authenticity from pretense. It allows us to determine more accurately another person's actual attitudes and corresponding intentions. Consequently, we can reliably predict behaviors not yet observed and—once we develop our facilitation skills (the focus of this chapter)—constructively respond, whatever that person's emotional state.

With experience, we can begin to discern subtle differences within the levels themselves. This further differentiation provides additional clarity about where and how we need to focus our attention, thereby enhancing our ability to make effective choices. This includes optimizing our communication in responding to any situation.

That awareness and ability helps us to begin moving toward more balance in our personal life as well as helping raise the resonance of others. Doing so on an increasingly regular basis is the foundation of personal and interpersonal growth.

EMOTIONAL STATES

We can separate our emotional states and the influences on them into categories of acute, chronic, and social. Understanding them, and the differences among them, helps us to assess and improve our—and others'—ability to constructively respond to life situations.

Acute Emotional States

An *acute* emotional state is the actual present-time emotion associated with a specific experience; in other words, how we are feeling at a given moment. We all have our acute ups and downs, day to day, moment by moment, that indicate to us (if we listen) how we are perceiving—and responding or reacting to—our environment. All of us, at different times, have experienced the entire range of emotions—from apathy and despair to fear and anger to contentment, enthusiasm, joy, and everything in between.

Chronic Emotional States

Our *chronic* emotional state is our *emotional home base*—where we spend most of our time emotionally—the one we return to when the emotional ups and downs settle out. Recurring attitudes and behaviors, beyond a person's social facade, such as "always angry" or "happy and positive most of the time" or "usually sad," reflect and are manifestations of a person's chronic state. Where our home base resides on the levels of emotional maturity is a very strong indication of our level of responsibility and, therefore, our resiliency and effectiveness in dealing with the circumstances of life.

Once we understand the emotional hierarchy and become familiar with an individual's home base, when we observe acute departures from that base—up or down—we can reliably predict the emotions and behavior the person will go through as he or she returns to home base. *The intensity with which and how fast or slow individuals move varies, but the emotions and associated behaviors and attitudes they go through do not.* The higher the home base, the more responsive (versus reactive), resilient, productive, and happier an individual is.

The higher an individual's emotional home base, the greater the person's real presence and, consequently, their responsiveness to and resiliency in dealing constructively with any situation. An increase in an individual's willingness to feel the entire range of emotions raises that person's emotional home base. *Facilitating movement that raises the emotional home base effectively raises the level of emotional maturity. This is true for both individuals and organizations.*

Social Demeanor

Both acute and chronic emotional states can be significantly different from the social demeanor we assume for public view. That social demeanor may be higher, lower, or the same as our actual acute or chronic emotional state.

Social competence and behavior depends largely on social background and personality. Different personalities exhibit different social interaction skills, but all can be more or less emotionally intelligent. Though social competence may have socially desirable aspects and benefits, it does not necessarily correlate to a person's level of emotional maturity. What does correlate is the degree to which the person engages in authentic communication and responsible behavior.

In a society that tends to cover up actual emotions, we often present a social demeanor or facade that broadcasts a message different from how we are actually feeling. *The ability to differentiate an individual's acute emotional state from a social demeanor, when they differ, is an important aspect of being emotionally intelligent.* That differentiation ability is key to understanding actual intentions and optimizing communication.

Cultural Influences

Cultural, political and social demands have an impact on what we think and how readily we allow ourselves to feel. Unfortunately, much of society not only condones but often encourages repression of feeling. Graciousness and consideration for other people's feelings are wonderful qualities. However, far too often, being polite or socially correct is not gracious or sensitive at all, but rather is a rationalization used to avoid honest expression of feelings.

Each culture, in various ways, limits some aspects of authentic emotional expression. This may have some seemingly socially desirable effects, but it always results in limitations that are, ultimately, detrimental to the individual and to society.

EMOTIONAL RANGE AND FACILITATION LEVEL

The ability to both assess and facilitate emotional maturity is key to creating a saner, more mature, productive, and happier environment where integrity is the norm, not the exception. Before we can facilitate anyone's emotional growth, we need to be able to accurately access, through any social facade that may be present, the individual's (group's) current emotional state. The charts in chapter 6 are designed to assist in that evaluation.

Facilitation level is the emotional communication that recipients can both relate to and be motivated by, given their acute emotional state. In any particular emotional state, people have a limited range of what makes sense to them. That range of emotional reality is typically no greater than one level away from a person's acute (not social) emotional state. People will be more or less receptive or motivated, depending on how much a communication falls within their emotional range. *Effective facilitation requires being willing and able to empathize and adapt our communication so as to relate somewhat above the other person's acute emotional state but within his or her emotional range.*

Attempting to relate to, influence, motivate, lead, or persuade when communicating outside a person's emotional range simply will not work. In other words, relating to people based on their social demeanor, when it is significantly different from their acute emotional state, is not effective. They will not be interested. At best, the resulting interaction will be superficial. Not only is the communication ineffective, but also tends to inhibit further communication because the person is turned off by how unreal the message seems. When this occurs, the recipient is likely to be even more negative toward the presenter, the viewpoint of the presenter, and whomever or whatever the presenter is representing—not a good foundation from which to position or persuade. This applies to written as well as oral communication. Developing skills applying the appropriate facilitation level is a *core competency* key to enhancing motivational and leadership effectiveness.

If you would persuade, you must appeal to interest rather than intellect.
—Benjamin Franklin

UNDERSTANDING FACILITATION DYNAMICS

A review of key points about emotions and communication lays the foundation for understanding the dynamics of facilitation:

- Emotions are frequencies of energy that act as messages from our subconscious about how well we are surviving. They are not good or bad, but they do indicate relative degrees of security or stress.

- Each emotion has a different filter of perception associated with predictable beliefs, perceived needs, attitudes, intentions, and behaviors.

- An individual's perception and interest are focused and have a limited range around their acute emotional state. He or she will respond or react from that state.

- Communication outside an individual's emotional range of perception is not real, interesting, motivating, or effective for that person. It tends to be the opposite.

- Communication at an emotional level just above an individual's acute emotional state or level and within the individual's emotional range of reality is real, interesting, motivating and effective for that person.

Lack of awareness of these points or unwillingness to apply them can lead to a canned, inflexible style of communication or presentation. *No matter how smooth or sophisticated the presentation may be, it will be effective only to the extent it falls within the emotional range and thus the reality of the recipient.*

To reiterate and emphasize this critical point: if our communication falls outside the emotional range and thus the reality of the person with whom we are attempting to communicate, it will not be effective in leading, motivating, or persuading that person. Furthermore, it will more likely result in the opposite. *If we end up getting what we want by communicating outside a person's (or a group's) acute emotional range, we were successful for other reasons and in spite of, rather than because of, our communication.*

To the degree that we can competently assess a person's acute emotional state, we have a powerful means to understand, more specifically, how they tend to perceive things, along with corresponding attitudes and behaviors. We then can determine much more easily how to most effectively communicate, relate to, and deal with that person.

Table 6.2, The Levels of Emotional Maturity, in chapter 6, page 220, describes attitudinal and behavioral characteristics associated with six levels of emotional maturity. The level where most of the observed current behavior occurs is a good initial indication of a person's probable acute emotional level. Observations over time will determine the person's chronic level or home base. Once the person's chronic level is established, we can predict with a high degree of accuracy and reliability other attitudes and behaviors not yet observed but highly likely to be present at that level.

Our acute behavior can range through all six levels, sometimes quite quickly. Acutely, we can be cheerful one moment, sad the next, and angry shortly thereafter. However, chronic behavior in specific areas, will seldom stray more than one level from home base.

When there appears to be more than a one-level difference manifested in a number of different behaviors, it is usually an indication that the higher level is an attempted social cover-up of the actual lower level. For example, observations of a number of behaviors over time—some of which appear to be at Level 5 or 6 and others at Level 2—strongly indicate an attempt to disguise negative intentions and behavior. High-level individuals are human and have their ups and downs; however, they do not *chronically* manifest low-level behavior in any arena. Personal growth—that is, becoming more emotionally mature and acting with integrity more of the time—is about raising one's home base to a higher level.

COMMUNICATING WITH REALITY

The human dynamic is complex and, as such, quick fixes and rote procedures seldom work. Developing skill in facilitating someone up the levels is not a rote procedure. It requires an ability to recognize, through social performances and pretenses as well individual human variations, the person's actual emotional state. Even with understanding the characteristics of and relationships among the emotional levels, developing facilitation expertise takes practice and persistence. However, for those willing to invest the effort, the rewards can be profound.

To the extent that we understand the attitudes and behaviors, including likely resistances, which correspond to each emotional state, we can more accurately understand an individual's perception of reality, including the individual's fears, motivations, and perceived needs.

Remember, the types of communication and the behaviors that will be most real to the person (or group) with whom we are communicating are those associated with the level on which that person (or group) is operating at the time. If we match the other person's emotional state when communicating, there will tend to be strong rapport: people like people who are like themselves. Conversely, the further our communication strays from the other person's emotional state, the less rapport we will have, and the less effective we are likely to be.

If we communicate at a slightly higher emotional level but within the other person's emotional range, the rapport will be slightly less, but respect and motivating influence will be greater. People are easily influenced by the next higher level. Why? Because, regardless of denials and pretenses, we all want more sanity, security, aliveness and happiness in our life. The higher the level, the more these are present as well as a sense of being more in control of our life. When someone communicates to us, or we to them, in a way that suggests these qualities may be more available, we are motivated to follow.

Observing where a person is within the emotional levels and facilitating his movement up them, without skipping any level, helps that person reach a less compulsive, more productive and happier emotional state. A person does not jump from apathy or fear, for example, to strong interest or enthusiasm. An individual's maturity and happiness is facilitated by going from where they are emotionally, through successive higher levels in sequential order.

Maturity is a process not a destination.

—Leo F. Buscaglia

APPLYING THE APPROPRIATE FACILITATION LEVEL

Consider the following example of applying an appropriate facilitation level. If a person is displaying generalized opposition with an angry tone, that individual is likely behaving at the lower end of Level 3. Our immediate goal is to get the generalized hostility more focused. Understanding that the Opposer's behavior is a defense against some perceived threat, we need, without accusation or attack, to help the person become more focused on the specifics of his anger. For example, ask, "What specifically happened?" "How many times—exactly?" "Who specifically?" Asking nonthreatening questions that narrow the focus of the person's anger to specifics provides him or her with an opportunity to ventilate hostility without being made wrong. Becoming more focused and specific also provides the person (and you) with something concrete to evaluate and do something about.

Continuing to ask for more, in a nonthreatening manner, helps to move a person into neutral, as he or she feels heard and acknowledged. Moving on by mentioning some facts that may be of interest to the person helps to move him or her to a state of curiosity. Providing relevant data interests the person even more. Continuing in this vein may even bring the person to a feeling of enthusiasm.

As another example, if we detect hints of covert behavior or subtle untruths (Level 2), an effective facilitating response is to display a willingness to use overt hostile force (Level 3) against the perceived problem. Why? Because the individual is feeling hostile to what he regards is a hostile world, but is too afraid to express it. He relates to the hostility and admires someone who is willing to overtly express what he is too afraid to express. The person communicating at the slightly higher level serves as a model, and effectively as a leader, encouraging more direct expression and action.

This is particularly effective when the overt force is directed toward a common enemy. However, it is also effective when directed at the frightened covertly hostile person. Why? For the same reason as above. The passive-aggressive person admires the courage of the person willing to use force. This is one reason dictators can be so effective in controlling a fearful population. They are not only afraid of the dictator but also hold that person, even if begrudgingly, in some degree of respect.

Note that we have attempted to raise the other person's acute emotional state gradually by doing the following:

- Understanding the behavioral characteristics of each emotion and the relationships among the levels of emotional maturity

- Being aware of the person's actual (as opposed to social), present-time emotional state

- Communicating (without judgment or attitude) from the emotions and attitudes of the level just above the other person's acute emotional state; communication from that slightly higher level tends to bring the person up to that level

- Shifting and communicating from the next higher level, once the person has come up to a higher level; repeating the process until the person is communicating at least at Level 4, preferably at Level 5 or Level 6

The same process is used at the lowest level. A person who is apathetic is emotionally below grief (see column C, Table 6.2, page 220). Helping to focus that person's attention on the loss, which is the focus of the person's grief, is actually positive and therapeutic. Why? Because in a state of apathy or despair, the person has a "why bother, don't care, nothing we can do anyway" attitude. If we can get the person to recall a time of loss, that person will have greater emotional involvement than before. Similarly, helping a person move from grief to feeling sorry for him or herself is a process of expanding the person's feelings and awareness. This process is therapeutic to the person, even if initially counterintuitive.

Continuing in this manner increasingly expands awareness. At Level 1, people are almost totally self-centered and emotionally introverted. Moving them into fear is the next step, as it directs their attention beyond themselves. By doing this, we help to make them aware of the dangers of staying where they were, and we help thaw their numbness. Only with this awareness can they hope to do something about the danger (at first covertly, as they are initially too afraid to be overt). As they become stronger, they become more willing to be open and direct with their hostility. At each progressive stage, individuals feel more able to influence their environment and change their circumstances. The lower emotional levels may not be pretty, but *"the way out is the way through.*" Understanding the levels of emotional maturity and their associated behaviors provides clarity on which way leads out.

WHAT MAKES LEADERSHIP POSITIVE?

Leadership is a dynamic process of keeping others reaching and moving beyond where they are. Persuasion and motivation are about addressing and meeting perceived needs. Leadership styles vary, but effective motivators have one thing in common: they have learned to relate at a level that meets their audience's need for and perception of something better. What that perception is depends largely on that audience's emotional state. Part of that process involves the leader accurately assessing the constituent's actual emotional level; communicating slightly above that level; and suggesting, offering, or modeling what that audience perceives as something better, thereby drawing them up.

A population in the lower levels feels overwhelmed, insecure and powerless, and wants and will follow virtually anyone who communicates a willingness and ability to deal with the perceived oppression/oppressors. For example, an angry, assertive speech can motivate an overwhelmed and dispirited population to move into action that feels so much better than the previous helpless inaction. Under some conditions, their sense of gratitude can become blind and fanatic allegiance.

The fact is that leadership can be positive or negative, constructive or destructive. The determining factor is the leader's own emotional level. An individual is only capable of leading others to his or her level of emotional maturity and no further.

Leadership stuck in the lower levels (disconnected from essence values) is inevitably destructive.

It is not possible for you to influence others to live on a higher level than that on which you live yourself.
—Leo F. Buscaglia

A classic example is the charismatic leadership of Hitler. Stuck in anger himself, he adroitly used fear-based messages and angry rhetoric and policies to motivate an overwhelmed population (loss of WWI, hyperinflation of the 1920s, depths of the depression) desperate for change. Hitler led the German people *from* the despair, grief and fear of Levels 1 and 2 (for which they adored him) *to* the aggression and overt hostility of Level 3—*and stuck them there—with devastating consequences.*

If we wish to motivate a person or group who is acutely in the lower levels, it is vital that we continue the facilitation process as long as it takes to attain a responsible level (Level 4 and above). If we stop the facilitation process prematurely (before being completely out of the lower levels), many of those facilitated will likely remain stuck in a lower level (irresponsible state), *only now more energized.*

Chronic low-level behavior, regardless of the person's socio-economic-political status or rank, is fundamentally insecure, and therefore self-centered and defensive. It is invariably accompanied by hostility (overt or covert), lack of compassion, and unethical and abusive behavior. *Individuals, groups, organizations, or nations stuck in the lower levels do hurtful and destructive things.*

Their negative behavior ultimately leads to their own destruction, but in the process, the collateral damage can be enormous.

Motivating people has consequences and responsibilities. The way out is the way through – all the way through to the higher levels where responsible behavior resides. *Only when individuals are emotionally mature (connected with and acting from essence values) will their leadership be positive and constructive.* Hence, facilitating emotional maturity throughout one's organization (and society) is a priority of enlightened leadership.

A MORE BENIGN EXAMPLE—BUYER'S REMORSE

Selling is also about leading and motivating others; therefore, the same principles apply. Understanding the dynamics of low-level behavior helps to lessen significantly the buyer's remorse problem. Buyer's remorse comes primarily from clients who were confused, in doubt, and in some way resistant to buying but felt forced into agreeing to the purchase. There may be many reasons why, but the point here is that they agreed when they felt under duress; i.e., they were, at least acutely, in the lower emotional levels and therefore more likely to say and do anything to remove the perceived pressure, including signing on the dotted line.

While in the lower levels of emotional maturity, people are reacting out of insecurity and their agreements and promises are not reliable or dependable. This is especially valid for those chronically stuck in a lower level. It is also true for those who are only momentarily overwhelmed. When they return to their higher home base, they too are likely to want to change any agreements made while in a more reactive and less rational state. With the pressure off, the individual reconsiders his irrational act and cancels the sale.

The foundation for lasting sales relationships is satisfied clients. People are not happy or satisfied when they feel pressured. Often when people buy when they are in the lower levels, they have been pressured, not sold, and the sale is less likely to stick, resulting in buyer's remorse. Pressure selling may move product in the short term but does not build trust, relationships, or repeat business. The astute professional does not move to close until the client is at least at a high Level 4 and preferably higher. That is where clarity and confidence in decisions reside.

Your professional purpose is to provide value to your client. Making a sale is not a purpose; it is a by-product—and an inevitable one if you provide real value as perceived by the client. This is too often forgotten, particularly when competitive and short-term pressures mount. For sustainable success, it is vital that providing real value is your conscious, senior purpose and that your priorities and actions correspondingly align. Understanding the levels and being able to apply facilitation dynamics can help to make this a positive and productive process for everyone.

THE LEVELS AND INTERVENTION EFFECTIVENESS

An understanding of the characteristics of emotional levels provides us with an increased ability to determine, for each individual, the potential effectiveness of various interventions. The higher the level of emotional maturity, the greater is an individual's sense of security, self-esteem, and self-confidence.

Correspondingly, an individual's ability to integrate and use new data and skills responsibly is greater.

A key point to remember is that, first and foremost, *all activities should be directed at raising emotional maturity to at least Level 4*. Only at level 4 and above are responsible results obtained. Be aware that concluding any agreement while any participant is below Level 4 is problematic.

Below Level 4, individuals are overwhelmed and, as they move to lower levels, increasingly unable to integrate new information. For this reason, most interventions, including training, conducted while the person is in the lower levels are an inefficient use of resources. The exception is competently conducted therapy (for those willing). Significant gains tend to occur primarily above Level 3. As the individual becomes healthier, therapy may no longer be needed and competent coaching, mentoring, training, or consulting take on increasingly effective roles. Figure 8.1 illustrates the effectiveness of competently conducted interventions with individuals at various levels of emotional maturity.

The DNA of Receptiveness

FIGURE 8.1 - Effectiveness of Interventions

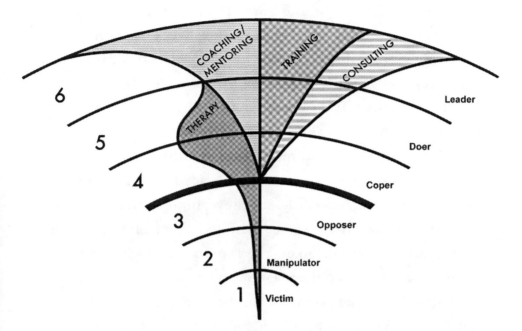

DEALING WITH CHRONIC LOW-LEVEL BEHAVIOR

Use of facilitation level can expedite chronically high-level people who are momentarily overwhelmed to more quickly regain their perspective and power. The higher the chronic level, the greater the resilience of the individual when acutely stressed and, therefore, the easier and more effective the use of facilitation level.

Individuals and groups overwhelmed and functioning in the lower levels want others to take responsibility. Be willing to do so initially as you help and insist that they take increasing responsibility for themselves, ensuring others are not hurt in the process.

If moving a person to the higher levels at the present time is not possible, then moving the person out of the current environment (including termination) should be considered. Why? Because, while in the lower levels, a person's behavior is more destructive than constructive, both to themselves and their surroundings. Because the person is reactive rather than responsive, present-time decisions and actions will be negatively skewed. If the person is at work, it is often better to send the person home and pay him or her rather than allow the person to continue to do more damage, which is being done even though it may not be immediately apparent. In addition, a change in environment can lessen the restimulation of whatever is causing the reactivity, more easily allowing facilitation. This change is often helpful, unless the stimulation originated in the environment to which the person is being sent.

As previously mentioned, skillful use of facilitation level can be markedly beneficial for those generally functioning on the higher levels but momentarily overwhelmed. However, using facilitation level to move individuals who are *chronically stuck* in the lower three levels is problematic and has, at best, a limited short-term effect. Remember, as dysfunctional as their behavior may be, people chronically stuck in a lower level have found, within that level, a way to survive. Consequently, they tend to be extremely reluctant to give it up.

Neurotics complain of their illness, but they make the most of it, and when it comes to talking it away from them they will defend it like a lioness her young.

—Sigmund Freud

.

We can provide a safe environment. We can encourage. We can communicate our concerns. We can initiate various interventions. Nevertheless, when push comes to shove, *no one changes until he or she personally makes the choice to do so.* Until that person does so, all outside attempts fail no matter how competent or well intended they are.

As long as people remain stuck in the lower levels, they act in ways that are destructive to themselves and their surroundings. They consume and waste resources that could otherwise be utilized much more productively. They depress the environment and everyone around them.

The best thing you can do for yourself and your organization is to not allow a chronic low-level individual to continue operating in your space. Do what is necessary to remove such individuals from the environment. This does not mean giving them a good evaluation or reference just to more easily get rid of them. Remove them responsibly. Do it with as much sensitivity as you are capable (remember all dysfunctional behavior is a distorted cry for love) and do it legally—*but do it!*

Once chronic low-level individuals leave or are removed from the environment, it is amazing how quickly seemingly unrelated problems disappear, productivity expands, and morale increases. If this change is not significantly noticeable, one or both of the following are likely to be present: 1) there are other low-level individuals still present and/or 2) you have removed the wrong person. Remember, low-level individuals (particularly Level 2) are often masters at directing responsibility elsewhere for problems they created. *Seeing beyond social facades and being accurate in assessing low-level behavior, is a core competency that is generally undeveloped to everyone's disadvantage.*

If we are to be responsible, effective leaders, managers, or just plain good friends, *it is imperative that we not allow or contribute directly or indirectly to the continuation of low-level behavior. By doing so, we effectively enable/reinforce dysfunctional behavior limiting both the individual and the organization.* Realize that being a "good guy," being reasonable or polite about ignoring, tolerating, or allowing chronic low-level behavior, is not doing anyone any kindness. It is just the opposite; it is cowardly and irresponsible.

Leaders who tolerate or ignore lower-level behaviors do so either out of ignorance or out of lower-level behavior themselves. If the reason is ignorance, then they need to be educated on the destructive consequences of their reasonable, nice-guy behavior. Chronic lower-level manifestation in any member of an organization needs to be corrected expeditiously or the individual's employment terminated. *Tolerating irresponsible behavior is always hurtful to all parties.*

UNDERSTANDING PERSONALITY, GENDER, AND CULTURAL DIFFERENCES

The levels of emotional maturity are the same for all people. However, differences in personality, gender and culture do affect how each person responds or reacts to various stimuli. The more we understand these factors and their variations, the greater the potential for meaningful interaction and effective facilitation.

Personality theories and models abound. A particularly useful model is the Enneagram of Personality. An ancient model who's origins are lost in antiquity, it was available for centuries only to an elite few. Since the mid-1980s, dozens of excellent books on the Enneagram have become available. A book specifically integrating the nine different personality types or drives with the six levels of emotional maturity, tentatively titled *The Integration of Personality and Emotional Maturity*, by this author, will be available in 2007. Excerpts are provided in the Appendix.

Men and women do have different perspectives on a number of issues, and it is helpful, sometimes critical, to understand those differences. You may want to start with John Gray's popular *Men Are from Mars, Women Are from Venus*.

Understanding and dealing with cultural differences is too broad a subject to specifically address here, but is vitally important and too often innocently or arrogantly ignored. Cultural norms, once imbedded in a group, die hard. Confronted with arcane traditions or policies that stifle legitimate needed changes, it is critical that *prior to attempting change*, we understand, acknowledge and address the specific confusions, doubts and fears *underlying* the resistance. The necessity for doing so seems obvious. Nevertheless, we continually violate it with the predictable result of even greater overt or covert resistance.

Table 8.1, following, summarizes the focus needed in facilitating people progressively up the levels. Table 8.2, on page 288, is a continuation of Table 6.2 and focuses on leadership and organizational aspects of the levels.

TABLE 8.1 - Facilitation Dynamics

LEVEL	Range of Emotional Behavior	Attitude/ Behavior	To Move From:
6	From cheerful to enthusiastic (very strong, focused interest)	Act with integrity above all else	Level 6 to integration
5	From mild to strong interest	Be conscientious and responsible	Level 5 to Level 6
4	From neutral to contentment	Do the minimum to get by	Level 4 to Level 5
3	From generalized, overt hostility to specific, overt hostility	Attack the enemy; "get them before they get us"	Level 3 to Level 4
2	From fear to unexpressed resentment	Manipulate the enemy; "con them before they con us"	Level 2 to Level 3
1	From "nothing anyone can do about it," through despair and grief, to feeling sorry for oneself	Appease the enemy or do nothing.	Level 1 to Level 2

Focus of Facilitator/Leader/Motivator	Reason for Doing So
Encourage an in-depth look at what truly turns them on—help them find their own passion/ambition versus those of parents or society.	Much of people's dissatisfaction, regardless of material/social success, is in living other people's dreams/ambitions rather than their own, or being practical rather than doing what they're passionate about.
Expand arena and degree of proactive, responsible interests and behaviors; encourage greater dialogue.	Joy, happiness, and aliveness are about being willing to face and experience more of life's richness and depth.
Encourage action from passive neutrality to increased proactive interests and behaviors.	Neutrality and contentment are static states; they inevitably deteriorate into frustration unless interests are proactively developed.
Encourage and request specificity in recognizing and communicating what the upset is about.	Increasing focus on specifics provides substance to deal with upset; communication about them ventilates hostility and helps move the person toward neutral.
Be direct; call them on their manipulative behaviors, e.g., "Stop the pretenses, I know what you're doing!" Encourage them to become more candid with their hostility.	Based in fear, they are afraid to be overt in their hostility but admire the bravery of someone who is willing to express the hostility they feel. Calling them on their covert manipulations often gets them overtly angry—a healthy movement.
Acknowledge the apathy, despair, grief, or self-pity present; bring them up to the fear that inaction will have even bigger consequences; encourage them to express the accompanying hostility.	Emotions at this level tend to be paralyzing; eliciting a fearful expression of hostility against the real or imagined oppressor starts movement.

TABLE 8.2 - The Levels of Emotional Maturity —Organizational Aspects

Level		AA Handling of Politics within Organizations	BB Reliability
6 Leader	True Power	Politics on this level means understanding that individuals and groups have unique needs. Also, that one needs to be aware of these differences and must have sensitivity and the appropriate communication skills necessary to get positive, ethical results for all concerned. Uses politics in the most positive sense of the word.	Delivers as promised or if no longer possible, makes appropriate restitution.
5 Doer		Less of above. Somewhat more reasonable in rationalizing and justifying behavior to accommodate personal positioning.	Usually dependable and reliable.
4 Coper	▼ ▼ False Power / "Power Over" / Powerless	The ho-hum, go-with-the-flow, noninvolved observer. The nonpolitician. Can't be bothered with playing politics at any level. Feeling they are above politics when they are actually simply nonresponsive and noncommitted about most things.	Marginal.
3 Oppo-ser		Blames own inadequacies on "those rotten politicians." Hostility and overt opposition often rationalized as, "I'm just frank and honest." Belligerence will turn off those at higher levels but a dynamic speaker at this level, can easily appear charismatic and persuasive to an audience in fear. (example: Hitler)	Generally unreliable. Will predictably use force or threat of force whenever feeling threatened or insecure.
2 Manip-ulator		Politician in the worst sense of the word. Can attain great heights in organizations through charm, manipulation, lies, claiming undeserved credit, and shifting responsibility for own shortcomings to others. Although always a major liability to the organization despite appearances, the total real costs are seldom apparent. No real loyalties except to self.	Will NOT deliver as promised. Artful cover-ups and excuses. Devious.
1 Victim	▼ ▼	Too weak and too much of a crybaby or yes-man to be really political. Rather, propitiates to the manipulator or apparent power hoping to get by. Sense that there is nothing one can do except go along.	Cannot be depended upon in any way.

CC Handling of Problems/ Degree of Overwhelm	DD Leadership and Management Potential and Contribution	EE Responsible Management Action (If behavior chronic)	Level
Views problems as challenges and opportunities to learn and grow. Emphasis on solution vs. problem. Resolutions often elegant and creative.	Outstanding. The emotionally wise leader. Should be given every organizational opportunity/ advantage possible.	Acknowledge. Reward. Support. Promote.	6 Leadership
Deals with most situations effectively.	Good to very good, especially with Level 6 coaching and mentoring.	Acknowledge/confront as appropriate. Support/Mentor. Coach/Train. Reward.	5
Problems are a bother. Ignores them if possible. Copes with them if can't be avoided. Camouflaged hole. "It's someone else's job."	Poor to Fair. Generally not managerial material, but potentially could progress with excellent leadership and coaching.	Confront. Coach/Train. If the individual moves to Level 5, acknowledge, reward and support; if not, terminate.	4
Feeling overwhelmed. Fights/rejects viable solutions. Refuses to take responsibility for their contribution to the problems, instead blames others.	Destructive. Leads and manages, by threat and intimidation. Weak leadership often ignores, allows, or condones such behavior, rationalizing "their numbers are up"—a short-term fix that doesn't confront the real costs of such destructive behavior.	Terminate. Be careful to distinguish between the behavior of a chronic Level 3 person and that of Level 5 or 6 person whose style/personality may be direct and overtly, but responsibly, demanding. The apparent similarities are superficial. The concerns and values are significantly different.	3 "Lack of" / Destructive Leadership
Heavy overwhelm, desperation often skillfully covered. Pretends to deal with problems, but doesn't. Covertly misdirects responsibility to others. Manipulates self into position to take credit for other's solutions.	Very Destructive. Threatened by and undermines those that are highly competent. Promotes/rewards incompetence. Should not be allowed to lead or manage under any circumstances.	Terminate. Retaining known chronic manipulators is an exercise in fearful avoidance, self-sabotaging rationalization, managerial irresponsibility, and organizational destruction.	2
Totally overwhelmed. "Nothing I can do about it."	Zero.	Terminate.	1

DEMOCRACY NOW?

Democracy by its very nature requires at least some degree of individual discernment and responsibility. Those qualities simply are not present when people are overwhelmed and insecure. Noble causes, freedom, democracy, et cetera are meaningless concepts to people whose immediate attention is on dealing with survival now!

Rushing to democracy while survival issues beset a population will be problematic at best. Those ruled by fear, are unable to discern or evaluate effectively. Their decisions and actions are highly likely to be reactive, not responsive, and therefore often irrational and dysfunctional rather than helpful or constructive.

Expecting/demanding people to be discerning and responsible, when they emotionally cannot, only exacerbates the situation. This generates more reactive behavior; including various forms of overt and/or covert resistance and misrepresentation of actual intentions and actions.

Frightened people, feeling incapable of having and/or providing appropriate safety and security, need and want some authority to take charge and "make it safe." Out of fearful desperation, they will follow (sometimes fanatically) whomever they perceive as willing and strong enough and to deal with the "threat/enemy." That is why insecure people will tolerate, support, even demand and elect authoritarian (and even abusive) leadership. (see "What Makes Leadership Positive?" page 276).

A foundation of safety and security is a prerequisite for democracy to function much less thrive. Without it, integrity is absent and touted "democratic processes" are little more than pretence and sham - misleading and dysfunctional.

Only when individuals attain some level of physical and emotional security, with its corresponding larger perspective and greater ability to discern, do they perceive concepts such as democracy and integrity as meaningful and valuable. Only then, they may be willing to act responsibly on them.

Insisting on democracy, before adequately handling safety and survival concerns, communicates lack of awareness, arrogance and/or incompetence in dealing with actual needs. Such perceived insensitivity generates and magnifies trust and credibility issues. It hinders, not expedites, the development of democracy.

We cannot ignore fundamental needs or their associated emotional states. Doing so will not get us where we say we want to go. The way out is the way through, patiently confronting actual emotional states and applying the appropriate facilitation level.

THE VALUE OF COMPETENT COACHING

The greatest good you can do for another is not just to share your riches, but to reveal to him his own.
—Benjamin Disraeli

Providing training and/or mentoring to and receiving it from emotionally mature individuals can have a huge and positive impact. To optimize that impact, having the right kind of coaching competence is essential. Coaching to evoke and instill a skill set works well in certain areas, such as emergency preparedness and sports. However, more complex is coaching with the goals of helping others to 1) determine what they really want, 2) access their inherent talents, 3) empower themselves, 4) bring their life into greater balance, and 5) be happier more of the time. It is a different process and requires different competencies.

Developing competence in this latter kind of coaching is one of the most effective and efficient ways an organization can improve both performance and morale. *Coaching competence is an invaluable tool for any supervisor, manager, or executive. It should be a key element of any comprehensive management or leadership development program.* It is especially valuable for people who mentor others. Without coaching competence, mentoring tends to deteriorate into little more than political sponsorship.

Coaching has many aspects, but most of all it is about helping individuals recognize and use more of their inherent strengths and talents. It is about facilitating people's growth and helping them manifest their potential. It is not about instructing people on how to do something or doing it for them. It is about facilitating other people's willingness to be more responsible, accountable and empowered. Coaching is about helping individuals help themselves and, in the process, enjoy life more.

Often, when individuals seek coaching, it is to acquire assistance in addressing some area of perceived limitation. The challenge of coaching is to refrain from letting the process focus on problem solving or conflict resolution. Certainly, problems need to be addressed and solved or resolved. However, that is not the purpose of coaching or the role of a coach.

The purpose of coaching is to help individuals better understand themselves—how and why they do what they do—

and thereby learn to responsibly resolve their own issues. It is to help them figure out how they create personal limitations, and how they can take increasingly more responsibility for their own condition and change it if they so choose. Coaching is about helping individuals focus on recognizing, understanding, and taking ownership of the causal factors that influence their behavior.

Frequently, the presenting issue is only a symptom of something more fundamental that the individual/employee/staff member/client has not yet observed or confronted. Fixing the symptom may provide temporary relief but seldom resolves the underlying issue. Competent coaching includes having the skills and flexibility to look beyond the obvious and use the presenting issue in such a way that the client learns and grows in the process. In fact, everything that comes up is part of the process and can be used to help the individual become more aware, more responsible and more powerful. Coaching is like peeling an onion, uncovering the layers of a social persona, going beneath the "shoulds and oughts," bringing to light the repressed or unspoken fears. It is helping the individual create a willingness to face his or her fears. Willingness enables an individual to develop the ability to move through and beyond fears and thereby discover and release more of his or her dormant capabilities.

Competent coaching recognizes individual differences in needs, communication abilities, emotional maturity, and personality. Understanding the human dynamics involved and how to deal with those differences is the key to effectively relating to, educating as needed, and motivating each unique individual.

The following process covers the important basics of effective coaching. Each step of the process lays a foundation for the next. Once we have laid the overall coaching foundation, we may return to and reinforce various steps. However, a coach's primary attention should be on the needs of the client, not on any blind adherence to a process. Being present and attuned to the client's needs and responsibly adapting to them is a coach's senior priority.

Coaching Process

1. Create a safe space where candor and confidentiality are the honored norm. Mutually determine the parameters of the coaching relationship.

2. Help the individual sort through what he or she truly needs and wants and clarify the individual's relationship to parental/societal/organizational requirements/demands/impositions.

3. Assist the individual to more clearly recognize and own the impact of his or her behavior.

4. Determine, assess, and prioritize the broader contributions that that person can and wants to make.

5. Facilitate expanded commitment to responsible proactive behavior.

6. Encourage greater responsibility and accountability for the person's own needs, actions and commitments.

7. Acknowledge and celebrate doing so.

As the coaching process progresses, personal consideration of what is wanted often evolves from initial attention on functional skills improvement to a deeper focus on determining, developing and aligning purpose and behavior with essence values. Improved interpersonal relations and increased personal satisfaction frequently are by-products of the process.

On occasion, this coaching process reveals that the needs of the individual and the organization are not in alignment. Unless they move into alignment, it is usually better for the individual to leave the organization so that he or she can get on with doing what is more fulfilling. The departure is better for the organization in that the job is now open to an individual potentially more aligned with the organization's needs. When individual and organizational goals and values are not in alignment, mediocre performance, at best, is the likely result. All parties are frustrated and unhappy. Consequently, a nonaligned individual is more of a liability than an asset to himself and the organization.

A coach is a facilitator, an ally, a cheerleader, a devil's advocate, and a trusted friend. His or her main purpose is to help the individual determine and attain more of what he or she truly wants and, as appropriate, to help the person align his or her desires and aspirations with the needs and goals of the organization. If they align, the result is a much happier, enthusiastic and empowered producer. That individual is much more likely to contribute in ways that optimize benefits to both the individual and the organization.

In summary, a coach's job is to help individuals become more of who they really are by helping them to do the following:

- Clarify their values, needs and aspirations
- Recognize, take responsibility for, and change limiting patterns of behavior
- Recognize, acknowledge and more fully develop their inherent strengths and talents
- Empower themselves to greater, more responsible actions
- Determine how they can (or cannot) better align with and contribute to an organization's needs and goals
- Challenge themselves to grow and hold themselves accountable for their own needs, actions and commitments

Suggested readings: *Co-Active Coaching* by Whitworth, Kimsey-House, and Sandahl; *Masterful Coaching* by Robert Hargrove; *Out of the Box: Coaching with the Enneagram* by Mary Bast and Clarence Thomson.

SUMMARY OF FACILITATION LEVEL

We can help an individual (or group) raise his or her emotional state by recognizing the individual's acute emotional level and consciously choosing to relate in ways that communicate aspects of the next higher level (facilitating level). Skipping levels usually is ineffective, as too high a jump seems unreal and out of reach to the other person.

Skillful, responsible use of the appropriate facilitation level can be amazingly effective in any supervisory, motivational, or leadership role, be it one-to-one or en masse. If we observe otherwise healthy individuals drop into the lower levels, competent application of the facilitation level may be the most helpful thing we can do for both the individual and the organization. The individual benefits because he or she is miserable in the lower levels, despite any denials, pretenses, rationalizations, or arguments to the contrary. The organization benefits because the individual in the lower level is being destructive, not only to himself or herself but also to the environment.

Competent and responsible use of the appropriate facilitation level to expedite a person's movement toward increased responsibility and emotionally mature behavior is a win for everyone. Implemented broadly, it helps create an environment and culture of integrity.

He who guides another to higher levels of awareness is noble indeed.
—Author unknown

THE POWER AND SCOPE OF FACILITATION DYNAMICS

The dynamics and applicability of facilitation level are universal and cross-cultural. The power and potential effectiveness of the appropriate use of facilitation level is by no means restricted to individuals or small groups. They apply to motivating huge populations as well as to individuals.

Facilitating principles and dynamics themselves are neutral. That is, when competently applied, they are effective whether the person using them is ethical, unethical, sane, or insane. They simply work and are applicable in virtually any context. Thus, like most powerful tools, they can be used or abused. We can abuse models that can enhance our discernment by superficial, cavalier, and/or inappropriate judgemental generalizations, that understandably generate reactions to being categorized or labeled. Even worse, partial understanding and use of powerful tools by insecure, power-hungry people can be and has been devastating, as Hitler and history have demonstrated.

On the other hand, having a deeper understanding of facilitation dynamics assists us in understanding what is actually taking place. We then have a much better chance of using those dynamics constructively. Our ability to assess the dysfunctional leaders and destructive despots of the world, as well as irresponsible people in our environment, expands. Such people can no longer easily seduce us with their manipulative rhetoric and exaggerated promises. Correspondingly, our ability to: discern and evaluate, communicate and relate, and reinforce and support responsible people and behavior grows significantly.

Responsible use of these facilitation tools provides a tremendous resource and aid to any interpersonal context—including family and client relations, coaching and mentoring, counseling and therapy, sales and negotiation, management and leadership, and diplomacy and international relations.

ON BECOMING A LEADER OF INTEGRITY

Truly great leaders know that real power is in helping others actualize their own power. They lead in ways that help others move to higher levels of awareness and personal responsibility.

If we desire to be a leader who creates a positive impact, we have to be emotionally mature ourselves. We have to choose to grow up—own and be responsible and accountable for everything we say and do. If we truly desire to help develop responsible leaders, we need the ability to assess and select those who have made that choice, or have the potential to make that choice, and provide them every support we can.

A way we can do so is to:

1. Develop competency in assessing a person's (our own and others) acute and chronic levels of emotional maturity.

2. Develop competency in facilitating ourselves and others up the levels.

3. Use these competencies to select, retain or remove, and motivate others to increasing levels of responsible proactive behavior.

Remember, we cannot lead anyone beyond our own level. However, *we can raise our level by consciously having essence qualities as our model and what we model—our standard and our stand.*

I don't know what your destiny will be but one thing I know. The only ones among us who will be truly happy are those who have sought and found how to serve.

—Albert Schweitzer

The creation of an emotionally mature environment of integrity is *the* measure of outstanding leadership and real contribution.

THE DNA OF WISDOM

THE DNA OF CONTRIBUTION

THE DNA OF ABUNDANCE

Epilogue
A Call to Leadership

Never doubt that a single person can change the world. For indeed it is the only thing that ever has.

— Margaret Mead

The history of the human race contains a continuing pattern of self-centered, hurtful and destructive behavior. We have decimated environments, annihilated species, and destroyed cultures—due to the influence of immature people who lack integrity. The Holocaust, Cambodia, Rwanda, the Congo, Liberia, Bosnia, Somalia, and Darfur are only some of the more recent and ongoing atrocities. By and large, most of us have been, and are continuing to be, complicit in such failures—choosing to rationalize turning a blind eye where courage and integrity are needed.

Passive acceptance of such tragedies is itself a lack of integrity and contributes to feeling separated, alone, powerless and afraid. The impact of integrity's lack is never isolated and rears its ugly head in many forms; from persisting corporate and governmental fraud to inadequate education and healthcare, to environmental degradation, terrorism and genocide.

The problems and consequences are accelerating at an exponential rate. Exsisting conditions, personal and global, are a direct reflection of the level of emotional maturity present and, correspondingly, the degree essence values are an actual priority (or not). We can no longer "let the next generation deal with it." Although our happiness and perhaps very survival demands mature adult judgement and action, we continue to react and behave like insecure self-absorbed adolescents.

Humanity and the planet can no longer tolerate our indifferent irresponsibility! *We must grow up!* We must wake up and realize that it is only when we start actually living essence values in all contexts of our lives, large and small, that we can hope to break the viscous pattern of individual and collective irresponsibility. When we do so, courage integrates with responsibility, love, and compassion—in other words—integrity. *Facilitate the maturity of willing individuals and one helps develop people who make more responsible, empowered choices laying the foundation for an environment of integrity.*

Integrity—personal and public—liberates forces for global change. Whenever anyone, prompted by compassion and conscience, faces one fragment of their hypocrisy and takes honest steps of individual transformation, that action communicates to others. It kindles an inspiration for initiatives to bring justice and dignity. This integrity could be the energy for social transformation in the 21st century—a growing momentum of people who become agents of change and reconciliation, forging relationships of trust across the world's divides.

— The Caux Initiatives of Change

Recent advances in understanding human perception, motivation and behavior provide more tools and opportunities than ever to influence the world positively. With these resources at their fingertips, enlightened, courageous leaders can generate a paradigm shift of enormous significance. How? By accessing such tools and using them to facilitate emotional maturity and integrity within their existing sphere of influence, whatever that may be.

Whatever you can do, or dream you can, begin it. Boldness has genius, power, and magic in it.
—Johann Wolfgang von Goethe

If even a few people in your immediate surroundings were more secure, happier, more responsible, what would happen? Imagine the possibilities.

Doesn't it behoove us to do whatever we can to facilitate ourselves, our loved ones, and our associates in that direction? Shouldn't we be doing our very best to create an environment that attracts, develops, supports, and requires emotionally mature people of integrity?

Isn't it obvious that integrity and emotional maturity are not only prerequisite to individual and organizational empowerment but that their presence is *vital* to the creation of a saner, more loving world?

For all the sad words of tongue or pen, the saddest are these: It might have been.
—John Greenleaf Whittier

For those up to the challenge of playing a truly purposeful game, *creating an emotionally mature environment of integrity is the ultimate leadership challenge—and—the ultimate leadership success.* The means are available. *Are you up for the challenge?*

THE DNA OF A SANE WORLD

Appendix
Understanding Personality

Only a life lived in the service to others is worth living.

—Albert Einstein

The Levels of Emotional Maturity apply to all humans. Their order and relationship is universal and cross-cultural. Personality is a vehicle we use to interact with our environment in our attempt to obtain our perceived needs. Understanding differences in personality can provide a valuable complementary tool to assess and facilitate emotional maturity. That awareness also helps to generate greater tolerance for and appreciation of those differences. The following are excerpts from the forthcoming book by this author, tentatively titled *Integrating Personality and Emotional Maturity*.

OUR BASIC DRIVES

Whether we are consciously aware of it, we all have energetic drives to do the following:

1. Live our values, do what's right, and make the world a better place

2. Be helpful; give and receive love

3. Achieve and have a sense of accomplishment and contribution

4. Create something special and be uniquely noticed

5. Know and understand how the world works

6. Have safety and security

7. Avoid pain, have fun, and pursue a dream

8. Be able to depend on ourselves, decide what the game of life is, and take charge and direct it

9. Find peace

Each of us has all of these energetic drives and in their totality they represent the essence and "bigness" of who we really are. However, when we experience trauma (birth itself can be traumatic) or are overwhelmed, we feel the need to focus our attention to survive. As we do so, we can lose touch with (but not lose) aspects of our essence, resulting in a false sense of separation and loss, and creating a sense of insignificance, of "not being enough." We feel that in order to survive we need to compensate for this delusion of insignificance. To do so we fixate primarily on one drive that has its own version of "not good enough" in the form of a false core limiting belief. Out of that belief, compensating survival strategies (personality) develop. This is how personality forms.

ABOUT PERSONALITY

The word *personality* comes from the Latin word *persona*, which means "mask." *Personality is a strategy we develop to compensate for our false sense of not being enough.* We put so much attention and energy into these compensations that we start to believe that the mask is who we really are; that is, we identify with, and as, the mask.

The ultimate human fear is the existential one of nonexistence. The more strongly we identify with our mask, the more any threat to this fixated compensation is perceived as a threat to our very existence. This helps explain why it is often so difficult for individuals to let go of old dysfunctional patterns of behavior, even when they know they are dysfunctional.

From the existential perspective, those dysfunctional behaviors and consequences are minor compared to the dread of potential nonexistence. In order to survive, at some point we felt we needed to create something that is the opposite of our believed deficiency, that can compensate for and hide the deficiency from the world and ourselves. Thus, survival itself is falsely believed to depend on that identity, that image, that personality being protected, defended and maintained at all costs.

In our need to protect our identity, we narrowed our focus and created elaborate defense mechanisms (strategies), which eventually became unconscious and automatic. *This narrowed focus keeps us from seeing and experiencing much of our potential. It is what keeps us feeling disconnected and sensing that something is missing in our lives.* Too often, rather than confronting those not-so-nice emotions and listening to their messages, we instead put more energy into reinforcing our compensations.

Since this entire compulsive mechanism is based on a false premise, the need is insatiable. The degree of compulsivity around maintaining, overtly or covertly, this identity, correlates inversely to one's emotional health and emotional maturity.

MOVING TOWARD EMOTIONAL MATURITY

We need to see the mask—our personality—for what it is: a *very* restricted misidentification of our true self—a false identity composed of an intricate set of limiting beliefs and corresponding compensations, of which we are mostly unaware. We need to understand the mechanism behind the mask. We need to recognize that we are not our personality, but instead that we have a personality drive. *It's necessary to bring to conscious awareness what have become unconscious and habitual compensatory patterns.* We need to see the false, limiting beliefs that underlie those patterns for what they are—false and limiting.

Having the ability to differentiate among the various personality drives, with their different false core beliefs, provides an opportunity to understand how and why individual strengths and weaknesses manifest. *Understanding personality drives can be a powerful tool to help us, if we so choose, to be more consciously proactive in changing dysfunctional patterns and reinforcing positive ones.* It can be a great asset in moving from simply fixing or even improving our automatic, compulsive behaviors, to opening the doors to accessing more of who we truly are.

Importantly, as part of that process, *understanding the differences among drives helps us to develop not only an allowance of, but also an appreciation for, differences in the perception and behavior of others.* This provides a foundation for enhanced objective discernment as well as more authentic, compassionate communication and relationships.

THE ENNEAGRAM OF PERSONALITY

The *Enneagram* is an ancient system for understanding personality. It describes in detail the nine fundamental ways various energies combine to drive our behavior. It has great depth, breadth, intricacy, and subtlety and provides remarkably accurate descriptions of the different ways human beings tend to compensate for their falsely perceived sense of deficiency. While the Enneagram of Personality does a brilliant job of differentiating and describing unique differences in behavior, its focus on underlying motivations is what makes it a uniquely powerful model and potential vehicle for real substantive change.

The Enneagram's origin is lost in antiquity, but some believe it goes back to ancient Greece and even before that to Persia and India. During most of its history, knowledge of the Enneagram was regarded as "too powerful and sophisticated for the common people." For thousands of years it was shrouded in secrecy and revealed only to a privileged few. The Enneagram was introduced to the West in the early 1900s by George Gurdjieff, a Russian mystic who apparently learned it from a secret Sufi school. It was greatly expanded upon by Dr. Oscar Ichazo and then taught to and further developed by Dr. Claudio Naranjo. Most of what is published today is by students of, or students of students of, those two men.

The word *Enneagram* is derived from the Greek word *ennea*, meaning "nine," and *gramma*, meaning "points." The term *drive* is used here to describe the various points, rather than the more commonly used *type*, as drive more accurately describes the dynamics of the Enneagram as well as indicates that *we are not a type, but rather have a drive.* Though we may have our behavioral preferences, no one personality drive is inherently any better than another.

It has been predicted that the Enneagram will be one of the significant twenty-first century models used to better understand our mental, emotional and spiritual processes. As such, it requires and deserves more than a superficial look. For those willing to look deeply, the rewards can be substantial.

We are all unique individuals, and no one exactly fits into any one of the drives. However, even being close enough in our assessments can be very useful in better understanding ourselves as well as understanding how and why others tend to perceive and relate to the world differently from, or similarly to, ourselves. It's important to keep in mind that *all* personality drives are compensations. They are masks created to hide, from the world and ourselves, some underlying—albeit false and misguided but nonetheless influential—sense of insignificance. Rather than try to improve our compensation, it's much more empowering to understand our compensation so we can recognize its inherent false basis and move toward lessening our dependence on it.

For those new to the Enneagram, both *The Enneagram Made Easy,* by Renee Baron and Elizabeth Wagele, and *The Essential Enneagram,* by David Daniels, M.D., and Virginia Price, Ph.D., are recommended. *The Essential Enneagram* provides an easy-to-use inventory that's helpful in determining one's drive. For educators, trainers, and parents, *The Enneagram Intelligences,* by Janet Levine, offers many insights. *The Wisdom of the Enneagram,* by Riso and Hudson, provides an excellent overview of the model. *Bringing out the Best in Yourself at Work: How to Use the Enneagram System for*

Success by Ginger Lapid-Bogda, Ph.D., provides an organizational perspective.

PRACTICAL APPLICATIONS

As we begin to understand our personality drive, we can be more consciously aware of the specific ways we rationalize maintaining suboptimal behavioral patterns. We thus are able to catch ourselves more quickly and make specific, conscious choices about which behaviors would be most helpful for us in our maturation and integration. Understanding our own personality drive can increase the probability of optimizing both our own growth and our facilitation skills.

Table A.1 on the following pages, "Leadership and Organizational Aspects of the Personality Drives," provides side-by-side comparisons of characteristics of the nine Personality Drives.

Table A.2, "Enneagram Personality Drives Integrated with the Levels of Emotional Maturity," (page 316) synthesizes the integration of the Levels of Emotional Maturity with the Enneagram of Personality for each personality drive.

Contemporary Enneagram theory acknowledges degrees of emotional health. It briefly refers to three levels—Healthy, Average, Unhealthy—but does little to address movement from one level to another. Integrating two powerful models, the Levels of Emotional Maturity with the Enneagram of Personality, provides dynamism to the Enneagram and adds greater specificity to the levels. Combined, they synergistically offer an even more powerful vehicle for expanded understanding and transformational change.

TABLE A.1 - Leadership and Organizational Aspects of the Personality Drives

	Feeling / Hostility / Image Triad			Thinking/
	Drive 2	Drive 3	Drive 4	Drive 5
GENERAL RANGE OF BEHAVIOR ▶	HELPER-MARTYR	ACHIEVER-PRETENDER	CONNOISSEUR-ELITIST	VISIONARY-RECLUSE
Speech Style/ Emphasis	• Helpful • Sensitive • Empathetic • Friendly • Considerate • Advises • Informal • Enthusiastic	• "Can do!" • High energy • Motivational • Persuasive • Self-promotion • Propaganda • Can be demanding	• Dramatic or elegant • Usually visual, aesthetic • Intuitive • Future desires or laments • Sad stories	• Master of facts • Scholarly • Intellectual • Treatises • Focused • In-depth • Detached • Quiet
Leadership Characteristics	• Personable, empathetic • Adept at determining other people's needs • Can spot potential in others • Appreciates and validates others • Encourages individual initiative • Befriends/coaches • Conveys confidence and sensitivity • Cheerleader	• Goal/task oriented • High expectations • High energy • High profile • Persuasive communicator/ presenter/ salesperson • Demands efficiency and results • Sophisticated net-worker • Image/status important • Bottom-line orientation • Pragmatic • Adaptable	• Elegant or dramatic • Invites imaginative approaches • Inspiring • Offers unique, creative ideas—sometimes impractical, sometimes ground-breaking • Demands artistic control • Intuitive/bold/ uncompromising • Dislikes rules, bureaucracy • Can be unapproachable	• Logical, often brilliant, thinking, visioning • Intellectual approach • Requires detailed information • Focuses on problems and solutions • Organized ideas • Shows little emotion • Pleasant but detached, often likes to be alone • Dislikes committees
Personal Emphasis	• Client/customer relations • Individual development	• Solutions/results • Image • Public relations	• Unique niches • Quality • Aesthetics • Innovative	• Information • Complex problems • Privacy
Task/ Organizational Emphasis	• Customer service/ satisfaction • Helpfulness	• Goals/results • Beating the competition • Efficiency • Market flexibility	• Creativity • Uniqueness • Originality • High-end quality • Integration	• Special knowledge • Secrecy • Information meritocracy
Leadership Style Most Appropriate/ Helpful When	• Empathy, help and caring are particularly important • Model of high levels of customer service is needed	• Quick decisions, actions, and results are needed • Ideas must be communicated effectively • Public relations important	• Distinctive, unique results are desired • Exploring creative solutions • Intuitive input is important	• Planning strategically • Clarity and precise logic are vital • High degree of certainty desired before taking action

Fear Triad		Doing/Relating/Aggression Triad		
Drive 6	**Drive 7**	**Drive 8**	**Drive 9**	**Drive 1**
PROTECTOR- WORRIER	ADVENTURER- DILETTANTE	LEADER- BULLY	PEACEMAKER- AVOIDER	REFORMER- CRITIC
• Devil's advocate • Concerns • Cautious (phobic) • Challenging (counter-phobic) • Setting Limits • Questions • Protocols	• Many positive possibilities/ opportunities • Charming • Cheerful • Anecdotes • Brainstorming • Storytelling	• Expansive presence • Direct, blunt • Challenging • Solid, certain • Humor • Confrontational • Imperatives	• Non-confrontational • Pleasant • Equal emphasis on everything • Accommodating • Indirect • Epic stories • Participatory	• "The right way" • Formal, precise • "Correct" • Intense • "Shoulds" • Sermonizing • Critical, judgmental
• Devil's advocate • Models diligence • Fosters team building • Reluctant authority • Practical, prudent • Cost conscious • Conscientious • Thorough • Reliable • Pragmatic • Organized • Encourages collaboration • Promotes loyalty and dependability	• Friendly • Positive plans • Big picture • Energizes others • Motivates enthusiasm • Encourages anticipation of positive results • Strong synthesizing skills • Keeps options open • Tends to avoid commitments • Dislikes/delegates details and follow- through	• Big presence • Respects openness and courage • Easily takes charge • Demands/gives directness • Tests for courage, dependability • Confrontational • Generous, loyal, honest • Demanding, but fair mentor • Delegates easily, once trust is established • Defends the underdog	• Listens calmly • Sees all viewpoints • Collegial, inclusive • Minimizes problems • Creates commonalities • Promotes teamwork • Accommodates • Difficulty deciding on relative importances • Hard to pin down • Determined/ stubborn • Prefers well-defined role	• Polite and formal • Reliable • Organized, detailed, exact • Relates in terms of rank and status • Follows strict guidelines • Demands quality • Authoritarian • Better at managing details than big picture • Duty before pleasure • Respect more important than admiration
• Safety and security • Problem solving	• Innovation • Positive, happy environment	• Dealing with challenges • Directing	• Collaboration • Global perspective	• Principles, rules • Prescribing • Directing
• Caution • Belonging • Loyalty • Tight management systems	• Versatility • Innovation • Satisfaction • Enjoyment • Global thinking	• Holding the vision • Overcoming resistance • Self-reliance • Action	• Keeping harmony • Avoiding conflict • Unity • Routine	• Quality • Precision • Procedure and controls • "Correct action"
• Caution, care is indicated • Wanting to build community • A clear chain of command is desired	• Desiring innovative strategies • Synthesizing complex issues is important • Bringing together diverse groups	• Prompt, tough decisions needed • Standing up to pressure is critical • Situation must be controlled • Injustice is an issue	• Situation requires diplomacy • Cooperation is critical • Harmonious team is desired • Getting routine work done	• Strict norms and protocols exist • Quality standards are exacting • Thoroughness is demanded • Deadlines must be met

	Feeling / Hostility / Image Triad			Thinking/
	Drive 2	Drive 3	Drive 4	Drive 5
GENERAL RANGE OF BEHAVIOR ▶	HELPER-MARTYR	ACHIEVER-PRETENDER	CONNOISSEUR-ELITIST	VISIONARY-RECLUSE
Attitude Underlying Problem Solving Approach	"Am I needed?" "Am I wanted?" "How can I avoid rejection and be appreciated?"	"Do I look good?" "Am I the best?" "How can I win and be acknowledged?"	"Is it unique?" "Am I special?" "How can I be special?"	"Do I know enough?" "Am I bright enough?" "How can I get more data?"
Focus and Concerns	• Who are the important, influential people? • How it would benefit others, particularly the leader? • What will be most appreciated? • How to meet others' needs so as to be appreciated and taken care of?	• Goal, task completion • Image/status • Short-term, tactical decisions can be based on "the end justifies the means" • Impatience with delays, group process, or extensive planning	• Individuality and aesthetics important in all decisions • Decisions primarily intuition based, won't necessarily make logical sense • Uniqueness of the item/task is important, if it is even to be considered	• Logical • Dispassionate • Abstract and strategic vs. tactical • Able to make tough calls—wants others to implement • Because of exhaustive research, decisions once made tend to be final, but responsive to legitimate new data
Leaders/ Personalities*	Mother Teresa Kathy Lee Gifford Dr. Albert Schweitzer Leo F. Buscaglia Barbara Bush Bill Cosby Mia Farrow Shirley Temple Danny Glover Mr. Rogers Many caregivers, support staff to powerful people	Oprah Winfrey Bill Clinton John F. Kennedy Johnnie Cochran Johnny Carson Tony Robbins Vince Lombardi O.J. Simpson Donald Trump Many CEOs, politicians, salespeople, promoters, performers	Michael Jackson Marlon Brando John Malkovich Judy Garland James Dean J.D. Salinger Jessica Lang Naomi Judd Edith Piaf Vincent Van Gogh Tennessee Williams Prince Charles Many artists, designers	Buddha Greta Garbo Lenin Thomas Edison Bill Gates Warren Buffett Bobby Fisher Meryl Streep Gov. Jerry Brown Albert Einstein B.F. Skinner Ebenezer Scrooge Many academics, researchers
Organizations*	Herman Miller Nordstroms Salvation Army	Federal Express McDonalds Oracle	Bergdorf-Goodman Neiman Marcus Ritz Carlton	C-Span CIA M&M Mars
Countries*	Argentina Bali Thailand	Hong Kong Taiwan USA	France Italy Traditional Japan	Tibet Traditional China

✱ *These examples are only intended to provide a flavor of the drive. Both countries and organizations have many subcultures within the generalized overall culture. For example, generally the US is considered an Achiever culture (Drive Three) which is exemplified by the business cultures of New York and Los Angeles. However, the Midwestern culture is much different—probably much more like the Six Drive. The culture of Mexico is often seen as somewhat macho, an Eight stereotype,*

Fear Triad		Doing/Relating/Aggression Triad		
Drive 6	Drive 7	Drive 8	Drive 9	Drive 1
PROTECTOR- WORRIER	ADVENTURER- DILETTANTE	LEADER- BULLY	PEACEMAKER- AVOIDER	REFORMER- CRITIC
"Is it safe?" "Am I safe?" "How can I avoid danger?"	"Is it exciting?" "Is it easy?" "Is it fun?" "How can I avoid pain/hurt?"	"What are the boundaries?" "Who's in charge?" "How can I avoid being vulnerable?"	"How can I avoid conflict?" "How can I keep the peace?"	"Is it correct?" "Am I right?" "How can I avoid being wrong?"
• Tends to doubt everything • Checks all possible downsides, other options • Often ambivalent • Initially some form of delay • Looks to outside authorities/ superiors: Bible, rules, experts • Looks for consensus	• Decisions based on avoiding emotional pain, unpleasantness —often disproportionately focused on fun • Rationalizer par excellence • Much time planning • Wants options open—avoids commitments • Can be impulsive	• Strategic • Focus on challenges • Decisive, but can also be impulsive • Open to outside input, but once decision made, expects immediate compliance • Willing to delegate but only after trust fully established	• Difficulty assessing priorities • "Fence-sitting" • Procrastinates "hoping" proper action will "emerge" • Rationalizes delays • Difficulty following through • Needs deadlines • Once truly committed, delivers	• Rarely impulsive • Quick decisions scary/difficult • Indecisive but seldom delegates • Can get bogged down in details • Decides on principle, by "the formula" of "correctness" • Difficulty making exceptions to formula—follows rigid guidelines
<u>Phobic</u> Richard Nixon George Bush Woody Allen Albert Brooks Diane Keaton Many analysts, accountants <u>Counter-phobic</u> Adolf Hitler Andy Grove Gene Hackman Mel Gibson Many police, firemen	St. Francis George W. Bush Will Rogers Larry King Robin Williams Goldie Hawn Carl Jung Tom Peters Malcolm Forbes Auntie Mame Howard Stern Elizabeth Taylor Jack Nicholson Many entertainers	Theodore Roosevelt General Patton Harry Truman Ann Richards Joseph Stalin Mao Tse-Tung Suddam Hussein Fidel Castro Dr. Phil McGraw Fritz Perls Humphrey Bogart Sean Penn Picasso Many CEOs, military leaders	Dalai Lama Gandhi Neville Chamberlain Eisenhower Gerald Ford Ronald Reagan Warren Christopher Carl Rogers Jerry Seinfeld Dean Martin James Stewart Peter Falk Many diplomats, mediators	Confucius Martin Luther Al Gore Pope Paul II Queen Elizabeth II Emily Post Hillary Clinton Ralph Nader William Bennett Martha Stewart Nelson Mandela Margaret Thatcher Many religious leaders
Banking CIA Toyota	Ben and Jerry's Ice Cream 3M	Anheuser-Busch Mafia Microsoft	Insurance Companies Public Utilities US Post Office	EDS Moral Majority Motorola
Germany Japan	Australia Brazil Ireland	Israel Mexico Serbia	India Netherlands Polynesia	England Singapore Switzerland

but the peasant culture of Mexico has more Nine characteristics. With regard to personalities, we can only generalize from their public image which may or may not be representative of their actual personality. As such, different Enneagram authors have various opinions as to the placement of public figures, organizations, and countries.

	Feeling / Hostility / Image Triad			THINKING/
	Drive 2	**Drive 3**	**Drive 4**	**Drive 5**
GENERAL RANGE OF BEHAVIOR ▶	**HELPER-MARTYR**	**ACHIEVER-PRETENDER**	**CONNOISSEUR-ELITIST**	**VISIONARY-RECLUSE**
Potential Leadership/ Managerial Weakness	• Can over-emphasize people aspect at the expense of task/ project/results/ bottom-line • Difficulty saying no even when overwhelmed • Doing too much for others, create dysfunctional dependencies; not meeting own needs • Can lose respect because of need to be liked and appreciated— difficulty being tough even when needed • Prefers supporting position versus direct leadership responsibility • Unwilling to confront/deal with sense of unworthiness	• Over-identification with job/position/ professional status • Results emphasis can dominate personal/other people's needs and create resentments and passive resistance • Can work self and others to burnout (Type A personality) • Overemphasis on short-term results, looking good • Willingness to cut corners to attain goals • Difficulty acknowledging failures, arrogance, shallowness • Underlying anxiety • Pretense and deception if threatened by failure	• Has difficulty with rules, routines, bureaucracy • Can depreciate value of ordinary interactions • Difficulty in accepting criticism/ correction/outside input • Difficulty in completing routine or mundane tasks • Many starts, few completions • Seldom satisfied with present environment • Tendency toward discontentment • Can come across as aloof, dissatisfied, condescending • Can be disproportionately and unpredictably misemotional • Often moody and depressed • Repressed sense of inadequacy	• Can be impatient and weak in interpersonal sensitivity and communication • Over-values and over-relies on intellectual and undervalues emotional, instinctual relationship components • Intellectually detached • Tends to be stingy/ stretch resources too far • Demands for complete understanding may cause unnecessary delays • Can overly minimize needs of self/others • Can be too much of an indifferent loner • Can be overly detached from outcome • Repressed fear of involvement
If Weaknesses Not Handled, Potential for A.) Deterioration B.) Disintegration	A. Martyr B. Tyrannical revenge; Manic-depression	A. Pretended performance, busyness B. Despair, Apathy, Paranoia	A. Manic-Depression B. Martyr; Self-Righteous criticism	A. Withdrawal, detachment B. Shallowness, Addictions; Tyrant
If Weaknesses Handled, Potential for Integration	Creating and providing something special from a position of caring	Positive, expansive results providing safety and security to all	Using unique talents to create significant improvement/ refinement	Strong, positive visionary leadership of breath and depth

Fear Triad		Doing/Relating/Aggression Triad		
Drive 6	**Drive 7**	**Drive 8**	**Drive 9**	**Drive 1**
PROTECTOR-WORRIER	ADVENTURER-DILETTANTE	LEADER-BULLY	PEACEMAKER-AVOIDER	REFORMER-CRITIC
• Sense that people are not to be trusted and all situations are inherently dangerous • Can be overly cautious and oriented to problems, and not see positives • Inflexible enforcement, tried and true procedures/structures • Often procrastinates • Overemphasis on loyalty, repressing dissent or critical thinking • Can become overly compliant or rebellious or may alternate between the two • Difficulty/confusion with delegation and unstructured situations • Wishes are not to be questioned (Counter-phobic)	• Can ignore real difficulties through absorption with planning • Tendency to "dump" versus delegate details, follow-through and routine • Doesn't want to hear problems • Avoids conflict, self-appraisal, or criticism • Avoids commitments • Difficulty working consistently with a team • Sense that success can be attained through charm • Ability to see endless possibilities along with the desire to avoid pain of loss can keep 7s in dysfunctional relationships • Represses underlying fear/panic	• Can be autocratic; insensitive to their impact on others; overly demanding without knowing it; impulsive • Continually testing for reliability, trustworthiness, loyalty, courage, strength, power • Difficulty: tolerating weaknesses in others or self; asking for help • Insistence on having things done his or her way • Can be overly attached to outcome • Unwillingness to take orders from or share authority or control with anyone unless respect and trust fully tested and established • Represses sense of vulnerability	• Over accommodates to avoid conflict, difficulty saying no • Can lose sight of priorities and own needs • Difficulty prioritizing and moving from concept to action • Tendency to compromise too quickly • Avoids change/decisions as that may create potential conflict • May slow implementation if confused or ambivalent • Passive resistance to authority • Procrastinates and justifies delays—needs deadlines • Repressed sense of being separated, alone	• Can be dogmatic and overly critical in holding self and others to exacting standards • Micromanages • Can get stuck in detail/be a quibbler when speed is needed • Constant self-critic • Often deferential to seniors but autocratic toward juniors • Wants respect, and can be demanding of deference • Sense of entitlement • Resents taking orders • Over-controls • Represses feelings of being wrong
A. Paranoia B. Frantic, unproductive, busyness; Apathy	A. Rationalized addictions B. Rigid Self-Righteousness; Aloof detachment	A. Tyrant B. Withdrawal, Paranoia; Martyr	A. Apathy B. Paranoia; Pretended performance	A. Self-Righteous perfectionist B. Manic-depression; Shallowness, Addictions
Accomplishing peace through dialogue and mediation	Intelligent, well thought out, in-depth, positive, options	Sensitive, compassionate, powerful, visionary leadership	Significant accomplishment providing security to all	Creating positive multiple options based in integrity

TABLE A.2 - Enneagram Personality Drives
Integrated with The Levels of Emotional Maturity

Name ▶	Drive 2 Helper-Martyr	Drive 3 Achiever-Pretender	Drive 4 Connoisseur-Elitist
Level 6 Leader	Unconditional love. Caring. Generous. Truly helpful. Altruistic. Empathetic. Clear sense of own boundaries. Integrates primarily to positive 4 and also to positive 8. *Mother Teresa*	Attitude of unlimited potential. Star Quality. Authentic. Self-accepting. Modest and direct. Gets things done. Charismatic leader. Integrates primarily to positive 6 and also to positive 9. *Oprah Winfrey*	Inspired creator. Manifests beautiful ambiance. Highly perceptive and intuitive. Enthusiastic. Elegant. Focus on substance. Integrates primarily to positive 1 and also to positive 2. *Thomas Merton*
Level 5 Doer	Individualized attention giving. Thoughtful. Warm-hearted caregiver. Alters/adapts self to meet other's needs. "Power behind the throne."	Adaptable. Exquisite social instincts. Constructive, capable doer, producer. Motivator. Ambitious. Works the crowd to attain leadership status. Efficient.	Refined. Aesthetic. Appreciates real humor. Expressive. Intuitive, ironic. Big dreams, some results.
Level 4 Coper	Talks more about generosity than actually being generous. Pleases to get something in return. Can lose sense of own real needs. "The good acts." Needs to be liked. Becomes "indispensable."	Image and status conscious. Needs praise. Wants to be noticed. Willing to cut corners. Chameleon. Looking productive rapidly becoming more important than being productive.	Aloof. Feels special. Wants fine things provided. Emphasis on appearance. Much dreaming, little doing. Attention on what doesn't have. Discounts what does have. Compares.
Level 3 Opposer	Possessive. Gossip. Jealous. Demands to be appreciated/ center of attention. "Saintly." Angry with those who didn't love/appreciate them enough.	Must avoid failure—success is everything. Kill the competition. Demands results at any cost. Exploits others. Arrogant. Explosive. Braggart. Showy symbols of material success.	Self-absorbed romantic. Complainer and critical. Never good enough. Demands immediate gratification. "Entitled." Melancholy. Unreliable. Affected. Condescending. Dauntless.
Level 2 Manipu-lator	Martyr. Pride. Manipulative. Hysteric. Vicious liar. Maestro of guilt. Hurtful. Deadly adversary. Gets even. Self-deceptive excuses.	Narcissistic. Self-deceptive. They "are" their last success. Hype. Malicious. Performers. Promiscuous. Vindictive. Artfully deceitful.	Introverted into own fantasy world. Envious. Self-indulgent. High maintenance. "Deserves" to be taken care of in high style. Little or no exchange. Depression.
Level 1 Victim	Extreme codependency. Scorned victim. Selflessly oppressed. Disintegrates primarily to negative 8 and also to negative 4. Zero responsibility for own vicious actions.	All busyness with no real results. Extreme Jealousy. Anxiety attacks. Feels worthless. "Poor me." Disintegrates primarily to negative 9 and also to negative 6.	Resents all obligations. Whiner. Feels totally unacknowledged. Self-pity. Shame. Deep depression. Despair. Disintegrates primarily to negative 2 and also to negative 1.
Level 0 Psychotic	Self-sacrificial martyr sacrificing others. Totally dependent. Hysterical aggressor.	Totally self-deceptive. Potentially homicidal. Disassociates. Catatonia.	Severe depression. Potential suicide or devouring/ explosive. Dissociation. Bipolar.

Drive 5	Drive 6	Drive 7	
VISIONARY-RECLUSE	PROTECTOR-WORRIER	ADVENTURER-DILETTANTE	▼ Level
Profound visionary. Unself-conscious. Able to transcend rational thought. Contemplative. Original. Brilliant. Learned. Humor. Integrates primarily to positive 8 and also to positive 7. *Albert Einstein*	Creator of security in and for others. Dynamic interdependence. Open. Perspective. Committed. Engaging. Playful. Integrates primarily to positive 9 and also to positive 3. *Krishnamurti*	True Renaissance Man. Enthusiastic, joyful appreciation of and for life. Grateful. Free-spirited. Vital. Optimistic. Models positive attitude. Integrates primarily to positive 5 and also to positive 1. *St. Francis*	**Level 6** Leader
Open-minded. Perceptive observer. Discoverer. Continual learner. Logical. Focused concentration. Innovative. Intellectual. Analytical. Private. Vigilant.	Highly practical. Organizationally effective. Analyses. Tenacious. Troubleshooter. Constructive critic. Devil's advocate.	Happy, uninhibited. Alert, quick mind. Open to experience desires and anticipates. Many projects, many friends. Jack of all trades.	**Level 5** Doer
Detached. Withdraws to avoid anxiety. Private space is important. "In the pursuit of knowledge." Endless study. Bookish. Highly specialized. Details. Compartmentalizes.	Dutiful. Cautious. Security oriented. Skeptic. Ambivalent. Indecisive. Evasive.	"Lets have fun." Gregarious. Last minute only commitments. "Grass may be greener." Expects to be entertained. Delegates.	**Level 4** Coper
Terse, cryptic, uncommunicative. Withdraws. Limits relationships. Monologues. Cynic. Avoids being controlled by becoming more seclusive. Uses thinking to numb feelings. Scattered.	Phobic: Anxious. Pessimistic. Defensive. Looks to authority figure. OR Counter-Phobic: Daredevil. Cynic. Blamer. Rebel. Antagonistic.	Constant activity and acquisition of new experiences to avoid anxiety. Hedonistic. "I want it all." Center of attention. Flamboyant. Hates routine. Manic. "Dumps" responsibilities. Critical.	**Level 3** Opposer
Isolated. "Go it alone." Narrows needs. Recluse. Neglects themselves. Repressed rage.	High anxiety. Immediately discounting of anything positive. Everything is a crisis. Self-disparagement. Denial.	Indiscriminate behavior. Superficial about everything. Avoids any real commitments or obligations. Big promises, no real results. Promiscuous. Hysteric. Rigid.	**Level 2** Manipulator
Terrified. Phobias. Strung out. Rigid. Cruel. Diabolical thinking. Disintegrates primarily to negative 7 and also to negative 8.	Whiner. Continual unsolvable problems. Masochistic. Persecuted persecutor. Projection. Disintegrates primarily to negative 3 and also to negative 9.	Burn out. Obsessive, compulsive addictions. Escapist. Caustic. Blamer. Disdainful. Deep depression. Disintegrates primarily to negative 1 and also to negative 5.	**Level 1** Victim
Hallucinations, disassociation, depression. Potential schizoid. Potential suicide.	Terrified of oblivion. Delusions of persecution. Paranoid. Potential suicide.	Delusional. Cruel. Obsessive/compulsive.	**Level 0** Psychotic

	Drive 8	Drive 9	Drive 1
NAME ▶	LEADER-BULLY	PEACEMAKER-AVOIDER	REFORMER-CRITIC
Level 6 **Leader**	Natural leader others look up to. Champion of under-dog. Innocence of manner. Decisive. "Can do." Exudes presence, self-confidence, and power. Integrates primarily to positive 2 and also to positive 5. *Theodore Roosevelt*	Dynamic and serene individual who can see all viewpoints and works to create a harmonious environment. Guileless candor. Empathetic. Integrates primarily to positive 3 and also to positive 6. *Dalai Lama*	Profound experience of beauty in all things. Truly wants to make the world better. Highly principled. Truth and justice primary values. Models integrity. Integrates primarily to positive 7 and also to positive 4. *Abraham Lincoln*
Level 5 **Doer**	Willing to take a stand, even an unpopular one. Vision. Direct and impassioned. Honorable and trustworthy. Straightforward. Resourceful. Commanding. Challenging.	Optimistic. Reassuring. Excellent mediator. Affable. Pleasant. Unpretentious. Easy-going. Accepting.	Conscientious. Strong personal convictions with strong sense of right and wrong. Self-disciplined. Very orderly. Efficient. Thorough. Responsible.
Level 4 **Coper**	Able to withstand pressure. "The Rock." Pragmatic. In-sensitive to other's needs. Expects own requests to be fulfilled.	Accommodates to avoid conflict. Emotionally detached. Diplomatic politician. Epic stories. Respectability important. Little or no sense of relative priorities. Promises/commitments forgotten.	High minded idealist. Picky. Opinionated. Expects "The Rules" to be followed. Notices error. Focused on detail. Sees glass half empty.
Level 3 **Opposer**	Demands support/compliance. Adversarial. In your face. "Don't mess with me or my people!" Arrogant pride. Explosive. Intimidations, threats. Potential ruthless, anti-social dictator, tyrant.	Projects hostility/negativity to others. Over extends. Many projects, few "dones." Lose self in "big picture." Nit-picking. Of all the types, 9s most "successfully" repress manifestations of rage.	Crusader. Zealousness. Critical. "How things ought to be." Perfectionist. Never satisfied. Indignant anger. Judgmental. Resentment. Rigidity.
Level 2 **Manipu-lator**	Projected anger. Disengaged. Of all the types, the 8s are the least subtle or covertly manipulative. To a large extent, "What you see is what you get."	Deeply repressed rage. Malicious apparent compliance. Lazy. Excuses. Chronic lies. Invalidating. Unable to differentiate self from others. Shallow.	Worry/anxiety. Moralizing. Must be right. Rationalized inflexibility and heavy control. Self-righteous put downs/invalidations.
Level 1 **Victim**	Apathetic frustration. Withdraws. Unresponsive. Indifferent. "I don't care." Disintegrates primarily to negative 5 and also to negative 2.	Doormats. Slothful. Disassociation. Self-abandonment/abasing. Morbid dependency. Neglectful. Nothing matters. Disintegrates primarily to negative 6 and also to negative 3.	Intolerant. Severe depression. Negates self and others. Obsessive/compulsive. Disintegrates primarily to negative 4 and also to negative 7.
Level 0 **Psychotic**	Paranoia. Potential schizoid. Implode.	Potential Multiple Personality Disorder. Dispassion.	Potential nervous breakdowns and suicide. Reaction formation.

Suggested Reading

Almaas, A. H., *The Pearl Beyond Price*, Diamond Books, 1988.

Baron, R. and Wagele, E., *The Enneagram Made Easy: Discover the 9 Types of People*, HarperCollins, 1994.

Bast, M. and Thomson, C., *Out of the Box: Coaching with the Enneagram*, NineStar Publishing, 2005.

Bossidy, L. and Charan, R., *Execution*, Crown Business, 2002.

Daniels, D. N. and Price, V. A., *The Essential Enneagram: The Definitive Personality Test and Self-Discovery Guide*, HarperCollins, 2000.

Hartman, T., *Attention Deficit Disorder: A Different Perception*, Underwood Books, 1993.

Charan, R. and Tichy, N., *Every Business Is a Growth Business*, Random House, 1998.

Collins, J. and Porras, J., *Built to Last*, HarperCollins, 1994.

Davis, R. and Braun, E., *The Gift of Dyslexia*, Berkeley Publishing Group, 1994.

DePree, M., *Leadership Is an Art*, Doubleday, 1990.

Dyer, W., *The Power of Intention: Learning to Co-create Your World Your Way*, Hay House, 2004.

George, B., *Authentic Leadership: Rediscovering the Secrets to Creating Lasting Value*, Jossey-Bass, 2004.

Goleman, D., *Emotional Intelligence: Why It Can Matter More Than IQ*, Bantam, 1995.

Gray, J., *Men Are from Mars, Women Are from Venus*, Harper Collins, 1992.

Hamel, G. and Prahalad, C.K., *Competing for the Future*, Harvard Business School Press, 1994.

Hanh, T. N., *Living Buddha, Living Christ*, Riverhead Trade, 1997.

Hargrove, R., *Masterful Coaching*, Jossey-Bass/Pfeiffer, 2003.

Hawkins, D., *Power vs. Force: The Hidden Determinants of Human Behavior*, Hay House, 2002.

Kouzes, J. and Posner, B., *The Leadership Challenge*, Jossey-Bass, 2002.

Kremeer, Ruzzuto and Case, *Managing by the Numbers*, Perseus Publishing, 2000.

Krishnamurti, J., *Total Freedom: The Essential Krishnamurti*, Harper, 1996.

Lapid-Bogda, G., *Bringing Out the Best in Yourself at Work: How to Use the Enneagram System for Success*, McGraw-Hill, 2004

Levine, J., *The Enneagram Intelligences: Understanding Personality for Effective Teaching and Learning*, Bergin and Garvey, 1999.

Mandela, N., *Long Walk to Freedom*, Little Brown, 1994.

Maslow, A., *Maslow on Management*, Wiley, 1998.

Nisargadatta Maharaj, S., *I Am That*, The Acorn Press, 1973.

Paine, L., *Cases In Leadership, Ethics and Organizational Integrity: A Strategic Perspective*, McGraw-Hill/Irwin, 1997.

Peters, T. and Waterman, R., *In Search of Excellence*, Harper & Row, 1982.

Rinpoche, S., *The Tibetan Book of the Living and the Dying*, HarperCollins, 1994.

Robinson, K., *Out of Our Mind: Learning to be Creative*, Capstone Publishing Limited, 2001.

Riso, D. R. and R. Hudson, T*he Wisdom of the Enneagram: The Complete Guide to Psychological and Spiritual Growth for the Nine Personality Types*, Bantam Books, 1999.

Spencer, L., *Winning through Participation*, Kendall-Hunt, 2001.

Senge, P., *The Fifth Discipline: The Art and Practice of the Learning Organization*, Doubleday, 1990.

Stansfield, B., *The Art of Focused Conversation*, ICA Canada, 1997.

Steil, L. and Bommelje, R., *Listening Leaders*, Beaver's Pond Press, 2004.

Talbot, M., *The Holographic Universe*, Harper Collins, 1991.

Tichy, N. and Devanna, M., *The Transformational Leader*, Wiley, 1990.

Tolle, E., *The Power of Now*, New World Library, 1999.

Wheatley, M., *Leadership and the New Science: Discovering Order in a Chaotic World*, Berrett-Koehler, 1999.

Whitworth, L., Kimsey-House, H. and Sandahl, P., *Co-Active Coaching*, Davies-Black Publishing, 1998.

Woodsmall, M. and Woodsmall, W., *People Pattern Power: P3: The Nine Keys to Business Success*, Next Step Printers, 1999.

GLOSSARY

The definitions included here are not intended to be comprehensive but limited to the meaning used in the text.

— A —

ACCOUNTABILITY: ownership of responsibility for the results of a particular activity or arena of control. Willingness to accept the consequences of both failure and success.

ACUTE EMOTION: actual emotional feeling experienced in present time.

ADOLESCENCE: the period between childhood and adulthood, where major hormonal changes generate a new and unfamiliar emotional need to break away from parental control and dependency and learn to become responsibly self-reliant. Compounded by a lack of experience, this change generates confusion, doubt and fear, often initially resulting in reactive, self-centered, defensive, often dysfunctional behavior. If the individual does not eventually learn the needed lessons (how to communicate and relate, increasingly living essence values—which is what growing up is all about), he or she will not move on to the emotional maturity of true adulthood. That individual will remain emotionally and behaviorally an adolescent occupying an older body—which, appears to be the case for a significant portion of the population as evidenced by the continuing worldwide presence of rationalized irresponsible, hurtful behaviors lacking in sensitivity or compassion.

Anger: an authentic emotion indicating the presence of some irresponsibility or injustice that needs addressing.

Artificial Emotion: a synthetic emotion, having no positive aspects, created by mankind to avoid dealing with real underlying emotions, most often anger, fear, shame, or hurt. Examples are guilt, martyrdom, and victimhood. Different from real or authentic emotions that have both positive and negative aspects or potential.

Anxiety: a lack of a sense of a positive future. The feeling associated with; expectation of error, anticipated rejection or humiliation, or trust erroneously placed. Undefined pain, anger, hurt or fear.

Arrogance: a façade of superiority attempting to mask a sense of inferiority.

Authentic Emotion: emotion actually present; characterized by the presence of both positive and negative potential. If both potentials are not present, it is not an authentic emotion but and artificial emotion used to repress some other emotion (see Artificial Emotion).

— B —

Blame: a hostile denial of responsibility and projection of cause.

Belief: a mental construct that forms the foundation of our perception of reality. A means to focus one's attention and/or maintain boundaries.

— C —

CHARACTER: the frequency or degree with which one lives his or her principles.

CHRONIC EMOTION: an emotional state present or consistently reoccurring over time.

COACHING: the process of helping an individual access more aspects of their passions and potentials.

CODEPENDENCY: dysfunctional and limiting mutual reliance.

COLLABORATION: involvement that considers the other's enhancement.

CONFRONT: the willingness and ability to face whatever is present.

CONTROL: the ability to start, continue, change, or stop something under one's own determination.

COOPERATION: involvement with another to enhance self.

CORE VALUES: the values from which an individual (or organization) *actually* functions. They may be essence values or social values or a combination of both.

COURAGE: the willingness to face one's fears and respond versus react.

COVERT HOSTILITY: hostility too close to fear for the person to be willing to express the hostility openly, so does so in a hidden manner often via invalidations, misdirection, lies, and/ or manipulation. Passive-aggressive behavior.

CRITICAL MASS: in training, the point that occurs when a program is sufficiently reinforced and delivered to enough people to attain the focus, maturation and synergy sufficient to create a new norm.

— D —

DETERIORATION: decreasing responsibility, within one's personality drive, to lower levels of emotional maturity.

DISINTEGRATION: The self-perceived failure of one's personality strategy to deal with life's conditions and the desperate shift to the negative aspects of other personality strategies.

DOMINION: power and the ability to share that power with respect, dignity and honor. Absolute ownership of responsibility. The opposite of domination.

DRIVES: refers to the unique combinations of energies that focus and propel attitudes and behaviors creating various strategies of survival, called personality. Used by the individual to compensate for and cope with perceived limitations in dealing with the vicissitudes of life.

DYNAMIC BALANCE: resilience in responsively dealing with the vicissitudes of life in a dynamic universe.

— E —

EGO: a vehicle to gather information created by humans as they evolved to compensate for the decline or loss of animal instincts.

EMOTIONAL INTELLIGENCE—having an awareness of: what emotions are; their purpose, meaning, and what they can tell us; the different behaviors and attitudes associated with each emotion; the relationship among emotions; and how we tend to misuse emotions.

EMOTIONAL MATURITY: living essence values. Willing, able and acting with integrity. Responsibly applying emotional intelligence. Responsible use of power.

EMOTIONAL RANGE: the emotional distance or difference one can be from a person's present emotional state and still be able to relate meaningfully. Communication and meaning becomes problematic more than one level distant (on the Levels of Emotional Maturity) from the individual's or group's present time emotional state.

EMOTIONS: feeling messages (energy in motion) from our subconscious indicating our survival potential.

EMPOWERMENT: giving oneself permission and assuming the authority (authorship) to act; power with responsibility.

ENNEAGRAM: An ancient system describing how people form different (nine) strategies (personalities) to compensate for considerations (false) of insignificance (not being enough).

ESSENCE VALUES: energetic qualities foundational to our very being characterized by 1) a presence that responsibly contributes to a more positive, loving environment; 2) inclusiveness rather than exclusiveness and 3) stability independent of circumstance, context, social mores or external sources of acceptance. Examples are love, honesty, authenticity, allowance, compassion, forgiveness, and generosity.

— F —

FACILITATION LEVEL: The emotional level from which one needs to communicate and relate in order to motivate/lead another to a relatively higher state of awareness and responsibility

FEAR: the emotional message of potential loss.

FIX: a way to avoid dealing with the difficult issues of change.

— G —

GREATNESS: Power used responsibly.

GRIEF: a feeling of having lost something of perceived significance.

GUILT: an artificial emotion used to avoid confronting some other emotion: usually anger, fear, hurt, or shame. An invalidating means to control others.

— I —

INTEGRATION: recognizing, taking responsibility for, and moving beyond self-created limitations. A quantum leap in the individual's, or organization's, willingness to be responsible for everything they say and do. Personal empowerment.

INTEGRITY: spontaneous assumption of responsibility. Living essence values.

INTENTION: focused direction with the appropriate energy to attain a desired outcome.

— J —

JUDGMENTS: conclusions based on ideas/beliefs previously formed and largely devoid of present-time input.

— L —

LEADERSHIP: the willingness and ability to motivate others to move beyond where they are mentally, emotionally, physically, and/or spiritually.

LEVELS OF EMOTIONAL MATURITY: Six groupings of associated emotions, attitudes, and behaviors, each indicating a different degree of responsible perception and intention. They represent relative degrees of acting with integrity; living essence values; responsibly applying emotional intelligence; being responsibly powerful. The higher the level, the greater the responsibility (and integrity) consistently present (chapter 6).

— M —

MATURATION—the process of growing up by assuming increasing responsibility for one's actions and attitudes.

— N —

NEGOTIATION—the process of determining and moving toward meeting, with integrity, all involved parties' legitimate perceived needs.

— P —

PAIN: a synergy of a sense of separation from and yearning for something: emotional pain—belonging; mental pain—understanding; physical pain—control.

PASSIVE AGGRESSIVE: covertly hostile behavior.

PERSEVERANCE: persistence in overcoming resistance and moving toward an intended outcome.

POWER: the ability and willingness to act.

PRESENCE: being in the moment with whatever is present.

PRINCIPLES: boundaries of behavior.

— R —

RAGE: a sense of powerlessness.

RAPPORT: harmonious congruence; sense of affinity, similar or mutual perspectives.

REACTIVE: acting from fixed ideas/beliefs of the past versus observing and responding to what is actually occurring in the moment.

REALITY: one's perception of what is; the greater the mutual agreement the more real (and solid) it tends to be. Thus reality changes with changing perceptions.

REMORSE: profound sadness of having been responsible for some loss that cannot be recovered.

REPRESSED EMOTIONS: emotions consciously avoided.

RESPONSIBILITY: the ability to respond in the moment to whatever is, "good" or "bad," doing one's utmost, with the resources available, to improve the situation.

RESPONSIVE: taking responsible action to deal with what is.

— S —

SCHIZOPHRENERGETIC: behavior that generates disorientation and confusion in others (crazy making).

SELF-CONFIDENCE: a sense that one is able to deal with, at least adequately, whatever occurs

SELF-ESTEEM: one's own evaluation of how well one is living essence values.

SELF-IMAGE: The consideration/belief one has of what they are actually capable of being, doing and/or having in their reality.

SHADOW: the psychological repository of everything (actions and non-actions, positive as well as negative) for which we refuse to take responsibility.

SHAME: a sense of being defective.

SILO EFFECT: the manifestation of a lack of responsible communication and activity between or among groups of the same organization.

SOCIAL DEMEANOR: the emotional and attitudinal display one puts forth to achieve some social purpose. It may be the same as, or used to cover, one's actual emotion at the time.

SOCIAL VALUES: values created by and learned from our environment of what will, and will not, be expected, acknowledged, admired, rewarded, and supported by a sizable part of the contemporary world.

STRATEGIC INTENT: the impeccable focus and intention that compels the vision to manifest.

STRATEGIC OBJECTIVE: a major focus whose attainment greatly assists and supports the strategic intent.

SUPPRESSED EMOTIONS: emotions unconsciously avoided.

— T —

TEAM BUILDING: collaborative, cocreative dialogue and action toward an agreed-upon goal/purpose.

TRAUMA: an incident so overwhelming that one cannot integrate all of what is occurring. A paralyzing sense of overwhelm.

TRUST: faith that what is promised or implied will be honored

— U —

UNDERSTANDING: awareness with the ability to apply that awareness to the circumstances of life.

— V —

VICTIM: the state of being unable or unwilling to deal with the circumstances of life.

— W —

WILLINGNESS: the attitude of openness to trying something.

WISDOM: living essence values. Acting with integrity. Being emotionally mature. Applied, responsible perspective. Awareness of the big picture without losing sight of the current situation.

Index

— F —

About the Author

EDWARD E. MORLER, M.B.A., Ph.D.

Dr. Morler is President of Morler International, a management training and development firm specializing in integrity based interpersonal effectiveness. His focus is the custom design and delivery of bottom-line, functional skill enhancement programs that simultaneously integrate the principles and dynamics of integrity, emotional maturity, motivation, and leadership. Examples are negotiation, sales, presentation skills, client relations, and leadership development. Dr. Morler conducts trainings for corporations and government agencies worldwide. He offers an unconditional guarantee of client satisfaction. Please visit www.Morler.com.

"*The Leadership Integrity Challenge* is *the* field manual for creating an emotionally mature environment of integrity—an invaluable resource for anyone in management or on a board of directors. Integrity is the foundation of trust. Emotional maturity is key to making discerning choices. This book eloquently clarifies the elements that facilitate their understanding and development."
    —John D. Santi Sr., CEO, The Santi Company, LLC

"Best business book I've read in years! Dr. Morler's mix of leadership philosophy and personal growth make for a fantastic combination. This book is extremely timely and a must read for anyone in management."
    —Chris Landwehr, CEO, Cal-Bay Mortgage

"*The Leadership Integrity Challenge* is a book I highly recommend. It is a brilliant synthesis of the archetypal and developmental psychologies of maturity. It is comprehensive, yet simple, elegant and wise. It challenges us and leads us forward. Particularly impressive is Dr. Morler's developmental schema of the stages of emotional maturity. He clearly demonstrates how to apply it individually and in an organizational setting to facilitate emotional maturity, integrity and leadership."
    —Andrew Hahn, Psy.D., Founder, Guided Self Healing

"*The Leadership Integrity Challenge* is the single most valuable book I've read in years…. There is no fluff in this book…. It deals directly and with unmistakable authority with the most important factor in all business dealings: people and their levels of emotional maturity…. It has changed the way I hire, lead, negotiate and sell. Most of all, it has given me considerably greater insight into human behavior and character."
    —Brooks Cole, CEO, Holocomos

Printed in the United States
65218LVS00005B/67-171